SOCIAL AND ECONOMIC ASPECTS
OF THE CHAIN STORE MOVEMENT

SMALL BUSINESS ENTERPRISE
IN AMERICA

Advisory Editors
Stuart Bruchey
Vincent P. Carosso

Research Associate
Eleanor Bruchey

See last pages of this volume
for a complete list of titles.

SOCIAL AND ECONOMIC ASPECTS
OF THE CHAIN STORE MOVEMENT

Harold M. Haas

ARNO PRESS
A New York Times Company
New York • 1979

381
H112

Editorial Supervision: RITA LAWN

———————◆———————

First publication 1979 by Arno Press Inc.

Copyright © 1979 by Harold M. Haas

SMALL BUSINESS ENTERPRISE IN AMERICA
ISBN for complete set: 0-405-11457-5
See last pages of this volume for titles.

Manufactured in the United States of America

———————◆———————

Library of Congress Cataloging in Publication Data

Haas, Harold Milburn.
    Social and economic aspects of the chain store
movement.

    (Small business enterprise in America)
    Originally presented as the author's thesis,
University of Minnesota, 1939.
    Bibliography: p.
    1. Chain stores--United States. 2. Grocery
trade--Indiana--Case studies. I. Title.
II. Series.
HF5468.H2 1979   381   78-18962
ISBN 0-405-11466-4

SOCIAL AND ECONOMIC ASPECTS

of the

CHAIN STORE MOVEMENT

A Dissertation Presented to the Faculty

of the

UNIVERSITY OF MINNESOTA

In Partial Fulfillment of the Requirements

for the

Degree of Doctor of Philosophy

By

Harold M. Haas

December, 1939

i

TABLE OF CONTENTS

11

LIST OF TABLES

APPENDIX TABLES

SUMMARY OF THE THESIS
" SOCIAL AND ECONOMIC ASPECTS
of the
CHAIN STORE MOVEMENT "

By

Harold M. Haas

December, 1939

Chapter I.

INTRODUCTION

One of the major developments in the business world
that has occurred during the past two decades is that of
a multiple-unit system of retail distribution, commonly
known as the "chain store." This type of concern, consisting of a number of separate units owned and controlled
by a central organization, has been in existence for many
years. History records the Hanseatic League, which appeared in northern Europe in the middle of the fourteenth century.[1] Like the modern chain store, its birth can be
traced to certain economic conditions which prevailed at
that time, and similarly it owed its growth in a considerable degree to the development of methods of accounting and
record-keeping. But the so-called "chain store movement"
did not assume significant proportions in the United States
until the decade immediately following the end of the World
War. Whereas the volume of chain store sales in 1919 was
estimated to have been approximately 4% of the total retail
trade, within three years of that date "chain store business
mounted to 6%; by 1926 to 8%; by 1927 to 12%; and by the end
of 1929 to 29% of our nation's total retail business."[2] According to the Census of American Business the ratio in 1933

1. See article by Frist Rorig in the Encyclopedia of the
   Social Sciences, Vol. VII, p. 266. Published by Mac-
   Millan Company, New York, 1932. Also see Appendix A,
   Supplement to Chapter I.
2. Nichols, John P., "Chain Store Manual," 1936 ed., p.11.
   Institute of Distribution, inc., New York, 1936.

was 25.2%.[1]

Alarmed at the rapid growth of the chain store organizations, those whose economic positions were threatened by the resulting changes in methods of distribution began to demand some form of governmental action that would check or control the growth of chain stores, on the ground that they constituted a threat of monopoly. In response to this demand, the Senate passed a resolution[2] in 1928 directing the Federal Commission "to inquire into the chain-store system of marketing and distribution," and to report back to the Senate any evidence of monopoly.

The first report of the Commission's investigation was submitted in December, 1931, and the final report was filed with the Secretary of the Senate on December 14, 1934.[3] But although the final report stated that "a study of the extent to which chain-store companies have invaded the general field of retail distribution of commodities does not indicate a monopolization of that field, taken as a whole,"[4] the "chain-store controversy" and the attacks on chain-store organizations by organizations of independent merchants still continue.

Since the end and aim of production and distribution are the satisfaction of human needs, it was inevitable that the consuming public would become involved in this contro-

----

1. "Chains and Independents and Other Types of Operation," p. 1-3. Census of American Business, Retail Distribution: 1933. Bureau of the Census.
2. Senate Resolution No. 224, Seventieth Congress, 1st session. See Appendix A, Supplement to Chapter I.
3. See bibliography for a list of these reports.
4. Federal Trade Commission, "Final Report on the Chain-Store Investigation." Senate Document No. 4, 74th Congress, 1st session, p.19. U.S. Govt. Printing Office, 1935.

versy, and that impartial investigators would seek answers
to such questions as the following:

1. Are the chain stores more or less efficient than
the independently-owned stores?

2. What are the effects of chain-store distribution
on the life and growth of the communities in which they are
located? Are there considerations more important than mere
money-saving?

3. To what extent has the movement toward greater integration and combination in distribution broadened or re-
stricted the opportunities for the individual to improve
his economic position?

To arrive at satisfactory answers to these questions,
definite standards of measurement must be established. But
these standards vary with different social groups. The
consumer is concerned with efficiency in distribution as
an important factor in lowering the prices he pays for goods.
the producer and distributor see it as essential to reducing their costs and increasing their profit margins. The
economic affairs of a community are involved with problems
of devising equitable systems of taxation; of obtaining
adequate leadership in activities and projects of common
interest; and of selecting effective methods for keeping
the community alive and growing. The individual is con-
fronted with the problem of making a living and at the
same time of finding opportunities for bettering his position, increasing his income, and giving himself and society
the full benefit of his abilities, whatever they may be.

Obviously this field of exploration is too vast for any
one investigator to cover, although a considerable amount of
data has been collected in widely scattered areas. Yet individual studies, even though relatively small, do have their
value. If certain facts are discovered about one market, a
basis is established for judging conditions in similar markets.[1]

The basis for this thesis is a study made by the author
in Bloomington, Indiana, the county seat of Monroe County.
In a later chapter the characteristics of this county will
be described in considerable detail. Data will then be presented showing the distribution of grocery stores in this
city classified according to sales volume, the typical operating expenses in the various classes, a comparison of
prices charged in chain and independently-owned stores, and
the effects of the chain store and the gross income tax laws.

Since this study should not only add to the existing
store of knowledge concerning the competitive situations of
chain stores and independently-owned stores, but should also
be evaluated in the light of what is already known, an attempt is made in the early chapters to summarize the relevant parts of the inquiry made by the Federal Trade Commission and of other studies similar to this one. This summa-
rization is necessarily brief, and omits many important
elements in the chain store controversy.

---

1. "In any study which requires observations from separate
sources too numerous or too widespread to admit of individual and complete coverage, it is customary in research work to rely upon data from a comparatively small
but representative segment of the field." "The Technique of Marketing Research." p.53. Committee on Marketing Research Technique of the American Marketing Society. McGraw-Hill Book Co. New York, 1937.

Chapter II.

THE REVOLUTION IN MERCHANDISING

When changes in methods of production and distribution take place slowly so that those affected by them have time to make the necessary adjustments, controversies as violent as the one under discussion here are not so likely to occur. But the great rapidity with which the chain-store organizations grew and developed was, in the minds of many, a cause for public alarm. In a letter of submittal accompanying one of its reports, the Federal Trade Commission stated that "the 'chain' has been popularly assigned an important role in reducing the number of independent stores, either through buying them out or by having them withdraw from business as a result of chain competition. This is perhaps the most important matter of public interest considered in this report. The question is raised, moreover, as to whether the future growth of the chains will be as rapid as hitherto."[1]

The Great Atlantic and Pacific Tea Company is usually accorded the distinction of being the first in the chain store field in the United States. Apparently there is some disagreement as to the exact year it was founded, but one investigator found that the name "Great American Tea Company" first appeared in the New York City Directory in

---

1. F.T.C. "Growth and Development of Chain Stores."
   Senate Document No. 100, 72d Congress, 1st session,
   p. ix. U. S. Govt. Printing Office. 1932.
   See Appendix A, Supplement to Chapter II.

1864.[2]   Palmer gives the year as 1859.[3]   Other dates given
by the same authority are as follows:

```
             Jones Brothers Tea Co.---- 1872
             Woolworth----------------- 1879
             Kroger-------------------- 1882
             Kresge- ------------------ 1897
             National Tea-------------- 1899
```

However it was not until about 1914 that large-scale
distribution began to attract the attention of manufacturers and merchandisers.   There had been a rapid development during the period from 1900 to 1915, but even then
the chain-store organizations were "hardly beyond adoles-
cence," and information about them is in many instances
difficult to obtain.[4]   The Federal Trade Commission's
study "was confined to 12 major classes of chains which,
with their subgroups, constitute a total of 26 types of
organizations."[5]   In these 26 fields the Commission received reports from or could trace only ten that existed
in 1890.   The increases after this year, in five year in-
tervals, were as follows:[6]

```
        1895----21          1915----505
        1900----58          1920----808
        1905---154          1925---1565
        1910---257          1928---1718
```

---

2. Bullock, Roy: "History of the Great Atlantic and Pacific Tea Company." Harvard Business Review, Vol.XI,
   No. 3, April, 1933, p. 289. Harvard University Press.
3. Palmer, James L.: "Chain Stores." An address delivered before the American Paint and Varnish Manufacturers'
   Association, October 16, 1928. Reported by Chain Store
   Age, 93 Worth St., New York.
4. "In many instances figures for the earlier years of a
   company's organization were not available, owing to the
   loss or destruction of the records."
   F.T.C. report, S.D. No. 100, p. 1.
5. F.T.C. report, S.D. No. 31, p. vii.
6. F.T.C. report, S.D. No. 100, p. 80.   See Appendix A,
   Supplement to Chapter II.

The opposition to the chain-store organizations resembles in some respects that which arose toward the mail-order houses and the department stores; two major developments in large-scale retailing which first appeared in their present form during the 1870's and the 1880's. The mail-order houses came into existence as the result of an extensive and dependable mail service which the construction of railways in all parts of the country made possible. With an increase in the circulation of periodicals, business houses began to use advertising both intensively and extensively. The growth of education, together with a much greater amount of reading by the consuming public, and in conjunction with a period of prosperity, created a demand for a wider selection and a better quality of goods than were available at most of the country stores. The mail-order houses developed in response to this demand. The department stores came with the increase in urban population and the building of rapid transit lines. Both the mail-order houses and the department stores could use large-scale buying methods effectively, and both were opposed by the independent merchants.

There are other types of distributive organizations that show a "growing tendency to decrease the number of successive steps in distribution." There have been mergers of laundries, cleaning and dyeing establishments, and linen supply houses; consolidations of chains of motion-picture theaters; mergers of companies manufacturing various kinds of branded and nationally-advertised food products; pro-

ducers' cooperatives for the marketing of agricultural
products; bank mergers; common ownership of storage companies, dry docks, and garages; and direct selling of
such articles as hosiery, brushes, toilet goods, flavoring extracts, cooking utensils, and men's clothing.[7]

It is difficult to identify any definite patterns
of distribution in all this intricate interlacing of the
lines along which goods move from producer to consumer.
Nevertheless such patterns do exist, and in the next
chapter those characteristics will be marked which distinguish one method of distribution from another; particularly the "orthodox" chain store from other types of
multiple-unit systems.

---

7. Hodge, A. C.: "Mergers and Marketing," American Management Association. Marketing Executive Series No. 63.
   1929.

Chapter III

DEFINITION OF TERMS

Before one can proceed far with any discussion, there
must be a clear understanding of the meanings of the words
used to express the nature of those things which are being
discussed. Here one must note carefully the use of such
terms as "national chain," "local chain," "local branch
system," "voluntary chain," "manufacturer's retail store,"
"producers' cooperative," "chain department store," "mail
order chain," "consumers' cooperative," and "company store."
All of these various forms of merchandising organizations
have certain distinguishing characteristics, but they also
have one in common, namely, that integration or combination,
or both, are present in some form or other.

Integration and Combination Defined

Marshall uses the word integration to describe "a growing intimacy and firmness of the connections between the
separate parts of the industrial organism."[1] In general, it
is the process of bringing the parts together into a whole.
When applied to the distribution of goods, this process has
one major consequence: there is an absorption of functions
and a lessening of the number of agencies involved in the
movement of goods from the producer to the consumer.

1. Alfred Marshall, Principles of Economics, p. 241.
London: Macmillan and Company, 1935.

This use of the term is in accordance with both the mathematical and the economic definitions. One can conceive of the marketing channel as consisting of a series of stages or steps extending from the producer to the consumer. There is differentiation in this marketing process to the extent that the marketing functions are performed by separate and independent organizations, each operating at one of the stages or steps, or engaged in some auxiliary function. The opposite of this must be integration.

Combination takes place when there is a consolidation or joining together, in one form or another, of agencies or units organized to perform one or more of the marketing functions. No fusion of "parts" takes place, because each unit is an entirety in itself. When used in this sense, combination takes place if a group of retailers join together for a common purpose; for example, to obtain the discounts usually allowed on purchases made in large-quantity lots.

Integration usually extends in a vertical direction, that is, from one stage to another, whereas combination occurs at the same level in the marketing channel. There are exceptions, however, to this general rule. To illustrate, when a firm absorbs certain of the auxiliary functions, as for example, when it finances its own installment sales, there is integration according to the definition given above. Also when a wholesaler organizes a voluntary chain but retains his separate identity, as do the retailer members, there is combination in a vertical direction.

These processes of integration and combination have been carefully defined in order to show their importance as factors in the development of large-scale retailing. They are especially useful as characteristics that enable one to distinguish between the multiple-unit system and the single-unit system. In the latter the independently-owned store stands alone, whether it belongs to an individual, a partnership or a corporation. The only tie it may have with some other organization is based on mutual interests that may exist.

A second characteristic which can be used as a basis for differentiation, although not so readily, is the volume of business done. A large unit store may do more business than a small chain. Nevertheless this characteristic is an important one, because many of the economies claimed for the multiple-unit system are based on operations made possible by a volume of considerably more than average size.

Definition of Multiple-Unit System

In this treatise, a multiple-unit system of distribution is defined as any method or system employed in the marketing and merchandising of consumers' goods which possesses the following characteristics:

1. There is an organization which embraces a multiple of units, and which may be either wholesale or retail, or both. Manufacturing processes may be included, but the establishment is organized primarily for the performance of the merchandising functions.

2. There is some form of central management and control of operations. The degree of centralization may vary between wide limits; from the cooperative buying of a retailers' association to the close and rigid supervision of the orthodox type of chain store. The term "orthodox type of chain store" will be defined later.

3. There is a definite attempt at uniformity in policies and methods of store operation. This uniformity may be obtained by contractual agreements, as in a wholesaler-sponsored voluntary chain, or by orders from executives holding absolute authority.

4. The major policies of the organization are based on a fixed determination on the part of the owners and executives to obtain the economies resulting from large-scale operations to the highest possible degree. What these operations are, and what economies are claimed because of them, will be described in chapters to follow.

5. Since size is relative, it is difficult to include this characteristic as one that is essential to a definition of a multiple-unit system. But by implication any organization to be so classified must be large enough to have caused changes in the marketing processes and in the relationships existing among organizations engaged in manufacturing, in distribution, or in the functions auxiliary to marketing. It is as different from that type of concern which has been termed a "multi-unit independent"[2] as a man is dif-

---

2. A term used in the Fifteenth Census of the United States, 1930. See Distribution, Vol. I, Retail Distribution, Part 1, p. 17. Also see Appendix A, Supplement to Chapter III, p. 202.

ferent from a small boy; although not necessarily in the
same sense, that is, in the sense of having "grown up." It
may have grown large by acquiring several smaller chains.

Definition of an "Orthodox Chain Store"

There have been many attempts to define a chain store.
Indeed, one difficulty which presented itself at the very
beginning of this study of the expansion of chain store
systems and their effects on patterns of distribution was
that difficulty arising from variations in the definition
of a "chain store."[3]

The term "orthodox chain store" will be used here to
designate an organization such as the Kroger Grocery and
Baking Company, the J. C. Penney Company, the Walgreen Drug
Company, or the Great Atlantic and Pacific Tea Company. Almost without exception, the orthodox chain store is a corporation; necessarily so because of the large amount of
capital needed for its operations. Regardless of whether
or not the stock is owned by a considerable number of widely
scattered individuals, or by a few, the control is highly
centralized. Although chain store organizations with as
few as five units might conceivably be included in the definition of the term, yet this discussion is concerned only
with those large enough to cause fundamental changes in the
methods of distribution and major disturbances in the competition for markets, and to be materially affected by the

---

3. See Appendix A, Supplement to Chapter III.

passage of state and federal anti-chain store legislation.

The orthodox chain store, of course, possesses all of the characteristics of the multiple-unit system as defined above. There is a high degree of standardization in methods of accounting, record keeping, and store control. Orders from the executives at headquarters are obeyed without question, and all merchandising operations are closely supervised. Problems of personnel training are of major importance. And within the organization itself there is specialization and a more or less minute division of labor. Indeed, the very nature of large-scale operations not only makes possible but also necessitates the employment of experts in the various phases of the marketing process.

Definition of a Voluntary Chain

In contrast to the orthodox chain is the "voluntary chain," or organization of independent retailers, which in the Federal Trade Commission's report is referred to as the "cooperative chain."[4] In this type of combination one can clearly distinguish two forms of organization: (1) the "wholesaler-sponsored cooperative," which consists of a "group of independent retailers affiliated with a wholesaler for buying and advertising activities;"[5] and (2) the

---

4. Federal Trade Commission. Cooperative Grocery Chains. Senate Document 12, 72nd Congress, p. xv. U. S. Government Printing Office, Washington, D. C. 1932. See Appendix A, Supplement to Chapter III.

5. Federal Trade Commission, Ibid., p. xv.

"retailer-initiated cooperative," where a group of retailers have voluntarily agreed to cooperate in buying, advertising, wholesaling, and other merchandising functions, in order to obtain some of the advantages of the orthodox chain. Examples of the first form are the Independent Grocers' Alliance at Chicago, Illinois, and the Red and White Corporation, with headquarters at Buffalo, New York. The Frankfort Grocery Company in Philadelphia, and the Allied Grocers' Company of Minneapolis are examples of the retailer-initiated cooperative.

Either of these three kinds of chains may be local, sectional, or national in its extent, and may be found in almost every retailing field. There are characteristics and problems common to both the orthodox and the voluntary chain, but there are also fundamental distinctions. The units of the voluntary chain are each controlled by its own individual management, although each retailer may have agreed to conform to certain procedures in order to become a member of the group. Store fronts may all be painted the same color; "specials" or "loss leaders" may be selected either by the wholesaler or by a committee representing the group; the same brands may be featured in all the stores; or advertising campaigns may be planned in which all of the members take part. But the independent merchants in a voluntary chain act in agreement, and not in obedience to orders.

Other Methods of Integrating or Combining

With the orthodox chain and the voluntary chain, the development of large-scale operations normally begins with the retail units. Wholesaling functions may or may not be absorbed, but they usually are if the organization attains any considerable size. Ordinarily, however, integration does not extend to the manufacturing processes in the voluntary chain.

On the other hand, a "producers cooperative" or a "manufacturer's retail store" is a form of distributive enterprise which starts with the producer and extends toward the retailing function. Here the emphasis is on the product, and on the desire is to market it as favorably as possible. The buying function is not nearly so important.

Although the "mail-order house chain" and the "chain department store" have certain differences which arise out of characteristics inherent in the parent organizations, yet they conform closely to the definition of a multiple-unit system. As will be shown later, they are on the side of the orthodox chains in the chain store controversy. A rather curious situation exists when an independently-owned department store leases one or more of its departments to an outside organization closely resembling an orthodox chain. This is often the case with the restaurants and tea rooms in the department stores.

A "local branch system" is formed when a large downtown store extends its operations by establishing smaller units in the suburban districts. The latter usually draw from the parent store's stock. If the downtown store is independently-owned, this type of distributive system is to be classed with the single-unit system rather than with the orthodox chain. The executives interests can be expected to be primarily with the community.

The "exclusive agency" is simply a contractual arrangement between the producer and a local merchant. It is not a form of large-scale retailing as defined above. "Consumers' cooperatives" and "company stores" are of importance in some districts, but are not yet significant as patterns of distribution.

Chapter IV

PRESENT SIZE AND EXTENT OF CHAIN STORE SYSTEMS

Prior to 1932 the number of chains and the count of
the individual stores within each organization were changing so rapidly that figures were out of date before they
could be compiled and published. One investigator in 1930
reported a total of 198,145 chain store units, with annual
sales in excess of $15,000,000,000.[1] As shown in Table
No. I, this number is considerably larger than those reported by the Bureau of the Census for 1929 and 1933. Such
variances are caused by differences in the definitions of a
chain store used by the enumerators. For example, in Table
No. II it is apparent that the Federal Trade Commission's
definition is different from that of the Bureau of the
Census.

Definitions of a chain store usually are based on such
characteristics as the number of units in the organization,
the plans of operation, and the degree of central ownership
and centralized management. Beckman makes a point of including in his tabulations of chains those organizations with
two or three units, and speaks of the "artificially concocted
definition of chains which covers only stores belonging to

---

1. M. M. Zimmerman, _Printers' Ink Weekly_, Oct. 2, 1930.
    p. 17.

Table I

Comparison of Retail Stores by Types of Operation

(Sales are stated in thousands of dollars)

	Number of Stores		Sales	
	1933	1929	1933	1929
U. S. Totals	1,526,119	1,543,158	$25,037,225	$49,114,653
Independents	1,349,337	1,375,509	$17,826,562	$38,081,504
Chains	141,603	148,037	6,312,769	9,834,846
Direct selling	7,026	1,661	187,368	93,961
Mail-order	311	271	244,381	515,237
Commissaries	2,719	1,347	95,578	115,583
Utility-operated	4,127	4,053	76,079	163,371
Other types	20,996	12,280	294,488	310,151

"In 1933 there were 26,000 fewer independent stores and 6,400 fewer chain stores than in 1929. On the other hand there were 5,400 more direct-selling (house-to-house) retailers, 40 more mail-order houses, and about 10,000 more stores of other types, including leased departments, cooperatives, etc.

"The sales of chains increased in relative importance to other types of operation during the four years since the previous Census. In 1929 chains did 20.0 per cent of the total of all retail business of the country; by 1933 the ratio had increased to 25.2. Independents, which did 77.5% of the total business in 1929, accounted for 71.2% in 1933. The sales of independents decreased 53.2%, whereas the sales of chains decreased 35.8%. . . . Much of the cause of the smaller aggregate decline in chain sales than in independent sales is the relatively smaller decline in the sales of those kinds of business in which chains prefer to operate—food, variety and drug stores, and filling stations."

From Census of American Business—Retail Distribution: 1933. Page 1-A. U.S. Dept. of Commerce.

Table II

Comparative Chains, Stores, and Sales Included in Census Figures for 1929 (4 Stores and Up) and Federal Trade Commission's Reports for 1928 for Chains of 6 Stores and Up

Kind of Chain	Number of chains		Number of Stores	
	Commission 6 Stores and Over 1928	Census 4 Stores and Over 1929	Commission 6 Stores and Over 1928	Census 4 Stores and Over 1929
Food	272	1,145	44,331	57,661
Drug	44	249	1,535	3,585
Tobacco	26	151	3,586	3,265
Variety	66	147	4,376	5,444
Clothing, furnishings, and accessories	139	669	2,114	6,900
Hats, caps, and millinery	42	204	1,264	3,754
Shoes	110	320	3,394	6,099
Department store and dry goods	58	202	2,088	3,904
General merchandise	20	312	247	2,661
Furniture	5	125	75	992
Musical instruments	8	66	104	663
Hardware	10	75	116	458
Total	800	3,665	63,230	95,386

Source: Federal Trade Commission's Report—Chain Stores—Scope of the Chain-Store Inquiry. Senate Document No. 31, 72nd Congress, 1st session. Page 33. U. S. Government Printing Office. Washington. 1932.

an organization having four or more units."[2] But the owner
of a "chain" of two units is more apt to consider himself
an independent operator, and to take sides with those who
are opposed to chain stores; that is, to favor legislation
aimed to regulate or destroy the chains.

Beckman also questions the use of the degree of centralized merchandising as a distinguishing characteristic
of chains, and in support of his argument he calls attention
to the Allied Stores Corporation as a chain of 34 department
stores in which the central office functions are limited to
the control of general policies, leaving the merchandise
management to the individual stores. He states further that
"voluntary chains are in reality not chains at all, because
the retailers who are members thereof preserve their individual ownership of the stores which they operate."[3] But
since the main consideration is not whether a particular
organization should be included in the count, but rather the
effects that the operations of that concern have had on
other business enterprises, the degree of centralized management appears to be an important characteristic. Moreover,
since anti-chain store legislation is aimed at those concerns with whom the independents have found it most difficult to compete, any definition should take into considera-

2. T. N. Beckman and H. C. Nolen, "The Chain Store Problem."
    p. 23. McGraw-Hill Book Company, Inc., New York. 1938.
    Also see Appendix A, Supplement to Chapter IV, for the
    census classifications.

3. Beckman and Nolen, op. cit., p. 23.

tion the extent to which the business operations of a concern would be affected by such legislation.

Ownership groups of department stores should also be classified as multiple-unit systems, even though they may not be so highly centralized as, for example, the variety stores. Moreover there is some degree of autonomy in the individual units of organizations that are always classified as chains. For example, in New York City there are two variety stores belonging to the same chain and located only a few blocks apart. One is in Harlem in the negro district; the other in the Spanish section. They do not stock the same goods, because the negroes are usually larger than the Spaniards, and have different ideas about the colors they like.

Beckman is right, of course, in his contention that a voluntary chain is not a "chain," if by "chain" he means what is defined here as an "orthodox chain." But voluntary chains can be identified as a part of the chain store movement, since they are one form of the multiple-unit system of distribution and contain the elements of integration and combination. Moreover recent developments in Colorado, which will be discussed in the chapter on chain store taxation, indicate that voluntary chains may be classed with orthodox chains by the courts and forced to pay taxes on the same basis.

The Census of Business for 1935 reports chain store organizations operating in nearly every business classification. The Federal Trade Commission in its inquiry excluded certain of the more highly specialized kinds of chains, such as gasoline filling stations, automobile accessories, and others, "because of the apparent intention of the inquiry."[4] But the Bureau of the Census included chain-store organizations of motor-vehicle dealers, lumber and building material, fuel and ice, liquor stores, tire and automobile accessories, electric appliances, jewelry, restaurants and cafeterias, dairy products, and filling stations.

There is, however, a very considerable variation in the growth of multiple-unit systems, both geographically and in these various types of businesses mentioned above. (See Tables III, IV, and V.) In the District of Columbia there are 234 chain store units to each 100,000 population, and only four times as many independent stores as chains. The next highest is Massachusetts with 170 chain stores per 100,000 persons and six times as many independents as chains. Mississippi is lowest in this listing with only 20 chains per 100,000 population and 35 times as many independently-owned stores as chain stores. The following tabulation shows the distribution based on the grouping of states commonly used by the Bureau of the Census:[5]

---

4. F.T.C. report, Senate Document No. 31, p. vii.

5. Based on 1930 population census and Census of Business, 1935.

Table III

Geographic Distribution of Chain Stores

Group	Population (1) (x)	Density per sq. mi. (2) (x)	Number of Independents (3) (y)	Number of Chains (4) (y)	No. Chains per 100,000 Population (5)	Ratio Independent to Chain (6)
New England	8,166,341	131.8	98,485	12,571	154	8
Maine	797,423	26.7	11,451	898	113	13
New Hampshire	465,293	51.5	6,401	593	126	11
Vermont	359,611	39.4	4,432	363	101	12
Massachusetts	4,249,614	528.6	46,899	7,239	170	6
Rhode Island	687,497	644.3	8,003	926	135	9
Connecticut	1,606,903	333.4	21,299	2,552	158	8
Middle Atlantic	26,260,750	262.6	352,202	34,318	131	10
New York	12,588,066	264.2	178,874	17,050	135	11
New Jersey	4,041,334	537.8	59,481	6,060	150	10
Pennsylvania	9,631,350	214.8	113,847	11,208	117	10
East North Central	25,297,185	103.0	301,877	28,696	113	10
Ohio	6,646,697	163.1	80,446	8,263	124	10
Indiana	3,238,503	89.8	38,142	3,241	100	12
Illinois	7,630,654	136.2	88,151	8,873	116	10
Michigan	4,842,325	84.2	54,711	5,600	117	10
Wisconsin	2,939,006	53.2	40,427	2,719	92	15

(x) Source: Statistical Abstract of the U. S. 1934, p. 3, 4.
(y) Source: Census of Business: 1935. Retail Distribution, Vol. IV.

Col. 5 = $\frac{\text{Col. 4}}{\text{Col. 1}}$ x 100,000   Col. 7 = $\frac{\text{Col. 3}}{\text{Col. 4}}$

Table IV

Distribution of Chains and Stores, According to Number of Stores per Chain on December 31, 1930.

(for 1,278 chains returning supplementary chain-store schedule)

Kind of Chain	Number of Stores in Chain															
	2 to 5		6 to 10		11 to 25		26 to 50		51-100		101-500		501 to 1,000		1,000 & Over	
	Chn	Str	Chn	Str	Chn	Str	Chn	Str	Chn	Str	Chn	Str	Chn	Str	Chn	Str
Grocery	25	79	19	145	15	247	11	434	8	610	16	3,250	6	4,788	1	1,382
Gro. & Meat	53	161	29	224	24	391	10	362	5	361	8	2,011	2	1,302	5	28,871
Meat	21	72	13	89	11	172	5	179	2	153	--	--	--	--	--	--
Confectionery	11	38	6	51	7	109	4	166	1	54	1	143	--	--	--	--
Drug	139	376	19	145	9	145	6	210	2	137	4	850	1	549	1	1,991
Tobacco	17	45	5	40	10	148	1	45	1	82	4	288	1	994	1	1,881
Var. ($1 limit)	25	67	16	122	8	119	7	261	5	401	7	1,739	1	678	--	--
Var. ($5 limit)	9	32	2	14	1	14	1	29	1	53	--	--	--	--	--	--
Var. (unlimited)	1	4	2	15	1	17	1	46	--	--	--	--	--	--	--	--
M. r'dy-to-wear	37	105	15	122	12	197	2	65	1	58	--	--	--	--	--	--
W. r'dy-to-wear	56	179	15	114	12	195	3	98	2	164	1	124	--	--	--	--
M. & W. R'dy-to-wear	21	63	16	131	6	109	4	155	3	180	--	--	--	--	--	--
M. furnishings	15	47	2	14	5	71	1	35	--	--	--	--	--	--	--	--
W. accessories	5	17	4	34	5	74	1	29	--	--	--	--	--	--	--	--
Hats and caps	6	18	2	19	1	19	4	136	3	166	1	117	--	--	--	--
Millinery	8	29	5	41	5	78	4	155	1	81	3	477	--	--	--	--
Men's shoes	4	12	2	15	1	22	1	44	3	224	1	117	--	--	--	--
W. shoes	14	53	5	40	3	52	4	156	1	51	1	115	--	--	--	--
Men's & women's shoes	53	173	28	220	21	347	7	271	4	346	4	939	--	--	--	--
Dry goods	12	34	--	--	1	15	1	34	--	--	--	--	--	--	--	--
Dry goods & apparel	48	157	17	124	7	118	5	210	--	--	--	--	--	--	1	1,452
Dept. store	13	50	4	27	3	58	2	61	--	--	1	347	1	560	--	--
Gen'l merchandise	22	70	7	54	3	58	--	--	--	--	--	--	--	--	--	--
Furniture	15	48	4	27	3	53	1	35	--	--	--	--	--	--	--	--
Musical instruments	7	26	4	25	3	55	--	--	--	--	--	--	--	--	--	--
Hardware	18	53	4	29	3	12	2	75	--	--	--	--	--	--	--	--
Totals	655	2008	245	1881	177	2895	88	3291	43	3121	49	10,517	12	8,871	9	35,577

From Report of Federal Trade Commission--Chain Stores-Scope of the Chain-Store Inquiry. Senate Document No. 31 72nd Congress, 1st session. Page 32. U. S. Government Printing Office. Washington. 1932.

(--) Dashes indicate none reported.

Table V

Comparison of Retail Sales Ratios by Types of Operation, 1935, 1933, and 1929

	Independents			Chains		
	1935	1933	1929	1935	1933	1929
All stores	73.1	71.3	77.5	22.8(1)	25.4	20.0
Grocery stores (without meats)	60.8	54.3	53.6	38.2	45.0	45.7
Combination stores (groceries and meats)	60.5	56.1	67.6	39.1	43.7	32.2
Beer and liquor stores (packaged)	48.0	x	x	1.8	x	x
Motor-vehicle dealers	95.6	94.6	x	4.4	5.3	x
Accessories-tire-battery dealers	50.0	x	x	50.0	x	x
Filling stations	77.8	64.3	66.0	21.5	35.5	33.8
Department stores	61.4	67.3	72.1	26.7	23.9	16.7
Variety stores	9.2	8.8	9.8	90.8	91.2	90.1
Man's clothing & furnishings stores	78.0	76.5	77.9	21.0	22.0	21.2
Family clothing stores	78.9	79.2	71.5	20.6	20.3	27.3
Women's ready-to-wear stores	72.3	74.5	74.3	25.2	23.3	22.7
Shoe stores	43.3	46.5	53.5	50.0	46.2	38.0
Furniture stores	86.0	84.6	83.9	13.5	14.2	14.2
Household appliance-radio stores	48.1	33.2	x	12.6	21.5	x
Radio dealers	75.6	82.7	79.0	23.1	15.6	19.1
Lumber & bldg. material dealers	75.6	x	x	23.8	x	x
Hardware stores & implement dealers	95.4	95.6	86.1	4.3	4.1	13.6
Restaurants and eating places	84.0	84.8	x	14.5	14.9	x
Drinking places	99.2	x	x	0.1	x	x
Cigar stores and cigar stands	61.1	65.1	73.5	35.8	33.9	25.1
Fuel and ice dealers	82.7	x	x	16.5	x	x
Drug stores with fountain	71.1	74.0	81.2	28.8	25.1	18.5
Drug stores without fountain	84.1	x	x	15.4	x	x
Hay, grain and feed stores	71.6	x	x	16.0	x	x
Farm and garden supply stores	75.0	x	x	4.7	x	x
Jewelry stores	90.3	93.6	93.0	8.9	5.9	6.4
All other stores	78.8	79.6	x	14.3	15.0	x

Source: Census of Business: 1935. Retail Distribution, Volume IV. Types of Operation. Page 9.
United States Department of Commerce. Bureau of the Census. January, 1937.

(x) No true comparisons available.
(1) Remaining amount of the total (4.1% in this case) goes to "other types" of stores.

26

Group	Number of Chains per 100,000 Population	Ratio of Independents to Chains
New England	154	8
Pacific	144	11
Middle Atlantic	131	10
East North Central	113	10
West North Central	96	14
Mountain	79	15
South Atlantic	76	14
West South Central	64	17
East South Central	48	18

The Federal Trade Commission received reports concerning the geographic distribution from 1,712 chain-store companies operating 62,810 stores on December 31, 1928.[6] "Approximately two-thirds of all chain stores reported in each of the six years are located in the three contiguous and populous divisions of the extreme North and East --- New England, Middle Atlantic, and East North Central -- although from 1919 to 1928 the aggregate proportion of stores reported therein is gradually diminishing."[7] "Approximately fifty per cent of the total stores reported for each year of the series are concentrated in five states --- New York, Pennsylvania, Ohio, Illinois, and Massachusetts --- and an additional twenty-five per cent in New Jersey, California, Michigan, Indiana, and Missouri. These are the ten leading

---

6. Chain Stores. State Distribution of Chain Stores, 1913-1928. Federal Trade Commission. Senate Document 130, 73rd Congress, 2nd session, p. ix. United States Government Printing Office, Washington, D. C. 1934.

7. Ibid., p. ix.

states."[8] The "six years" are 1913, 1916, 1919, 1922, 1925, and 1928.

The history of the development of chain stores shows clearly a correlation between the number of chain-store units and the density of population.[9] Beckman found this correlation when he analyzed the statistics compiled for the Census of American Business, 1933, and the Census of Business, 1935.[10] Moreover, both his analysis and the findings of the Federal Trade Commission seem to establish beyond question the fact that "the chain store is still essentially an urban institution."[11]

Although chain-store organizations are found operating in almost every kind of business, they are much more important in some lines than in others. The Federal Trade Commission found Ohio to be the only state in which all of the 26 types of chains reporting were operating.[12] Beckman advances

---

8. Ibid., p. x.

9. "Among the many factors determining the concentration of chain stores within various states, undoubtedly that of a numerically large population is fundamental, owing to the large potential market it affords. Related factors include density of population as well as the comparative proportion of urban dwellers included in the population." F. T. C. report S.D. 130, p. xi.

10. Theodore N. Beckman and Herman C. Nolen, The Chain Store Problem, p. 36 ff. New York: McGraw-Hill Book Company, 1938.

11. Beckman, Ibid., p. 38.
"Close correlation is indicated between the distribution of chain stores among the states, urban population, and personal income-tax returns." Federal Trade Commission report No. 130, p. xi.

12. Federal Trade Commission Report No. 130, op. cit., p. xi.

the following conclusion:[13]

A correct measurement of the significance
of chain stores cannot be obtained by dealing
in totals. The analysis must be made by lines
of retail trade in which chains actually operate. It seems that chain stores prefer to concentrate in a few kinds of retailing where operations can be fairly standardized. In those
lines of business in which they concentrate, the
proportion of business attracted by chains runs
very high and results in keen competition with
independents. In some of those fields, notably
the variety store business, they have attained a
virtual monopoly.

Dr. Beckman compiled from the Census of Business for 1935

the following national averages of chain sales ratios for

five lines of businesses in cities of more than 500,000

population:[14]

Grocery Stores	Drug Stores	Shoes	Filling Stations	Variety Stores
38.83	25.7	50.0	21.5	90.8

These figures show clearly the variation in importance of

chains in the marketing of different kinds of commodities,

which raises the question as to whether or not the degree

of vertical integration in any particular line of business

is affected by the type of product sold. This question

will be discussed in Chapter VI, in connection with the re-

lation of large-scale merchandising to manufacturing.

Size of Multiple-Units Systems

A very important consideration as a major development

---

13. Beckman, op. cit., p. 40.

14. Ibid., p. 39. See Appendix A, Supplement to Chapter IV.

in large-scale retailing is the tremendous size of some
chain store organizations. One grocery chain, the Great
Atlantic and Pacific Tea Company, was reported as having
more than 17,000 stores in operation at the beginning of
1930. Another chain, the Kroger Grocery and Baking Company,
had in addition to more than 5,260 retail outlets with
$207,000,000 sales for 1928, ten bread and cake bakeries,
three meat packing plants, four dairies, four coffee roast-
ing plants, one sausage plant, and a general plant for
packing candies, spices, teas, coffees, and extracts.[15]
Statistics on other chains are given in the tables in
Appendix B.

The effects on our methods of distribution of organizations as large as these, which can market quickly huge crops
of agricultural products or the entire output of large manufacturing plants, will be discussed in chapters to follow.
In the next chapter the bases for comparing multiple-unit
with single-unit systems will be outlined.

---

15. The Magazine of Wall Street. June 1, 1929, p. 230 ff.

Chapter V

THE ELEMENTS OF THE CHAIN STORE CONTROVERSY

It is a trait of human nature for men, either as individuals or in groups, to first determine what is advantageous to their own interests, and then seek to control
or dominate the social body, so that they may obtain the
desired advantages. When taking such action, they are
governed by their own habits of thought and by the conven-
tions of society. But they must have the approval of the
public, and therefore they must appear to have the public's
interest at heart. In any controversy, however, in order
to clearly mark the contestants it is necessary to know or
at least be able to judge the desires that motivate their
actions.

Those who favor the chain-store system of distribution
are naturally the chain-store organizations, manufacturers
with their own retail outlets, large agricultural producers'
cooperatives, manufacturers who sell chiefly to the large
retail organizations, newspapers and advertising agencies
who profit from the chains' advertising, and others who
benefit from the business operations of the chains.

The strongest opposition to the chain-store movement
comes from the independent wholesalers. Aligned with them
are the independent retailers who are unable to meet chain-
store competition successfully (this does not include all

independent merchants); owners of real estate whose rentals
have been adversely affected; brokers whose services are no
longer needed because of the shortening of market channels;
business men located in towns that are losing business to
nearby cities where chain-stores are operating; and others,
not identified by groups, who for various reasons have become antagonistic to the chains.

The consumer is affected by this controversy, not only
because costs of distribution are a considerable part of
the prices he pays for goods, but also because both sides
have actively enlisted his support and their appeals have
influenced his thinking and his judgments. Often he has
been lead to take sides, and to give aid to those who favor
or oppose anti-chain store legislation.

It is interesting to note that the same charges are
being made against the chains today which were made ten
years ago.[1] None of the many investigations seem to have

---

1. The following summary of these charges appears in a
   1929 publication:

   "The principal charges that have been leveled against
   the chains are the following:

   (1) They take money out of the local community, and
       thus tend to bring about its impoverishment.
   (2) They drive out of business local retailers who
       are desirable citizens, and whose interests
       should be protected.
   (3) They destroy the flavor of local community life
       by their policies of standardization, and tend to
       'depersonalize' the community.
   (4) They concentrate ownership in the hands of a few
       absentees, as a consequence destroying opportunities
       for young men.

settled the issues even though they have to a considerable
extent replaced conjecture with factual evidence. The
arguments and contentions as presented are classified according to the social and economic groups which they concern. This classification will help to identify these
groups.

Arguments Concerning the Manufacturer

Those opposed to the chain store organizations charge
them with invading the manufacturers' field, either by
setting up their own factories or by following practices
which tend to force the manufacturer to operate under conditions dictated by the chains. These practices include

---

1. (continued)

"(5) They are tending to produce a 'nation of clerks'
       as a result of centralizing control at the home
       office.
(6)   They pay low wages.
(7)   They do not bear their full share of the local
       tax loads.
(8)   They practice unfair competition in order to
       destroy the independent merchant.
(9)   They tend toward monopoly, and, if allowed to
       develop, will be able to control prices.
(10) They disorganize distribution, forcing readjust-
       ments all along the line, thus raising the costs
       of marketing.
(11) They exert undue influence in buying, thus com-
       pelling manufacturers frequently to sell at less
       than cost.
(12) They do not save money for the consumer, the
       popular impression that their prices are lower
       than those of the independent being a result of
       the use of 'leaders' and not based upon actual
       fact."

James L. Palmer, "Economic and Social Aspects of Chain
Stores." Journal of Business, Volume II, 1929.
Page 276. The University of Chicago Press, Chicago,
Illinois.

driving hard bargains and obtaining prices which permit the
manufacturer little or no profit; forcing him to assume
functions which properly belong to the distributor, such as
warehousing, grading, shipping, delivery, and advertising;
requiring that the manufacturer put the chain's private
labels on his own products, thereby taking away the intangible value of his good will and reputation, and substituting
that of the chain store; demanding advertising allowances,
special discounts and other unfair concessions; refusing to
assume any of the risks of marketing new products, and selling only standardized merchandise; and dictating to the
manufacturer what he shall produce.

The chain-store organizations answer those charges with
the statement that they are illogical and unfounded. The
chains say it would be folly to destroy the sources of the
merchandise which they must have if they are to stay in
business; that it is only fair to expect the manufacturer
to bear some of the cost of the tremendous volume of advertising which the chains can offer; that their huge buying
volume permits manufacturing economies which they should
share; that lower prices move masses of goods which could
not be sold at higher prices; that the chains give valuable
assistance to the manufacturers, not only by their prompt
payment of bills with elimination of credit losses and
collection costs, but also by sending their buyers to deal
directly with the manufacturers, thus making their selling
costs negligible.

Arguments Concerning the Independent Wholesaler and Retailer

It is to be expected that the chief competitors of the chains would be their most bitter critics. This group charges that the chains are driving toward a monopolistic position, and are threatening the independent merchant's existence with unfair competitive practices, such as selling at prices below cost in one locality to eliminate competition while making up their losses with higher prices in other localities; making secret agreements with manufacturers to supply goods at lower prices than the independent wholesaler can obtain, and selling in retail stores at prices lower than the independent retailer can buy from the wholesaler; using the standard, nationally advertised brands for loss leaders while selling their own brands of inferior quality or, at least, of lower cost at higher prices; forcing the independent dealer to assume the risks of introducing new products, and at the same time robbing him of his market for standard merchandise; and undermining the reputation and good will of the independent dealer by subjecting him to the suspicion of the public because of his apparently higher prices.

The chain store organizations answer these charges with counter-charges. They say the independent dealers, both wholesale and retail, have long been using antiquated and inefficient methods of merchandising; that their margins of profit are much higher than their expenses warrant; that the chains have few if any advantages either in buying or

in operating which the independent dealers cannot have if
the latter will adopt modern methods of merchandising; that
records show the high mortality rate among independent
dealers to be due to incompetency rather than to unfair
competition, and that this rate is no higher now than it
was before the attacks on chain stores began; and that independent dealers who are using modern business methods
are meeting the competition of the chains successfully.

Arguments Concerning the Consumer

When considering the arguments directed to the consumer
by these opposing groups, it should be borne in mind that
this controversy is really a fight to control the market
which the consumer represents. This struggle is of long
standing, and pervades our entire economic system, both
national and international. Its characteristics and motives
are the same as the price-cutting tactics of two competing
dealers in the same city block, or of two warring nations.
The importance of such struggles is proportionate to the
size of the groups engaged in them, since this determines
the number of individuals affected.

Those opposed to the chains charge that the latter are
deluding the public with their claims of lower prices; that
they lure customers into their stores with below-cost prices
on standard articles, and then short-weight and short-change
the customer; sell from canned packs that are two or three
years old; sell smaller-sized cans and packages than the in-

dependent dealers; use tricks with adding machines to trap
the customers into overpayments; advertise for one price
and sell for another; give no credit or delivery services
and no personal attention to the customer's needs; and try
in every way to regiment and standardize the public's tastes
and desires.

The chain store organizations contend that their claims
to lower prices have been substantiated by every price
survey that has been made. They deny the charge of short-
weighting and short-changing, and not only point to their
policy of instantly dismissing any employee found guilty of
such practices, but retaliate by calling attention to the
need of city inspectors to prevent the independent dealers
from cheating the public. They frankly admit to having
some smaller-sized packages in stock, but explain this by
saying that when prices advance it is the practice of many
manufacturers to reduce the size of the package rather than
increase the price, and that having these smaller sizes in
stock is prima facie evidence that their goods are fresher.
The chains also claim that their lower prices are due mainly to a reduction in overhead costs obtained by the elimination of expensive services which a large portion of the
public does not demand, and that those dealers who supply
these services are serving an entirely different market
from that to which the chains cater.

Arguments Concerning the Community as a Whole

　　1. Problems of Taxation. The chain-stores are accused

of evading their share of the local tax load. It is said
that they do not own their locations and therefore pay no
tax on real estate; that they deliberately reduce their inventories to a minimum during the periods when assessments
are made; and that their tax payments in no way represent
the true value of the government protection they receive in
relation to the amount of business they do.

The chains answer this charge with the claim that they
not only pay higher taxes on real estate because of their
higher rent schedules, but that they also pay many more
direct taxes and in larger amounts than do the individual
independent stores. An officer of a chain store association
makes this statement:

"A few of the taxes now paid by chain stores include
state and municipal license, occupational, excise, and sales
taxes; real estate and improvement taxes; personal property
taxes; corporation income taxes; capital stock taxes; excess
profit taxes; corporation franchise taxes; and unemployment
and old age pension taxes."[2]

2. Problems of Civic Development. It is charged that
the chains take no responsibility for the welfare of the
community; that they contribute to local enterprises only
when forced to do so by public opinion; that they come into
a community when it is prosperous and take the cream of the

---

2. John P. Nichols, Chain Store Manual, 1936 edition,
   page 93. Published by Institute of Distribution, Inc.,
   New York.

business away from the local merchants, but that when hard times come, they close up their stores and leave.

The chains' answer to this is that "the first and most important service of any business to its community is efficient performance, elimination of waste and direct aid in making consumers' dollars go farther."[3] They say that many so-called community enterprises are really promoted by some individual who is seeking a profit for himself, and that opposition to such schemes is in the interests of the community; and that the chain store manager is in a much better position to offer this opposition than the local merchants, who are afraid of the criticisms of their neighbors.

The chains contend that the presence of a chain store in a rural community attracts trade and lessens the amount of business lost to competing cities, and also reduces the trend toward concentration of population in urban centers. They deny the charge that chain store managers do not share in the community life, and present figures showing that these managers take a very active part in civic affairs.

3. Problems of Community Leadership. Opponents of chain stores contend that the very nature of the chain store organization inhibits the development of those qualities of leadership which are so essential to the success of community enterprises; that even the manager of a chain store unit is merely a glorified clerk; and that employees of concerns with

---

3. Nichols, op. cit., p. 89.

a highly centralized management are moulded into a sort of standardized human being who is unable to act on his own initiative.

The chains' answer is that standardization of goods and methods of procedure does not connote standardization of human beings; that the former is simply the application of scientific knowledge to practice; that leadership qualities are just as important in a large organization as in a small one; and that when present in an individual they are bound to show up regardless of the situation in which he is placed. They assert that just as many leaders are found among chain store managers as among independent merchants.

4. <u>Problems Relating to Opportunity for Individual Development</u>. The arguments listed in this section are close-ly related to those concerning community leadership. Oppo-nents of the chain stores contend that the employees of the chains are not hired because of their intelligence, but be-cause they are the type that is willing to obey orders blindly; that the chains pay their employees low wages and work them long hours; that the practice of forcing the manager to make up stock shortages for which he is not responsible encourages dishonesty; and, in general, that the chains stifle individual initiative and destroy the opportunities for individual development.

The chains deny these charges categorically. They claim that the wages they pay are not determined by them, but by the market price of labor; that their employees not

only have unusual opportunities for training in merchandising, but also have chances for promotion to positions that
pay higher salaries and are more permanent than positions
with independent owners, and offer greater security than
independent ownership. They contend that their systems of
stock control are merely a part of their modern methods of
merchandising, and that the store managers are simply required to be better merchants because of them.

     5. <u>Problems Relating to Public Welfare</u>. Many of the
arguments already given can be repeated in this section,
since society is made up of individuals, and is affected in
the mass as its members are affected singly. In brief, the
American public is urgently warned by the enemies of chain
stores to be suspicious of big business in any form, because of the danger of misuse of power. This attitude is
well illustrated in the following statement:

    "Even when chains lend the original producer a hand --
as in recent campaigns to stimulate consumer-buying of over-
produced crops -- the ease with which they combine forces
and the tremendous pressure they put on the market are
ominous. If they can get together so readily to do one
kind of job, heaven help us when they decide clandestinely
to get together for another kind of job."[4]

    The chains say that such statements are merely attempts
to create an unfounded fear in the minds of the public; that

---

4. "Pro and Con. Shall We Curb the Chain Store," <u>Reader's
Digest</u>, December, 1938, p. 85. See Appendix A, Supplement to Chapter V.

the chain-store movement is only one phase in the great process of nationalizing the business of the United States, a process which is being brought about by forces which were set in motion when the states were prohibited by the Constitution from setting up tariff barriers against the products of other states; that a national distributing system is necessary for our nationalized systems of production, transportation, and communication. They contend that the growth of the chain-store system of distribution is a part of an economic revolution, similar to the Industrial Revolution.

The arguments for and against the chain-stores suggest some of the many problems found in distribution, using the term "distribution" to include all marketing processes.[5] Some of these problems can be solved by the application of engineering principles, but goods will not be purchased unless there are people who are ready, willing, and able to buy. Thus there is another set of problems, which have to do with the division of the social income. A comparison of the chain-store system of merchandising with the manufacturer to wholesaler-to retailer system must consider not only physical facilities, but also relative efficiencies

---

5. Ralph Borsodi, The Distribution Age, p. 19. New York: D. Appleton and Company, 1927.
"There are two uses of the word "distribution, . . . first, the use of the word to describe physical distribution such as transportation and storage; second, the use of the word distribution to describe what is better termed marketing. . . There is a third use of the term -- the special and technical sense in which it is used in pure economic science -- which might be called income distribution."

measured in terms of volumes, varieties, and prices of products made available to the consuming public. The chapters to follow will treat of these considerations.

Chapter VI

THE CHAIN STORE AND THE PRODUCER

Webster's Dictionary defines a "producer" as "one who produces or manufactures articles of consumption." The term is used in that sense in this chapter, and includes both the producer of agricultural products and of manufactured goods.

The Chain Store and the Farmer

At the present time there is little if any controversy between the large food chains and the agricultural producers' cooperatives. These two groups are working closely together, because they have found a common bond in the need of the chains for a dependable source of farm products in large amounts, and the need of the producers for a highly organized system of distribution extending over the entire nation.

Chain stores have been buying foods in large amounts from producers' cooperatives for many years. But only recently this local or sectional production-distribution relationship has become national in its scope through an agreement between two organizations representing the food chains and the farmers' cooperatives.

The National Association of Food Chains is composed of corporations owning 37,000 chain stores which serve 30,000,000 consumers. The National Cooperative Council is said to represent 1,500,000 farmers. In 1936 these two groups met and

agreed on a marketing plan which, it is claimed, "has
materially benefitted agriculture, has been a real cooperative movement looking to the improved economic situation of
a large segment of our farm population," . . . the success
of which "has not been achieved at the expense of the consumer or any other group."[1]

There are other evidences of a cordial relationship
existing between organizations of agricultural producers
and the chain stores. In a meeting at Indianapolis in 1938,
the Indiana Canners' Association passed the following resolutions:

> BE IT RESOLVED That the Indiana Canners' Associa-
> tion go on record as being opposed to any legisla-
> tion which is obviously written, not for the pur-
> pose of taxation for revenue only, but apparently
> for the purpose of discriminating against, or
> destroying, the business or industry so indicated
> in such legislation as may be introduced either
> by the state or nationally, and that copies of
> this resolution be forwarded to the governor and
> to all members of the legislature of the State of
> Indiana and to all members of the House and Senate
> of the United States from Indiana.

The same attitude was expressed in a resolution passed
by the American Farm Bureau Federation at its meeting in New
Orleans in December, 1938:

> We condemn discriminatory and punitive taxes
> of all types designed to favor or penalize a se-
> lected group. The enactment of such legislation
> results in further efforts by other groups to ob-

---

1. Practical Farm Relief - One Year of Cooperative Progress,
    p. 1. Published by National Association of Food Chains.
    Washington, D.C. April, 1937. See Appendix A, Supple-
    ment to Chapter VI, for examples of sales campaigns con-
    ducted under this cooperative plan.

tain special privileges. Such unnecessary taxes and restrictions have a damaging effect by increasing costs of distribution, increasing costs to consumer, reducing total consumption and limiting production in agriculture as well as industry. We oppose all such tax proposals.

According to a pamphlet just issued by Carl Byoir and Associates,[2] public relations counsel for The Great Atlantic and Pacific Tea Company, resolutions opposing punitive chain store taxes have been passed by the following organizations:

National Canners' Association
National Grange
Farmers' Educational and Cooperative Union of America
National Wool Growers' Association
National Creamery Buttermakers' Association
Georgia Association of Peach Growers
Georgia Association of Vegetable Growers
Idaho State Dairymen's Association
Hudson Cooperative Dairy Association (Iowa)
Massachusetts Fruit Growers' Association
Upper Peninsula of Michigan Milk Producers
Minnesota Association of Local Creameries
New York State Horticultural Society
Pennsylvania Horticultural Society
Pennsylvania Potato Growers' Association
South Carolina Peach Growers' Association
Virginia Horticultural Society
Oklahoma State Grange
Nebraska Farm Bureau Federation
Montana State Farm Bureau
Washington Cooperative Council
Washington State Farm Bureau Federation
West Virginia Horticultural Society
Wisconsin Buttermakers' Association
Nebraska Farm Bureau Federation
Arkansas State Grange
Colorado Wool Growers' Association
Eastern Connecticut Poultry Producers, Inc.
Idaho Creamery Operators' Association

One of the most important phases in the cooperative marketing of agricultural products is the system of pooling

---

2. Current Trends in Chain Store Taxation, p. 17, 18. Published by Carl Byoir and Associates, Inc., New York City.

shipments.[3] This system is necessary because of the inherent difficulties in the handling and marketing of a large
number of small lots of produce as separate units. But
car-lot shipments, particularly of perishable products, require an immediate outlet to the market, and the multiple-
unit system of distribution meets this need. On the other
hand, the demand of the food chains for farm products in
large volumes has had a stimulating effect on the growth of
producers' cooperatives. Thus one development supports the
other, and as long as this relationship continues it is to
be expected that the agricultural groups will remain friendly to the chain store organizations.

<u>The Chain Store and the Manufacturer</u>

It is doubtful if there is any real conflict between
the chain store organizations as one group and the manufacturers as another. While in a considerable number of lines
the development of the chain stores disrupted the existing
patterns of distribution, many manufacturers have become

---

3. Henry H. Bakken and Marvin A. Schaars, <u>The Economics of
    Marketing</u>, first edition, p. 430, 432. New York:
    McGraw-Hill Book Company, inc., 1937.
    "Pooling is a distinctive cooperative practice, so much
    so in fact that the term is incorrectly applied by some
    to any form of cooperative marketing."
    "Pooling involves (1) the physical mingling of the prod-
    ucts, (2) lumping together of the sales returns and ap-
    portioning the net returns among those who contributed
    products to the pool, and (3) combining the expenses of
    operations, both direct and overhead expenses. Products,
    sales receipts, and expenses are pooled before patrons
    receive their individual shares of the net returns.
    Pooling is an averaging process."

completely adjusted to the changes which have occurred.
Nevertheless certain charges have been made against the
chains which involve the manufacturers and cause them to
appear to be aligned with those groups which make these
charges.[4]

Are the chain store organizations invading the manufacturers' field? The report of the Federal Trade Commission states that "purchase from manufacturers is by far the
most important source of chain store merchandise, accounting for approximately 70 per cent of the aggregate supply
of all chains".[5] This indicates that chain stores supply
the outlets for a tremendous volume of manufactured goods
which they purchase from other concerns rather than produce
themselves. Nevertheless, since many chain store organizations do engage in manufacturing, and since this discussion
is concerned with the extent of integration and combination
in retailing, an examination of the fields in which vertical
integration is found should be relevant.

Does integration in the large-scale retailing organizations follow any definite pattern? Some chains do not manufacture at all; others make almost all the goods they sell.
"Confectionery are for the most part of the completely integrated type, while in wearing apparel lines manufacturing

---

4. See Chapter V, p. 33.

5. Chain Stores - Sources of Chain Store Merchandise.
    Federal Trade Commission. Senate Document No. 30, 73rd
    Congress, 1st session, p. viii. U.S. Government Printing
    Office, Washington, 1932. See Appendix A, Supplement to
    Chapter VI.

appears to be a more important activity than retailing for
a considerable number of the manufacturing chains."[6] "Information received from drug chains reveals no instance in
which the integration of manufacturing and retailing has
developed primarily from the manufacturing side. Drug
chains began and apparently have remained primarily retail
organizations." "The manufacturing activity of food chains
is distinctly subordinate to retailing." "Commodities most
frequently reported as manufactured, processed, or packed
by the food chains are bread and other bakery products,
coffee, tea, various kinds of packaged dry groceries, mayon-
naise, dried and smoked meats, and flavoring extracts."
"All of the department store and dry goods and apparel
chains furnishing detailed information are engaged primarily
in retailing. Among the variety chains only 3 out of 71 do
any manufacturing whatever, and only one of the larger
chains in this field manufactures any of its merchandise."
"No manufacturing was reported by any of the $5 - limit
variety, men's furnishings, dry goods, general merchandise,
or hardware chains." "The largest numbers of manufacturing chains are found in drugs, confectionery, men's ready-
to-wear, men's and women's shoes, grocery and meat, and
grocery."

---

6. All of the quotations in this paragraph are taken from
    the Federal Trade Commission's report. Chain Stores.
    Chain Store Manufacturing. Senate Document No. 13,
    73rd Congress, 1st session, p. x, U. S. Government
    Printing Office, Washington, D. C. 1933.

In its report on Chain-Store Manufacturing, the Federal Trade Commission classified the "reasons for and advantages of manufacturing as stated by 76 chains" under the
following heads:[7]

> Higher quality and control of quality
> Exclusive sale of the brand, goodwill
> Lower cost, elimination of middleman
> Lower retail prices
> Better value to customer (quality and price)
> Larger profit
> Control of supply, more rapid turnover
> Manufacturers' quality uncertain, prices unsatisfactory
> Control prices, avoid the cut-throat competition of
>   national brands
> Historical reasons
> Special product, cannot be purchased
> No advantages
> Miscellaneous statements not elsewhere classified

A study of these various reasons given by the chains
for engaging in manufacturing does disclose some definite
patterns of integration. One is found in those retail businesses handling a product that is highly perishable. For
example, the report from the Mary Lee confectionery of over
50 stores contained the following statement:[8]

> We sell through our own retail stores be-
> cause our product is perishable and other deal-
> ers do not handle it in such a way that it
> reaches the public in a fresh condition.

Similar statements were received from the Fanny Farmer confectionery chain of almost 150 stores, and from smaller
chains; also from a number of food chains, both large and
small.

---

7. Federal Trade Commission report No. 13, op. cit., p. 42.
8. Ibid., p. 45.

Another pattern is identified where some reason exists for a very close control of the quality of the merchandise. Chains dealing in specialty lines, particularly wearing apparel, frequently integrate their manufacturing and retailing operations. The following statement to the Federal Trade Commission by a shoe chain illustrates this situation:[9]

> Our principal reason and advantage for manufacturing shoes for ourselves is that we are certain to continually keep the standard of construction that we desire. Too often manufacturers who have not the 100 percent interest of the retailer at heart will deviate even if only slightly from the standard if necessity compels them to.

Included in this group are chains selling men's shoes, men's ready-to-wear clothing, women's shoes, men's and women's shoes, and women's accessories. The Federal Trade Commission found that chains of this type manufactured more than 74 per cent of the merchandise sold in their stores.[10]

Sometimes integration occurs as the result of an historical accident. The spirit of enterprise may have led a manufacturer to venture into the field of merchandising; or a merchant may have been offered the opportunity of obtaining a controlling interest in a factory which had been supplying him with its products; may have even been forced to buy it to keep it going. An illustration is the Regal Shoe Company, "which originated as a special type of re-

---

9. Federal Trade Commission report No. 13, *op. cit.*,
   p. 45.

10. *Ibid.*, p. 25.

tailer, became a regular retail company, developed into a
chain, combined with the manufacturing company which had
been its chief source of supply, and more recently discon-
tinued its sale to outside dealers and became a fully integrated organization."[11]   "Out of 25 shoe chains that
give information throwing light on the manufacturing-retail-
ing relationship 16 can be described as engaged primarily
in manufacturing if the classification be based upon the
historical development of their combined activity in the
two fields as well as upon their present practice."[12]   Such
a type is the shoe chain of I. Miller and Sons, Inc., which
developed from a business engaged solely in the manufacture
of theatrical shoes, but which sells less than half of its
total output through its own stores.[13]   Or the manufacturing
and retailing may "have been developed as complementary
factors with primary importance attached to neither one,"[14]
as in the case of the Richman Brothers Company, which has
been engaged in manufacturing and retailing men's clothing
for more than 25 years. Another case in point is that of
The Great Atlantic and Pacific Tea Company, which found that
its sources of private-brand merchandise were closed by the
withdrawal of manufacturers from that business when their

---

11. Federal Trade Commission report No. 13, op. cit., p. 9.

12. Ibid., p. 7.

13. Ibid., p. 8.

14. Ibid., p. 9.

own nationally advertised brands became better known.[15]
This case is also significant to the discussion below of
manufacturers' brands versus chain-store brands. Other
reasons given by companies interested primarily in manufacturing for operating their own retail stores were:

> Next to impossible to get any representa-
> tion in the large trade centers without putting
> in our own retail outlets.[16]

> The indirect advertising benefits due to the
> operation of exclusive shops under our trade name,
> the promotional work in the introduction of new
> style features, and the direction of manufactur-
> ing policies through the intimate contact with
> the reaction of the consumer, we have found to
> be of material benefit to us as manufacturers.[17]

> Stores were opened in New York City for the
> purpose of creating an outlet for some of the
> excess manufacturing capacity, and to establish
> ourselves in the New York market where we had no
> large outlet.[18]

"The reasons most frequently expressed by drug chains
for their manufacturing operations are those that have to
do with lower costs and higher profits, with control of the
quality of their products, and with the good will or repeat
order value that attaches to goods sold under their private
brands."[19] To illustrate, the Walgreen Company stated

---

15. Federal Trade Commission report No. 13, op. cit.,
    p. 51.

16. Ibid., p. 54.

17. Ibid., p. 54.

18. Ibid., p. 55.

19. Ibid., p. 45.

that:[20]

> The principal reason and advantage of en-
> gaging in the manufacture of commodities sold
> in our stores is that it does away with the
> usual manufacturer's selling cost, including
> national advertising and it permits us to put
> quality items in the hands of our retail cus-
> tomers at a comparatively low price.

"The close relationship of private brands to manufac-

turing among chains is indicated by these replies."[21] "The

benefits attaching to the control of private brands are

named by 18 chains as an advantage of manufacturing."[22]

"Approximately 80 percent of the manufacturing chains re-

port that they own private brands, while only 20 percent of

the non-manufacturing chains own such brands."[23] "The aver-

age mark-up on manufactured private brands is greater than

that on competing standard brands in each of the 20 commod-

ity classifications included."[24]

Here is one important cause of conflict between chain

stores and manufacturers of nationally-advertised brands.

It is not essentially a conflict between groups, because

many manufacturers have found it advantageous to manufacture

for the chains, and the latter have often found it to their

advantage to buy from independent sources. Reasons given

---

20. Federal Trade Commission report No. 13, op. cit.,
     p. 46.

21. Ibid., p. 42.

22. Ibid., p. 43.

23. Ibid., p. xi.

24. Ibid., p. xiii.

by the chains for handling privately-branded merchandise
include the ability to give the consumer better values,
higher profits obtainable, lower purchase costs, lower
costs of distribution, better quality, and the ability of
the chain to control, standardize, and improve this quality;
also the benefits received from advertising, the creation
and promotion of good will, and the development of repeat
business.[25] The report of the Federal Trade Commission
substantiates the following conclusions:

1. Chain store organizations are not at all
   unanimous in their advocacy of private
   brands. Many prefer to sell the nationally-advertised brands, rather than to
   expend the extra advertising and selling
   effort necessary to overcome consumer
   resistance to private brands.

2. The quality of privately-branded goods
   compared favorably with the nationally-
   advertised brands.

3. The larger the chain, the more certain it
   is to have its own private brands.

4. Private-brand business is more important
   in some lines, particularly in confection-
   ary and men's shoes, than in others.

5. The proportion of sales of private brands
   to total sales is increasing.

6. There is no significant difference in the
   mark-up of private and standard brands as
   sold by many chains, but this conclusion
   cannot be generalized to apply to all
   chains. But private brands are generally
   priced lower than standard brands chiefly
   because of lower cost to the retailing organization.

---

25. Chain Stores. Chain-Store Private Brands. Federal
    Trade Commission. Senate Document No. 142, 72nd Con-
    gress, 2nd session, p. xiii. U. S. Government Print-
    ing Office, Washington, D. C. 1933.

Factors causing conditions unfavorable to integration of manufacturing and merchandising are clearly indicated in the report of the Federal Trade Commission. These are listed below, with accompanying illustrative statements:

1. Where a large investment in fixed assets is required.

Statement of the United Cigar Stores Company of America:[26]

> One of the principal reasons for not manufacturing has been the necessity for a large investment in fixed assets; another is the ability to buy trade-marked items at prices sufficiently advantageous to yield a small profit, which, coupled with the manufacturer's advertising, obtain rapid turnover.

2. Where diversification is necessary to meet the varying demands of the trade.

Statement of a chain selling men's and women's shoes in over 150 units:[27]

> Because we carry a general line of shoes for the entire family, including men's, women's, children's felts and rubbers, etc., it would require a special factory for each of the types of shoes we sell. As it is, we are able to place our orders in anticipation for various seasons and help to operate the factories which sell us at a time when they can do so to the mutual benefit of both themselves and ourselves by keeping their overhead down during their slack season.

3. Where an additional risk due to price changes must be assumed which is out of proportion to the profits obtain-

---

26. Federal Trade Commission report No. 13, *op. cit.*, p. 66.

27. *Ibid.*, p. 63.

able.

Statement of a large millinery chain, operating more
than 100 stores at the close of 1930:[28]

> We find that under the present conditions
> and present prices, we are better off to buy
> merchandise for our own consumption rather
> than try to manufacture and compete with the
> present market conditions.

4. Where the sales volume of an article is too small
to make manufacturing profitable. This suggests a fundamental difference between large and small chains, that is,
the significance of size as a factor affecting the extent
of integration between manufacturing and retailing.[29]

Statement by a dry goods and apparel chain with nearly
50 stores:[30]

> The disadvantages (of manufacturing) are
> that we have to sometimes manufacture goods we
> really do not need in order to keep the plant
> in operation.

5. Where the interests of the officials lie almost
entirely in one field, manufacturing or retailing.

Statement in the report submitted by the Woolworth

---

28. Federal Trade Commission report, No. 13, op. cit.,
p. 59.

29. Ibid., p. 81. "While the manufacturing chains comprise
only 15 percent of the total number, they operate 60
percent of the stores and make 57.9 percent of the
sales of all reporting chains. In other words they are
approximately four times as large as all chains combined in point of average number of stores operated
per chain, and only a little short of that in point of
average sales per chain."

30. Ibid., p. 61.

Company:[31]

> We have not nor do we consider engaging
> in the manufacture of any commodity which we
> sell in our stores, the principal reason being
> that this was adopted as one of our earliest
> policies by Mr. Woolworth. It was always his
> contention that he preferred to go into the
> open market to buy goods rather than manufac-
> ture them.

The Federal Trade Commission found that whereas variety

chains have almost a monopoly in that line of business,

they engage in manufacturing to a very limited extent.[32]

The difficulty of trying to do two essentially differ-

ent things was pointed out in the statement by an official

of another variety chain:[33]

> Manufacturing requires an entirely differ-
> ent line of thought than distribution. I worked
> in manufacturing fields for five years before I
> came into the distribution field, and know the
> men there think in different terms than we do.
> They think in terms of hours and costs of materi-
> al. We do not primarily think in terms of hours,
> costs of material, and so on, but in terms of
> customer demand and sales. These statements are
> not intended to indicate that in other lines of
> merchandising it might not be highly desirable
> for retail distributor to go into the manufactur-
> ing business.

All of these examples seem to warrant the general con-

clusion that while integration of manufacturing and retail-

ing appears to be natural and logical with some commodities

and in some lines of business, in many cases integration

---

31. Federal Trade Commission report No. 13, op. cit.,
     p. 65.

32. Ibid., p. 17.

33. Ibid., p. 65.

has been the result of a particular combination of circumstances. There have even been instances of integration
followed by differentiation. One department-store chain
reported to the Federal Trade Commission:[34]

> We had a wall-paper factory, which we owned
> ourselves and was a very profitable arrangement
> for us, but we found it was more profitable to
> sell that mill to the _____ Co. and let them
> operate it and we take stock in the company.

Movements toward integration are motivated, of course,
by the desire to obtain profits through the control of the
markets. But where satisfactory profits can be obtained
without this control there will be no tendency to integrate.
In other words, many cases of integration can be traced to
the inability of the chains to locate satisfactory sources
of supply.

The competition between the manufacturer's nationally-
advertised brand and the chain store's brand is, of course,
one very important phase of the chain store controversy.
But the competitive struggle between brands permeates our
entire retail business structure. It is not confined to
chain store competition. Manufacturers who continue to
depend solely upon advertising to force distribution, and
who refuse to make any effort to protect the profits of
their retailing outlets, are finding it more and more difficult to meet the competition of the private brands.

The position the larger chains take with regard to

---

34. Federal Trade Commission report No. 13, op. cit.,
    p. 61.

their purchases from manufacturers is that they offer a
ready-made market to the manufacturer because of the number
of stores they operate and the large number of customers
they serve. The manufacturer is not compelled to enter into
extensive promotional activities entailing heavy expenditures to develop and maintain a market. Therefore the chains
expect price reductions equivalent to the savings represented
by these services. If the manufacturers will agree to sell
to the chains on this basis, they can continue to supply
them with merchandise. As one chain store executive reported
to the Federal Trade Commission:[35]

> We would rather cooperate with the manufac-
> turing companies to try to help them do a better
> job than to go into the business of manufactur-
> ing ourselves, because manufacturing and distrib-
> ution are two entirely different types of en-
> deavor.

But as will be shown in the next chapter, these price
concessions to the chains by the manufacturers are the very
core of the controversy between the wholesalers and the
chains. One independent wholesaler, in an interview with
the author, made the following statement:

> We shall never know the truth about chain
> store practices until we can get these manufac-
> turers on the witness stand and make them testi-
> fy under oath about the prices of the goods they
> sell to the chains.

Do the chain store organizations use coercive and unfair buying practices to drive down the prices they pay for
products? Chain store officials vigorously deny this

---

35. Federal Trade Commission report No. 13, _op. cit._,
    p. 66.

charge. The author personally interviewed a number of
chain store officials and executives of manufacturing
plants to obtain their opinions, and their respective attitudes are indicated by the following replies.

Statement of the manager of a large store operated by
Montgomery, Ward, and Company:

> Those who make such a statement are talking
> about conditions as they existed in some businesses
> twenty years ago. We have instances in our records
> where the price to the manufacturer stipulated in
> the contract was actually higher than the price he
> originally offered. Our buyers are instructed at
> all times to make contracts which will enable the
> manufacturers to operate at a profit. In one in-
> stance a buyer with our firm was discharged be-
> cause he insisted that a certain manufacturer
> carry out the terms of a contract which would have
> involved the latter in a heavy loss.

Statement of a sales manager for a furniture factory
in Southern Indiana, which last year (1938) sold more than
$600,000 worth of furniture to Montgomery, Ward, and
Company:

> We have sold to the mail order houses for
> years, and have always made money on our contracts.
> They are quite willing to make price adjustments
> to meet changing conditions. It takes a long time
> for a large firm like Montgomery, Ward, and Company
> to teach a factory how to make furniture just the
> way they want it, and to pack it for shipment ac-
> cording to their very minute specifications. They
> cannot afford to be constantly changing their
> sources of supply.

Statement of the president and owner of a factory in
Indianapolis which manufactures wrought iron specialties:

> The first real money I ever made was on a
> contract with Kresge's. The chains are fine
> people to do business with.

In his annual report to the stockholders of Sears,
Roebuck and Company for the period from January 30, 1936 to
January 31, 1937, the president of that company made the
following statement:

> The best test of your Company's fairness to
> its merchandise sources is shown by the length of
> association with it. This Company is dealing with
> 6,641 manufacturers. Of this number 294 manufac-
> turers have been selling to the Company for 25
> years or more; 1,292 have been selling to the
> Company for more than 15 years; 3,045 for more
> than 10 years; 4,460 for more than 5 years. Busi-
> ness relationships like this with companies not
> financially connected with Sears, Roebuck and
> Company do not endure in this way unless the re-
> lationship is a mutually satisfactory one.

Are the large chain store organizations driving toward
a monopolistic position in the retail trades? This question is raised here because the Federal Trade Commission's
report on integration of manufacturing and retailing bears
directly upon it.[36] Apparently the Commission found no
tendencies among the chains to achieve a monopoly. The
United States Supreme Court accepted this as a fact, at
least so far as food chains are concerned, in a decision
handed down on May 2, 1932. Acting on a petition of five
large meat packers for modification of the Packers' Consent
Decree, the Court stated in its decision that "few of the

---

36. Federal Trade Commission, op. cit., p. xi.
"The expansion of chain store companies in the manufacturing field and of manufacturers into the field of retailing also raises questions as to concentration of
industrial control and monopoly concerning which the
resolution directs the Federal Trade Commission to in-
form the Senate."

chain stores produce the foods they have for sale, and then chiefly in special lines. Much, indeed most, of what they offer they are constrained to buy from others."[37] The report of the Federal Trade Commission appears to bear out this conclusion with regard to chain store organizations as a group.[38] Information on the question about the amount of manufacturing engaged in was supplied to the Commission by 1,066 chain store companies. Of these, 162 or 15.2 per cent reported that they manufactured part of the goods sold by them in their stores in the year 1930.[39] But these 162 chains operate 60.4 per cent of the total number of stores, and their sales were 57.9 per cent of the total sales in that year. This group of 162 must evidently include the large chains. Yet the retail value of the goods manufactured by this group in 1930 was approximately only $350,000,000 as compared to the $4,304,000,000 value of the total sales. In other words, there was integration only to the extent of about 8 per cent of the total volume of retail sales. Considering the fact that this was divided among 162 separate organizations, it does not appear that the public's interest is threatened by integration and centralization of control resulting from the development of the chain stores. Moreover, assuming that such integration is motivated by the

---

37. United States v. Swift and Co. et al. 286 U. S. 106.

38. Federal Trade Commission, op. cit., p. 13 and 14.
    See Appendix A.

39. Ibid., p. xi.

desire for profits, it would seem that no menace exists as long as present conditions continue, because the Commission found no marked advantage, measured in terms of return on business investment, of the manufacturing over the nonmanu-facturing chain.[40]

---

40. Federal Trade Commission report No. 13, op. cit., p. xiv.

Chapter VII

THE CHAIN STORE AND THE INDEPENDENT MERCHANT

The Wholesaler

The chain store controversy centers around the competitive struggle between the chain store organizations and the independent merchants, both wholesale and retail. There are three main elements in this conflict: 1, the wholesaler's fight to prevent the chains from obtaining special price concessions from the manufacturers; 2, the attempt of both wholesalers and retailers to maintain retail price levels; and 3, the continual struggle of both chain stores and independents to reduce their costs of doing business. The first two elements require a separate discussion dealing with such subjects as advertising allowances, quantity discounts, and the purposes and effects of price legislation.[1] The third element is the subject of this chapter, particularly with reference to the wholesaler.

Historically, the orthodox producer-wholesaler-retailer channel of distribution developed naturally, and under past conditions performed satisfactorily. But there came a time when the wholesaler occupied a dominant position between the producer on the one hand and the consumer on the other. The producer was small, far from his market, and

---

1. See Chapter XIII.

wholly dependent on the wholesaler for market information
and retail outlets. The retailer had to rely upon him for
goods, credit, and information about sources of supplies.
The wholesaler, in this position of dominance, was able to
bring pressure on the manufacturer for lower prices, but
was not compelled to pass these along to the retailer. This
pressure had effects on manufacturing which were as drastic
as those which the multiple-unit systems have had on distribution.[2] The manufacturer, like the wholesaler today,
was forced to find ways to reduce costs. This led to the
invention of labor-saving machinery, the standardization of
raw materials, and finished products, and the development
of elaborate systems of cost-accounting.

As manufacturers grew in size and power, they began to
compete with the wholesaler for control of the markets.
Here was the origin of the conflict between the nationally-
advertised brands and the private brands. When a manufacturer by the use of advertising can create a consumer demand
for his products so that the wholesalers and retailers must
stock the products or lose business, the manufacturer can
force the middlemen to operate on a very narrow margin of
profit. Indeed, the latter become virtually agents for the
manufacturer.[3]

---

2. Willard E Atkins and collaborators, Economic Behavior,
p. 297. See Appendix A, Supplement to Chapter VII. New
York: Houghton Mifflin Company, 1933.

3. Ibid., p. 300.

Then, with the growth of the chain stores, came a further threat to the economic position of the wholesaler. He was faced with a competitory struggle far more serious than that between the nationally advertised brand and the private brand. His very existence was endangered, because his outlets, that is, the retailers who were his customers, were menaced by the success of the multiple-unit systems. He was forced to change many of his policies, to eliminate unnecessary expenses, and to adopt the methods of merchandising developed by the chain store organizations. Those independent wholesalers who are alert to the changes in distribution have been able to meet chain store competition successfully. Indeed, one might argue that the coming of the chain stores was the salvation of the wholesaler; that had he not been forced to modernize his plant, organize and train the retailers to whom he sold, and aggressively merchandise his own private brands, his independence would have been lost forever. Of course, many wholesalers protested at being compelled to meet this competition, because it is human nature to try to protect vested interests and established institutions when they are imperiled by new developments.

Yet in spite of what the wholesaler can do, there are certain phases of chain store competition which he finds very difficult to meet. A study by Dr. Eldon Wittwer in 1930 of a wholesale hardware business[4] discloses many of

---

4. Eldon Wittwer, "Allocation of Costs in Wholesale Distribution, with Special Reference to Hardware," 1927-1929. A doctoral dissertation. Cornell University, June, 1930.

the competitive disadvantages of the orthodox or service
wholesaler. Since the wholesaler's success is dependent
upon that of the retailer, a large part of the former's
efforts must be directed toward making the retail merchandising operations profitable. The chain store has the advantage over the independent wholesaler of being able to
concentrate its efforts on retail outlets, because retailing is its most important function. But the wholesaler
must bear the burden of his own problems in addition to
those of his customers. This discloses the fundamental
weakness of the single-unit system, namely, the lack of a
close coordination of the steps in the marketing process.

If there is to be a close linking of wholesaler and
retailer, there must be intelligent cooperation between
them to a very high degree. But, for a number of reasons,
this is difficult to obtain. One or the other may not
appreciate the importance of this relationship; one or the
other may not be willing to give to his business the time
and effort and study that scientific merchandising requires.
For example, many wholesalers in the wholesaler-sponsored
voluntary chains are giving much time and attention to the
preparation of effective advertising programs for their
retailing groups, but their greatest difficulty is that of
getting the retailers to carry through the programs energet-
ically. This situation was mentioned to the author by the
wholesaler-sponsor of a large voluntary chain in the Pacific
Northwest. On the other hand, the division manager of

Kroger's in a large Midwestern city stated:

> When we get orders to carry through one of
> these big selling campaigns, we know it is up to
> us to get busy immediately.

Wholesalers can obtain the same quantity discounts
that the chains get when the former buy in comparable
amounts. Nevertheless, two points of contention have arisen
because of the development of large-scale retailing; one,
the smaller wholesalers cannot buy in comparable amounts,
and two, the integrated organizations (integration of wholesaling and retailing) appear to be able to operate on a
smaller spread between the manufacturer's price and the
price to the consumer than do the single-unit systems. The
business man, of course, naturally considers this spread as
consisting of two margins, the wholesaler's and the retailer's, and he is convinced that the spread should be large
enough to permit both to make a profit. From the social
point of view, it is simply a question of the total costs
of distribution. These fundamental differences of the
multiple-unit and the single-unit systems are important, because they are evidences of the advantage to society of integration in retailing. They will be discussed in more
detail in Chapter IX, which deals with the comparative costs
of distribution in the two systems.

There are other kinds of discounts, however, which the
independent merchants contend are a form of unfair competition. Legislation such as the Robinson-Patman Act is intended to outlaw discounts which are in excess of those

which could be justified by the economies of integrated
distribution, and to eliminate any discrimination in prices
on the part of the manufacturer.[5]

Chain stores and wholesalers who operate cooperative
buying groups are in a much better position to predict the
requirements of the retailing units which they supply than
are those wholesalers who have no affiliations with their
retailer-customers such as exist in the voluntary chains.
The former can plan their orders in advance of sales on the
basis of past sales records. As pointed out above, the independent wholesaler in the past was in a dominant position
because of his ability to forecast customers' demands for
the manufacturer. But in the multiple-unit systems, whether
orthodox chain or voluntary chain, this forecasting can be
done much more accurately. This is an important advantage,
because more and more the consumer is taking command of
production, and success in business is to an increasing
degree dependent upon the ability to forecast the consumer's

---

5. N. H. Engle, "Implications of the Robinson-Patman Act
   for Marketing," The Journal of Marketing, October, 1936,
   p. 75. The first section of this Act, which amends the
   Clayton Act, declares it to be unlawful for any person
   to discriminate in prices between purchases of like grade
   and quality of a commodity in interstate commerce within
   the jurisdiction of the United States, where the effect
   of such discrimination may be: 1, substantially to lessen
   competition; 2, to tend to create a monopoly; 3, to
   injure, destroy or prevent competition.
   "The independent merchant will benefit only to the extent
   that chains have in the past derived substantial advantages from concealed or hidden rebates."

demands.[6]

Independent wholesalers are also at a disadvantage in having to assume credit risks. This disadvantage extends to some extent to the manufacturer, because if the wholesaler is unable to collect from the retailer, the manufacturer may be unable to collect from the wholesaler. In any case, the capital requirements of the latter are increased. Chain stores do not have the credit losses that the wholesaler has, nor his expenses of making collections.

Dr. Wittwer presented in his thesis the following figures which he compiled from the data supplied by the Brookings Institute of Washington, D. C., showing the relative costs of wholesalers in the grocery trade:[7]

Table I

Operating Costs of Performing the Wholesale Functions
by the Regular Service Wholesaler, Chain Stores
and Retailer's Cooperatives

	Per Cent of Net Sales		
Expense Items	Regular Service Wholesaler	Chain Stores	Retailer's Cooperatives
Sales expense	4.07	0.00	0.00
General expense	4.13	3.07	1.64
Administrative expense	1.97	2.37	2.03
Interest and discount	2.00	0.03	0.02
Bad debts	.54	0.00	0.01

6. Donald M. Hobart, "The Value of Consumer Purchase Surveys to Management", The Journal of Marketing, July, 1939, p. 23. . . "The study of consumers is of vital importance to management. We realize that the future of any business lies in the hands of consumers. As a result, we constantly study their abilities to earn, their capacities to consume and the changeableness of their habits and desires."

7. Ibid., p. 6.

These figures show that the chains and the retailers' cooperatives in the grocery trade operate at a much lower cost than the regular service wholesaler. Two important disadvantages of the latter are clearly shown in this table: 1. his high selling expense, and 2, the high cost of granting credit.

Wholesalers with a considerable number of unprofitable accounts are at a tremendous disadvantage in the performance of the wholesaler's functions as compared to chain store organizations. This situation in the hardware business is clearly indicated in the following quotation from Dr. Wittwer's thesis:[8]

> Small customers who buy from hand to mouth are very expensive for the wholesaler to carry. With 29.5 percent of his customers purchasing less than $100 worth of merchandise per year and 72.3 percent purchasing less than $500 worth of merchandise in a year, the wholesaler faces a difficult problem. The average size of orders and average sales per item from small customers are much lower than those from large ones. Over 80 percent of the customers with poor credit ratings are among those giving the wholesaler a small volume of business.

The elimination of selling expenses in the multiple-unit system of distribution is a very important advantage, both to the orthodox, centrally owned chain and the voluntary chain. Chain stores have no need for traveling salesmen. They are replaced by supervisors whose expenses can be pro-rated to the stores which they supervise. Moreover, these supervisors can be busy all the time, whereas the

8. Wittwer, op. cit., p. vi ff.

traveling salesman must wait until his customers are ready
to see him. Also, the traveling salesman must accommodate
his route and his calling time to the wishes of his customers. The supervisor is free to arrange his own route, to
study the needs of the individual stores with the managers,
and to instruct and advise them, knowing that they will
follow his instructions and advice to the best of their
abilities. Wholesalers are also concerned about retaining
the good will of the retailers. Chain stores with their
own retail outlets have no such problem. They need only to
concentrate their attention on obtaining the good will of
the ultimate consumer.

In their endeavor to increase their volume of sales,
some wholesalers, particularly those classified as "local
wholesalers," (as distinguished from the national and sectional wholesaler) frequently solicit trade from retail
stores located outside the radius of economic distribution.
Not only does this practice increase transportation costs,
but from a social viewpoint it is costly competition.[9] The
distant wholesaler, unless business warrants his establishing a branch warehouse, is at a disadvantage in competing
with the nearby jobber. The percentage of small orders and
unprofitable business is increased, and often a more inten-

---

9. In an interview the author had with a wholesaler in
    Indianapolis, the latter stated that wholesalers often
    send their best salesmen into the most unprofitable mar-
    kets, keeping their poorer salesmen in the nearby mar-
    kets which should be cultivated intensively. One whole-
    saler stopped soliciting in 112 cities, reduced his
    volume one-third, and increased his net profits.

sive cultivation of the wholesaler's own territory is
neglected.

Chain stores and wholesalers with their own cooperative organizations do not have this disadvantage, that is,
of having to solicit business from distant points in the
effort to reduce the percentage of overhead costs. They
can place their warehouses at strategic points, and thus
obtain the most economical distribution. For example one
chain store organization operating in Indiana supplies the
retail outlets in that state from warehouses at Louisville,
Indianapolis, Fort Wayne, Terre Haute, and Chicago. Transportation and warehousing are confined to the particular
district which each warehouse services. There is no need
for going into distant sections for business.

Independent wholesalers may in the near future find it
expedient to combine with wholesalers in other areas in
order to obtain buying and operating advantages, and to
eliminate wasteful competition. This is a plan already in
use by groups of department stores.[10] As long as there are
a large number of small independent retailers, there will
be a need for the services of the local wholesaler, but the

---

10. C. W. Barker and Melvin Anshen, Modern Marketing,
    p. 137. New York: McGraw-Hill Book Company, 1939.
    "A number of independent department stores have com-
    bined into ownership groups, stores operating under
    single financial control but usually with independent
    merchandising management . . . Ownership groups have
    experimented with group buying, whereby the buyers for
    one department in the several stores make purchases
    together, thus securing increased advantages from
    their tremendous quantity buying."

latter must necessarily shape his policies and methods of
operation to meet the competition of the large-scale retailing organizations.[11] If they do adopt such a plan, it will
be just another example of the significant changes occurring
in distribution as a result of integration and combination.

Dr. Wittwer concludes that:[12]

> The final solution of the problems facing
> the wholesaler must come through the joint
> efforts of the three interested parties: name-
> ly, the retailer, wholesaler, and manufacturer.
> It should begin with a careful study of the
> consumer's demand, to determine as nearly as
> possible the kind, quantity, and quality of
> the goods desired. Then a united effort should
> be made to meet these demands in the most effi-
> cient and economical way.

Adjustments which wholesalers have made in their opera-

---

11. T. N. Beckman and N. H. Engle, _Wholesaling Principles
and Practice_, p. 513, 514. New York: The Ronald Press,
1937.
"There are three major types of wholesaling establishments which constitute the battleground of competition
within the field. These are the independent wholesale
merchants, still the dominant type; the wholesale
branches of manufacturers who have sought to eliminate
wholesalers; and the chain store warehouses, or the
wholesaling departments of integrated wholesaling-re-
tailing chain systems, which deal directly with the
manufacturer and primary sources of supply. . . Of
these three types, the chain store warehouse has the
lowest operating ratios in all lines save the hardware
and the furniture and house furnishings trades."

"In recent years there has been a pronounced trend
away from that type of wholesaler who sold throughout
the entire country, the national wholesaler. . . At
the present time the interest of retailers is in getting quick deliveries of small orders from wholesalers.
The type of wholesaler best prepared to offer this
kind of service to retailers is the local wholesaler
who serves the small area around his warehouse."

Ibid., p. 82.

12. Wittwer, _op. cit._, p. 10.

tions to meet changing conditions include revamping of
packing rooms, analysis of customers' desires, commodity
analysis, selection selling, improvement in selling methods,
improvement in physical operations, increased emphasis on
service to retailers, reduction of the cost of orders,
stricter collection practices, and the establishment of
adequate bad debts reserves. Wholesalers who have made
these adjustments, and who have surrounded themselves with
an efficient group of retailers, are today successfully
meeting chain store competition.

Chapter VIII

THE CHAIN STORE AND THE INDEPENDENT MERCHANT
(Continued)

The Retailer

To speak of a controversy between the chain store and
the independent retail merchant is to fail to recognize the
distinction between one who merchandises intelligently and
another who simply "keeps a store." There are many retail
merchants who are meeting chain store competition successfully, and this group is far more concerned about the inefficient merchant than it is about the chain store. In a
recently completed survey of the grocery business in Indiana,
in which replies from a total of 300 proprietors of independently-owned grocery stores were received to the question,
"Where do you find your most severe competition comes from?"
One hundred and sixty-four or more than one-half stated
that it came from other independent merchants, rather than
from the chain stores. (See Table VI.) One grocer described the situation as follows:[1]

> We don't worry about chain stores. The
> fellows who cause us trouble are those that
> come into the business with a little money
> and no experience, and want to be "big shots."
> We have had two or three in our locality who
> thought that they were going to show us how

---

1. From a personal interview with a grocer. This Indiana
survey was directed by the author, who also did a considerable amount of the field work and tabulating, edited
all of the questionnaires, and wrote the final report
(not yet published).

the grocery business should be run, and they
started in by giving goods away. They lasted
until their money was gone, and they caused us
a lot of trouble while they were here.

As stated above, the chain stores are charged with
forcing many independent retailers out of business. The
latter, however, fail not only because of chain store competition, but also for a number of other reasons; because
they are in a locality that does not supply a volume of
business that will produce a gross margin large enough to
cover the necessary expenses; because they undertake a job
that requires special skills and technical training which
they do not possess;[2] because they enter the retailing
business without sufficient capital; or because of changing
conditions in the areas they serve, for example, the closing

---

2. For example, Professor Vaile, of the University of Minne-
    sota, found in his study of the Twin City area (Minnea-
    polis and St.Paul) that over 50 per cent of the people
    entering the grocery business did so merely because they
    were out of work and had to do something. Most of the
    men who entered the grocery business were more than 40
    years of age, and approximately half of them had had no
    previous experience. Of those entering the grocery busi-
    ness in any given year, only 55.3 per cent would be ex-
    pected to survive for more than one year, 42.4 per cent
    for more than two years, 34.3 per cent for more than
    three years, and only 28.6 per cent for more than four
    years. For the same periods the survival expectancy for
    voluntary chain units is respectively 83.6 per cent,
    79.5 per cent, 77.7 per cent and 77.7 per cent; for the
    ownership chains, 91.5 per cent, 90.4 per cent, 79.6 per
    cent and 64.8 per cent. Professor Boer, of the Univer-
    sity of Pittsburgh, found much the same conditions pre-
    vailing in that city.

    R. S. Vaile, "Grocery Retailing--With Special Reference
    to the Effects of Competition", University of Minnesota
    Studies in Economics and Business. No. 1, p. 16, 37.
    The University of Minnesota Press, Minneapolis, April,
    1932.

    A. E. Boer, "Mortality Costs in Retail Trades", The
    Journal of Marketing, July, 1937, p. 52 ff.

down of a factory, and so on.

In the study by Indiana University, referred to above, 300 cases were interviewed, and of these, 69 were stores with annual sales below $10,000. Some reported sales as low as $2,400 a year. Such stores are not businesses in the broad sense of that term. The proprietor does not pay himself a salary; often he owns the building and lives in the back; many times he has an outside job and his wife and children "run the store." If records are kept at all they are meager and do not follow accepted principles of accounting. Moreover, his attitudes and interests are not typical of a business man. One proprietor of such a store said:

"I don't care whether I make any money here or not. I live on my savings. I just run this store because it keeps my wife busy, and gives me a place to sit."

Factual material dealing with this type of store will be presented in the chapters to follow. Like many small farmers, the owners of these tiny stores struggle along as best they can, usually getting a bare subsistence, or supplementing the meager income from wages earned in other work by members of the owner's family. Some saving in household expenses is possible by obtaining food supplies at wholesale prices. Often the work of keeping the store is shared by the wife who receives no wage. While the volume of business done by this group is small compared to the total volume, many of these small proprietors and of those who sympathize with them condemn the chain stores be-

cause they believe or have been told that the latter are the
cause of their troubles. It appears logical to them that
if the chain stores did not exist, they would be getting a
bigger share of the total volume of business. Therefore
they support anti-chain store legislation, and they will
vote for those legislators who promise them relief.

Retailing is becoming more and more an occupation requiring a high degree of intelligence and ability, and
there are so many retailers of ordinary ability that the
value of their services to society is too small to permit
them to receive any considerable amount of compensation.
The operation of the economic principle which determines
the return they receive for their labor is the same as with
any other kind of work. With a slowly expanding population,
there is a limited amount of distribution of goods to be
done. If too many undertake to perform the functions of
distribution, the reward of each must be correspondingly
less. It is the same condition that would exist (and does
exist) if there are too many farmers, laborers, draftsmen,
railway engineers, or doctors. When railway building
stopped, many civil engineers found themselves out of a
job. No one thought of passing a law to stop the building
of concrete highways and the manufacture of automobiles so
that there would have to be more railroads in order that
these engineers would have work. But when improvements in
merchandising methods began to make the situations of many
independent merchants very difficult, the public was, and

is, urged to support legislation that would help them stay
in business.

The efficient independent merchant has found ways to
meet chain store competition successfully. One of these
ways is to become a member of a buying group or voluntary
chain. In Indiana, for example, one organization known as
the Clover Farm Stores has weekly meetings which the members
are required to attend. At these meetings all the various
phases of grocery merchandising are discussed; experts are
employed to arrange stock, trim windows, install accounting
systems, and plan advertising campaigns. This organization
has a number of private brands which are sold in no other
stores. One grocer, a member of this organization, when
interviewed by the author, stated that he had no fear of
chain store competition. He was very enthusiastic about
the methods and policies of his organization. He was
located in a middle-class residence district where he could
build up a personal following, and where there was small
chance of a chain store coming in to compete with him.

So much has been written about the voluntary chain
that no lengthy discussion will be included here. It has
many characteristics in common with those organizations
which are managed almost entirely through a central office.
The fundamental difference, of course, is the independence
of the individual members. Yet it is clear that in order
to obtain the competitive advantages of the voluntary chain,
the members must be willing to surrender some of their
independence.

It has already been pointed out that there is the retailer-owned wholesale house, which may be termed the re-
tailer-cooperative, and the wholesaler-sponsored chain. In
order for either to succeed, there must be an individual in
the group with initiative and enthusiasm. The retailer
group is reluctant to pay the salary required to obtain the
services of such a man. The wholesaler-sponsored voluntary
chain is, therefore, likely to be the stronger of the two,
because the wholesaler's strength depends upon his retailers,
and his interest in their success motivates his efforts to
promote the merchandising of the retailers in various ways,
such as supplying market information or organizing discussion groups to study merchandising methods. Thus an important advantage to the retailer member in the wholesaler-
sponsored group is the leadership of the wholesaler. There
is weakness in this type of organization to the extent that
the retailers are indifferent to this leadership. There is
also a conflict of interests, since the wholesaler desires a
profit from his transactions with the retailers.[3] The
weakness of the retailer-sponsored group is the lack of

---

3. Beckman, op. cit., p. 561.
    "Retailer-owned cooperatives in the grocery and drug
    trades, and buying groups in the several shopping goods
    trades, are basically buying organizations. Being or-
    ganized and controlled by retailers, their main desire
    continues to be that of eliminating the wholesaler, his
    net profits, and as much of his costs as possible."

leadership.[4] Its strength lies in the fact that it permits
a greater feeling of independent action among the members.

Geographically, voluntary chains do not appear to have
developed according to any definite pattern. For example,
membership in voluntary chains among retailers in the

Table VI

Comparison of Numbers of Grocery Chain-Store Units and
Retailer-Members of Voluntary Grocery Chains
on Basis of Population

| State | Number per Each 10,000 of Population | |
	Chain Store Units	Retailer-Members
Minnesota	9	152
Oregon	35	141
Vermont	48	135
Maine	55	122
Washington	26	121
New York	65	112
California	41	112
Pennsylvania	56	99
Massachusetts	88	95
District of Columbia	101	89
Connecticut	90	71
Illinois	44	69
Wisconsin	24	68
Michigan	54	67
New Jersey	94	67
Indiana	37	65
Ohio	50	61
Tennessee	25	22
Mississippi	7	14
Florida	36	25
Louisiana	14	7
Idaho	20	8

4. Ibid., p. 568.
"The members of a retailer-owned cooperative chain
serve in a dual capacity as part owners of retail stores
establishers with the full powers, if any conflict
arises between the interests of these two organizations,
the individual will normally react as a retailer, not
as a wholesaler."

grocery trade is much more general in some states than in others. Illustrations of this variation are given in Table VI.[5]

There appears to be no correlation between the amount of competition from chain stores and membership in voluntary chains.

The Indiana survey obtained information about membership in voluntary chains from 295 grocers. Of this number, 98 belonged to a wholesaler-sponsored association, 4 to a retail group owning and operating a warehouse, and 4 to a loosely federated retailer organization. The balance, 189, stated that they did not belong to any type of voluntary chain. This ratio of approximately 35 per cent holding membership to 65 per cent non-members held fairly closely in all of the sixteen counties scattered throughout the state where interviews were made; although it appeared that in the northern part of the state there was a slightly higher percentage of membership.[6]

Whether or not a retailer belongs to a voluntary chain

---

5. See Table 3 , Appendix A, Supplement to Chapter VIII for a more complete tabulation.

6. "The cooperative chain movement is so new and changes are taking place so rapidly that any classification is only temporary. Variations in both types, but particularly the wholesaler-retailer type, are limited only by the ingenuity and zeal of the promoters of the organization and the extent of cooperation given by retail members."

Chain stores. Cooperative Grocery Chains. Federal Trade Commission. Senate Document No. 12, 72nd Congress, 1st session, p. 12. U. S. Government Printing Office, Washington, 1932.

may depend upon the presence or absence in a district of an
aggressive and enterprising wholesaling organization. Also,
since frequent meetings and discussions are essential to intelligent cooperation in a voluntary chain, distance to the
meeting place might affect a retailer's decision about joining a chain. For example, the grocer mentioned above who
belongs to the organization known as the Clover Farms Stores
must drive fifty miles and back every Monday night to attend
the weekly meeting.

A second way in which independent merchants can meet
the competition of the chain stores is by catering to a
market that is different from that which the chain stores
usually serve. The price differential between service and
non-service stores found in Bloomington (see Chapter IX)
may be explained partly by the indifference of the higher
income groups to savings that appear small on individual
articles, and partly by their desire for credit and delivery
services. Moreover, judging by information obtained in a
study of the shopping habits of residents of the University
District, Seattle, Washington,[7] convenience, habit, and
friendship are important factors affecting retail trade.

In the next chapter a comparison will be made of the
grocery stores in Bloomington that are representative of
the various types. The chapter following will contain in-

---

7. Made by an advanced class in Marketing, at the University of Washington, and sponsored by the University
   Commercial Club. Report written by the author and
   printed for private distribution.

formation about their operating expenses. Conclusions concerning the present competitive situation of chains and independently-owned grocery stores will be stated in a later
chapter. Some of these conclusions will pertain specific-
ally to this business; others may be applied to retailing
in general.

PART II

ECONOMIC ASPECTS

of the

CHAIN STORE MOVEMENT

Chapter IX

COMPARATIVE PRICES OF CHAINS AND INDEPENDENTS

A number of studies have been made of comparative prices
in chain stores and independently-owned stores, and these
will be summarized in this chapter. One must use care, however, in drawing conclusions from these studies for three
reasons:

1. Because of the difficulty of comparing the quality
of goods of different brands[1]

2. Because price is affected by the presence or absence of "service," which is defined as "the performance of
labor for the benefit of another or at another's command."
In the grocery business "service" includes the granting of
credit, delivery of goods without extra charge, taking
orders over the telephone, and often special favors to retain the good will of customers.

3. Because of the danger of generalizing about all
market areas from conclusions based on data obtained from
relatively small districts or from relatively small samples

---

1. For a detailed discussion of comparative qualities of
merchandise in chain stores and independently-owned
stores, see the following:

Roland S. Vaile and Alice M. Child, "Grocery Qualities
and Prices." University of Minnesota Studies in Economics and Business No. 7. The University of Minnesota
Press, Minneapolis. 1933.

Federal Trade Commission. "Chain Stores. Quality of
Canned Vegetables and Fruits. (Under Brands of Manufacturers, Chains, and Other Distributors.)" Senate Document No. 170, 72nd Congress, 2nd session. U. S. Government Printing Office. 1933.

of larger areas. Market areas have more or less clearly
definable characteristics such as population, source and
variability of income, and buying habits of customers, and
may therefore resemble each other to the extent that such
characteristics are similar. But they may differ in other
respects to such a considerable degree that an attempt to
judge conditions in one from data obtained in the other may
lead to erroneous conclusions.

In Table VIII are summarized the results of a number of
studies of comparative prices in chains and independently-
owned grocery stores, which have been made in various parts
of the country during the past ten years. Table IX shows
the results of the Federal Trade Commission's price study.
Only two of the cities in which these studies were made,
namely, Durham, North Carolina and Lexington, Kentucky, have
marked resemblances to Bloomington, Indiana, where the price
study discussed in this chapter was made. Both of these
studies were conducted nearly ten years ago. Both of these
places are university towns in the south. Bloomington was
founded and the country round about was settled by pioneers
who came up from Kentucky. It is located in southern
Indiana, which resembles in a number of ways the southern
districts bordering on it.

The study in Durham, North Carolina was made under
Professor Malcolm D. Taylor's direction. All the stores
studied were visited on one specified day, and prices were
obtained across the counter. Sixteen nationally-advertised

staples were selected, and loss-leaders were eliminated. A total of 93 stores were investigated, 24 of which were chains, and 69 independents. The average prices of all chain stores showed 14.79 per cent lower than the average prices of all independents.

The study made in Lexington, Kentucky was directed by Dr. Edgar Z. Palmer, who obtained prices on forty-nine articles from 44 independent stores. Every effort was made to carry out the study on the basis of equality in the matter of weights, size and quality of goods. Dr. Palmer found that chain prices averaged 14.3 per cent lower than individual prices.

The differential of 14 per cent found in Bloomington, Indiana checks closely with the findings of these two investigators. It also seems to be more than a coincidence that the study made by a graduate student in Gainesvile, Florida showed a differential between chains and independents of 14.4 per cent.[2]

Dr. Converse of the University of Illinois, has made two studies in Champaign-Urbana, one in 1931 and one in 1937. It is interesting to note that a smaller differential was found in the latter study, which suggests the possibility that as the independents become more and more equipped to meet the competition of the chains, the differentials

---

2. Not published. Material obtained by the author from the professor who directed the study.

found in earlier studies, which ranged from 10 per cent to 14 per cent, have become steadily smaller. It also indicated that changing conditions invalidate market data in a relatively short period. One who wishes to judge market conditions by comparison is on safer ground if he makes the comparison within an area small enough to be homogeneous in physical economic conditions, and operating under the same set of laws. Taxes levied in Indiana, such as the gross income tax and the chain store tax, may affect business operations and cause important differences between that state and other states.

Studies made in Indiana[3] indicate that the 92 counties can, for purposes of comparison, be grouped into four classifications: Industrial, Semi-Industrial, Semi-Rural, and Rural. This classification was used with satisfactory results[4] in the survey of grocery stores referred to above.

---

3. For example, a recent vocational survey made by the Works Progress Administration, Indianapolis. Report not yet published, but original data examined by the author.

    See also "Industrial Development of Indiana." Indiana Studies in Business. Indiana University, School of Business Administration, Bureau of Business Research. September, 1937. Particularly note charts showing relative distribution of manufactures, e.g. Chart 14, page 49, "Value of Product, 1930;" Chart 21, page 59, "Total Wages Paid, 1930;" and Chart 28, page 66, "Number of Wage Earners, 1930." Also see Chart 44, page 97, "Agricultural and Industrial Income, County Distribution, 1930."

4. "It is interesting . . . to consider some results of a survey conducted by Professor Harold M. Haas under the auspices of the Indiana University Business School in 1938. In the survey were included independent and chain grocery stores in sixteen counties of the state ... It

Starting with this assumption, it follows logically that
the conditions in any particular type of business in one
county also exist, to a considerable extent at least, in
other counties in the same classification. Furthermore, a
study of counties in other states may disclose a similarity
of market characteristics which will enable one to judge
conditions in these counties with a fair degree of accuracy
by comparing them with the one county studied.

There are in Indiana 38 counties out of the total of
92 that are listed as having population of between 20,000
and 40,000, and an addition 33 with between 10,000 and
20,000. Bloomington, the city in which the price study described in this chapter was made, is the county seat of
Monroe County, which, according to the United States Census
of 1930, has a population of 35,974. Industries located
there include the quarrying and milling of limestone and
the manufacture of furniture. Agriculture is another
source of income, although the topography is hilly, not the
rich, level farm lands found in the northern part of the
state. Monroe County is classified as "semi-rural."

---

4. (continued)

may be noted that the average percentage of taxes to
sales arrived at by Professor Haas for the entire group
of independent grocers is almost identical with the
percentage we secured for individual grocers as shown in
another section of this study." (Much of the information collected came from Federal Income Tax reports.)
The Report of the Indiana Tax Study Commission, page 161.
(Authorized by Chap. 317, House Concurrent Resolution
No. 7, 80th Session Indiana General Assembly.)

Bloomington has a population of approximately 20,000,
and according to the 1930 Census there are 17 cities in
Indiana with population between 10,000 and 25,000, and 26
with a count of between 5,000 and 10,000. It appears reasonable to assume that these 43 cities have at least some
market characteristics in common with Bloomington. There are
differences, of course, Indiana University is located at
Bloomington, and supplies the retail groceries with customers who have a steady and sustained income.

This price study represents the buying of a family of
four, over a period of several weeks, and includes 51 nationally-advertised brands of food products which are commonly
found on the pantry shelves of the faculty families in
Bloomington. Some error may be present in this study, because the prices were not obtained from all the stores on
the same day. This error, however, cannot be large, because retail prices change slowly. It is compensated for
by the fact that the buying was not done in one store at
one time, with two exceptions, but as far as possible was
distributed evenly among the various stores during the
entire period. These exceptions should not affect the results materially, because one is in the independently-owned
service group, which is well represented; the other, the
general country store which, as will be seen, is apparently
not in direct competition with the Bloomington stores.

The prices quoted (See Table X   ) were obtained by
bona fide shopping and purchasing, not by mere inquiry. Ten

combination (groceries and meats) stores were included in the study. They were selected as being typical of the classifications which they represent. The descriptions of these stores and of their patrons are based on personal observations and inquiries by the author.

Store No. 1. An independently-owned, single unit, service store. It is located in a residential district, one block from the campus. The only business establishments near it are two lunch rooms with soda fountains which cater to the student trade.

Store No. 2. Independently-owned, single unit, service. This store is very similar to No. 1, except for its location. The proprietor has a filling station adjoining his grocery, which is near a corner that appears to be developing into a secondary shopping center. The new University combined grade and high school, which is used for educational demonstrations and practice teaching, is located nearby. The street itself is one of the main state highways, and the traffic at this corner is heavy during the hours when the children are going to and from school. The proprietor is an agressive merchandiser, and does a considerable amount of advertising.

Store No. 3. Independently-owned, single unit, service. This is a long-established store, patronized by long-time residents, both faculty and townspeople. (Both Bloomington and Indiana University were founded over 100 years ago.) It is a busy store, with four full-time clerks, in addition to the proprietor.

Store No. 4. Independently-owned, single-unit, service. This store is located in the downtown business district, one block from the court house. In many respects it resembles the "old-time" grocery store, with baskets of vegetables, brooms, and other merchandise displayed on the sidewalk in front of the store.

Store No. 5. Independently-owned, single unit, non-service. This store was opened less than two years ago. The proprietor is aggressive and is making a determined effort to get established by advertising "special prices" in the local newspapers.

Store No. 6. A local chain, limited service. Deliveries are made without extra charge, but credit accounts are not solicited, although a small amount of credit is given. One who desires credit must arrange for it through a personal interview with the owner. This chain also sells at wholesale to other retailers, but does not actively promote this end of the business. Although most of the purchases were made at the chain's Number 1 store, located in the downtown business district, comparisons were made with some of the other units in the same chain. Prices were the same, the only difference being that stores in this chain located in some of the poorer sections of the city did not carry all of the articles priced in this study, indicating differences in customer demands. The proprietor stated that his strongest appeal was made to the medium ($2,000 - $4,000) and low (below $2,000) income groups.

Store No. 7. Chain store, (Kroger's) non-service,
located in the downtown business district, in the square
surrounding the court house. In Bloomington, as in many of
the county seats in Indiana, the court house and the lawn
surrounding occupies an entire block, and retail businesses
are located around it on all four sides. In the same block
with Kroger's store are three variety chain stores, a J. C.
Penney store, and a Hook's drug store, one of a chain with
headquarters in Indianapolis. This store seems to draw a
large portion of its trade from the country folk. The latter
throng the sidewalk in front of these stores on Saturday
afternoon; the men standing out in front in groups, the
women in the stores shopping. Townspeople try to avoid buying in this block on the days the farmers are in town, because of the crowds and the difficulty of getting the attention of the sales-people in the stores.

Store No. 8. A cash-and-carry supermarket, located in
an old warehouse, about two blocks from the court house and
back from the street alongside the railroad tracks. It was
opened less than two years ago by Karsell's, a grocery wholesaler who had supplied the local retail grocers with merchandise for many years.

Store No. 9. The Atlantic and Pacific Tea Company's
cash-and-carry supermarket, opened less than two years ago.
This company formerly had a unit similar to Kroger's, but
located on the opposite side of the court house square.
This store was closed when the supermarket was opened. The

site of the latter is a corner about two blocks from the
court house square, on a street that runs between the railroad and an old residential section. Judging from the age
of the automobiles that stand out in front, and from the
types of people seen in the market, this store draws much
of its trade from the lower income groups, although it is
also patronized some by members of the faculty.

Store No. 10. One of a small chain of five general
stores called the "Rainbow Stores." It is located about
eight miles west of Bloomington on a state highway, at a
"cross roads shopping center" named Stanford. This firm
also engages in country buying to a considerable extent,
and much of its business takes the form of trading with
the farmers.

The price indexes used as a basis of comparison were
prepared in two ways: the prices of individual items were
converted into relatives for each item separately. For one
table these relatives were based on the average of all
prices quoted, and for the other table the base used was
the lowest price on that item found in any store. (See
Tables   IX   and   X   ) To illustrate, the lowest
price found in any store on Kellogg's cornflakes was 2 for
17¢, or 8.5¢; the average for all stores was 10.8¢. Each
of these in turn was used as a base to compute a price
relative for that article, and from these relatives an
index was computed for groups of related food products and
also a general index. (See Appendix A, Table ᴸ , Supplement to Chapter IX, for a complete list of articles and
prices.)

An examination of these data leads to the following
conclusions concerning comparative prices and the competitive situation of chains and independents in the grocery
business in Bloomington:

1. Prices in the Atlantic and Pacific Tea Company's
supermarket are 14 per cent _lower_ than the average of all
stores on nationally-advertised brands of foods.

2. Prices in the independently-owned, single unit
service stores average 6.75 per cent _higher_ than the average of all stores on nationally-advertised brands.

3. The three highest independents average 5 per cent
higher than the fourth independent (Store No. 2), and the
prices in these three are approximately the same.

4. Using the average price as a basis for comparison,
the local chain which delivers and gives a limited amount
of credit is 9 per cent _higher_ than Kroger's cash-and-carry
chain store, and 17 per cent _higher_ than the A. and P. supermarket.

5. Every nationally-advertised brand purchased in the
independent groceries was found on sale at the A. and P.
supermarket. This was not true of most of the other stores.
Only one of these brands was not carried in Stores No.'s 3
and 6; two were missing in Stores No.'s 2 and 5; three in
Store No. 4; six in the supermarket operated by the independent wholesaler; and eighteen in the country general
store. These omissions may indicate either a manufacturer's price that is not acceptable to the retailer, a difference in customer demand, or the desire to build up a

customer acceptance of a private brand.

6. If buyers were always able to buy individual articles at the lowest prices quoted in any store in the city,
they could purchase for $1.00 a supply of food that would
cost them $1.02 at the A. and P. supermarket and $1.11 at
Kroger's chain store, but they would have to pay cash and
do their own delivering. They can have their supplies delivered by paying 23¢ more at the local chain, but for this
same amount they can have their groceries both charged and
delivered if they trade at the lowest-priced independent
store.

7. With a few exceptions, the relative position of
the individual stores, that is, high or low with respect to
prices, as indicated by the general index, is the same in
each of the five groups of products. In other words, there
is a high degree of consistency within the tables.

The general conclusion is that when independently-owned
stores are competing side by side with the chain stores and
supermarkets, they are supplying different markets. It is
not so much a question of comparative prices as it is of
finding out what people want and what they are willing to
pay. Some want credit and delivery and others do not. Those
who want both the commodity and the service make up one market, while those who want only the commodity make up another. There is one demand curve for commodities and a separate demand curve for services.

These demand curves are influenced by the personal
characteristics of the customer. There is one type of

shopper whose sense of importance is magnified by the feeling that she makes her own selections, serves herself, and gets the most for her money. There is another type that prefers to get her buying done with as little effort as possible and to use her time for other activities. In other words, the customer can buy groceries with services or without, just as one may often obtain a room in a hotel with or without adjoining bath. Certain alternatives are offered to the buyer, and the choice is determined by the buyer's income or preferences.

The effects of habit, convenience, and friendship for the proprietor on retail trade have already been mentioned. To illustrate, a family moves into a community, and since groceries are an immediate requirement one of the first things done is to find the nearest store. Perhaps the costs of moving have been high and the supply of cash has run low. A charge account, therefore, relieves the immediate burden of financing the household expenses.

The family continues to trade at the same store and gets on friendly terms with the proprietor. Perhaps the latter's wife helps in the store, and the lonesome newcomer welcomes the chance to chat with her while making the daily purchases. In this way a relationship springs up which will make the housewife reluctant to change to another store for the sake of a small price saving. She knows a pleasant relationship adds to the pleasure of trading, and that she would be embarrassed if she did not like the new store and came back to the old one.

In a large city, friendly relationships with the store
personnel may not be so important. It is interesting to
note (see Tables IX and X) that the 14 per cent[5]
differential found in Bloomington between the A. and P.
supermarket and the average of all stores checks closely
with the studies made by Professor Taylor in Durham, North
Carolina, and Professor Palmer in Lexington, Kentucky, in
1930, but is higher than the differentials found in the
large cities by the Federal Trade Commission.

Some investigators have raised the question as to
whether or not these differentials have grown smaller in
the last five years. For example, Professor Converse reported in 1931 a differential of 8.4 per cent existing in
Champaign-Urbana, Illinois, but a study in 1937 found a
difference between chains and independents of only 6.5 per
cent. One who is well acquainted with Bloomington might
explain the higher differential by pointing out how slowly
habits and customs change in this old town, located not
far from the Mason-Dixon line, and with what reluctance
modern business methods are adopted. This explanation of
continuing price differentials is supported by the fact
that the differential between the chains and the most
aggressive proprietor of the four independent stores studies is 7 per cent lower than the highest of the four.

---

5. Average index of 3 highest-price
              full-service independents   108
              Kroger chain   94
                                             ————
                                              14

The evidence given above supports strongly the conclusion that in the retail grocery trade, at least in Bloomington, there is a strong and persisting element of monopoly. Residents of Bloomington will patronize their favorite stores, regardless of such price differentials as exist. This preference or favoritism may be based on convenience, friendship with the proprietor, an income level high enough to make the customer indifferent to possible savings, a desire to trade at the same store with friends or with those who rank high socially, or simply habit and inertia. Where such a situation exists there is imperfect competition between the chain and the independent.

Table VII

Prices and Margins of Chain and Independent Distributors

City	Independents Amount	Index	Small Chain Amount	Index	Large Chain Amount	Index
(Grocery)						
Cincinnati[1]	$23.35	106.38	$22.08	100.6	$21.95	100
Detroit[2]	35.66	105.98	---	---	33.26	100
Memphis[3]	38.11	105.98	---	---	35.96	100
Washington[4]	58.03	107.30	---	---	54.08	100
(Drug)						
Cincinnati[5]	143.34	109.81	---	---	130.54	100
Washington[6]	130.09	110.72	---	---	117.49	100

1. Federal Trade Commission Report. "Chain Store Prices and Margins of Chain and Independent Distributors. Cincinnati--Grocery." Senate Document No. 88. 73rd Congress, 2nd Session. Page VIII ff. United States Government Printing Office. Washington. 1933.

2. F. T. C. Report. S.D. No. 81. Page X ff.

3. F. T. C. Report. S.D. No. 69. Page VIII ff.

4. F. T. C. Report. S.D. No. 269. Page X ff.

5. F. T. C. Report. S.D. No. 95. Page VIII.

6. F. T. C. Report. S.D. No. 98. Page VIII ff.

Table VIII

Results of Studies of Comparative Prices in Chain
and Independently-Owned Grocery Stores

Reference Number	City	Year	Number of Stores Studied	Number of Articles Compared	Average Saving in Chain Stores
1	New York	1929	1,022	50	4.6%
2	Chicago	1930	305 Independents 4 Chain Cos.	75	11.39%
3	Durham, N.C.	1930	36	60	13.79%
4	Lexington, Ky.	1930	44 Independents 5 Chain Cos.	58	14.3%
5	Atlanta, Ga.	1930	88	60	8.7%
6	New York	1930	*	*	10.71%
7	Albuquerque, N.M.	1931	14	30	10.00%
8	Champaign-Urbana, Ill.	1931	84	61	8.4%
9	New York	1932	95	48	8.53%
10	Minneapolis-St. Paul	1932	*	33	9.3%
11	Durham, N.C.	1934	79	60	11.0%
12	Canastota Canzenoria Earlville Hamilton Sherburne New York State	1935	*	52	10.02%
13	Champaigne-Urbana, Ill.	1937	110	66	6.5%

* Not specified.

See following page for sources. For summaries of other studies, See Appendix A, Supplement to Chapter XI.

104

References for Table VIII

1. R. S. Alexander, "A Study in Retail Grocery Prices."
   Published by The Journal of Commerce, New York, 1929.
   See Appendix A, Supplement to Chapter XI.
2. James L. Palmer and Einar Bjorklund, "A Study of the
   Prices of Chain and Independent Grocers in Chicago."
   Studies in Business Administration. Volume I, No. 4.
   The University of Chicago Press. 1930. See Appendix
   A, Supplement to Chapter XI.
3. Malcolm D. Taylor, "What Price Chain Groceries?"
   Harvard Business Review, Volume VIII, No. 4. Page 413.
   July, 1930. See Appendix A, Supplement to Chapter XI.
4. Edgar Z. Palmer, Reported in Journal of Commerce, July
   19, 1930 and August 2, 1930, and in Chain Store Progress,
   September, 1930. See Appendix A, Supplement to Chapter XI.
5. Maurice Ray Brewster, "Price Differentials in Chain
   and Independent Grocery Stores of Atlanta, 1930."
   Georgia School of Technology, Bulletin No. 10, July 25,
   1932.
6. Charles F. Phillips, Colgate University. Reported in
   Chain Store Progress, May, 1931. See No.
7. Myrtle Rush, "A Study of Chain Grocery Stores in
   Albuquerque, N. M." University of New Mexico, 1931.
   Reported in Chain Store Progress, November, 1931.
8. Paul D. Converse, "Prices and Services of Chain and
   Independent Stores in Champaign-Urbana, Ill." University of Illinois. NATMA Bulletin No. 4, October,
   1931. Published by National Association of Teachers
   of Marketing and Advertising, New York.
9. Dorothy Dowe, "A Comparison of Chain and Independent Store Prices." Journal of Business, University
   of Chicago, April, 1932. See Appendix A, Supplement
   to Chapter XI.
10. Roland S. Vaile and Alice M. Child, "Grocery Quali-
    ties and Prices." University of Minnesota Studies
    in Economics and Business No. 7. The University of
    Minnesota Press, Minneapolis, 1933. See Appendix A,
    Supplement to Chapter XI.
11. Malcolm D. Taylor, "Prices of Branded Grocery Commodi-
    ties During the Depression." Harvard Business Review,
    July, 1934.
12. Charles F. Phillips, "Chain, Voluntary Chain, and
    Independent Grocery Store Prices." Journal of Busi-
    ness, University of Chicago, April, 1935.
13. Paul D. Converse, "Prices and Services of Chain and
    Independent Stores in Champaign-Urbana, Ill."
    Journal of Marketing, January, 1938.

Table IX

Average Savings in Chain Stores Reported by
The Federal Trade Commission

City	Number of Stores Studied	Number of Articles Compared	Average Saving in Chain Stores
(Grocery)			
Cincinnati[1]	608	120	8.1%-9.0%
Detroit[2]	2,264	183	9.5%
Memphis[3]	437	193	7.7%
Washington, D.C.[4]	570	274	6.0%
(Drug)			
Cincinnati[5]	262	268	16.9%
Detroit[6]	534	256	14.9%
Memphis[7]	171	212	17.1%
Washington, D.C.[8]	180	226	18.5%

1. Federal Trade Commission Report. "Chain Store Prices
    and Margins of Chain and Independent Distributors.
    Cincinnati--Grocery." Senate Document No. 88. 73rd
    Congress, 2nd Session. Page VIII ff. United States
    Government Printing Office. Washington. 1933.

2. F. T. C. Report. S.D. No. 81. Page X ff.

3. F. T. C. Report. S.D. No. 69. Page VIII ff.

4. F. T. C. Report. S.D. No. 269. Page X ff.

5. F. T. C. Report. S.D. No. 95. Page VIII.

6. F. T. C. Report. S.D. No. 96. Page VIII.

7. F. T. C. Report. S.D. No. 97. Page VIII.

8. F. T. C. Report. S.D. No. 98. Page VIII ff.

For detailed information of the results of a study
of comparative selling prices of chain and independently-
owned grocery and drug stores in Florida, see Beckman,
Theodore N., and Nolen, Herman C. "The Chain Store
Problem." Pages 102 ff. McGraw-Hill Book Company, New
York and London. 1938.

Table X

Comparison of Prices in Chain and Independently-Owned Grocery Stores in Bloomington, Indiana

(Indexes Based on Average Prices of all Stores)

	No. 1		No. 2		No. 3		No. 4		No. 5		No. 6		No. 7		No. 8		No. 9		No. 10	
	Number of Items	Index	Number of Items	Index	Number of Items	Index	Number of Items	Index	Number of Items	Index	Number of Items	Index	Number of Items	Index	Number of Items	Index	Number of Items	Index	Number of Items	Index
Breakfast Foods	5	109	5	104	5	103	5	108	5	94	5	97	5	88	5	88	5	86	5	113
Soaps	8	112	8	103	7	114	8	106	8	96	3	107	3	38	6	95	7	82	7	108
Laundry Supplies	5	108	5	94	5	110	5	108	5	96	5	97	5	95	5	97	5	89	5	105
Canned Foods	8	104	8	108	7	109	8	108	8	96	8	99	8	97	8	94	8	83	5	101
Miscellaneous	25	110	24	104	23	106	23	106	24	98	24	104	24	95	21	97	11	87	11	100
General Index	51	109	49	103	47	108	49	107	50	97	50	103	45	94	51	95	33	86	33	104

Stores No.'s 1, 2, 3, and 4--Independently-owned, single unit, service.
Store No. 5--Independently-owned, single unit, non-service.
Store No. 6--Local chain, limited service.
Store No. 7--Kroger's.
Store No. 8--Marsell's Supermarket.
Store No. 9--Atlantic and Pacific Supermarket.
Store No. 10--Country General Store--Local chain.

Table XI

Comparison of Prices in Chain and Independently-Owned Grocery Stores
in
Bloomington, Indiana

(Indexes Bases on Lowest Prices Quoted in Any Store)

	No. 1		No. 2		No. 3		No. 4		No. 5		No. 6		No. 7		No. 8		No. 9		No. 10	
	Number of Items	Index	Number of Items	Index	Number of Items	Index	Number of Items	Index	Number of Items	Index	Number of Items	Index	Number of Items	Index	Number of Items	Index	Number of Items	Index	Number of Items	Index
Breakfast Foods	5	129	5	123	5	122	5	128	5	110	5	114	5	102	5	102	5	101	5	134
Soaps	8	136	8	126	8	139	7	130	8	117	8	132	6	107	8	117	8	103	7	130
Laundry Supplies	5	122	5	105	5	123	5	120	5	108	5	110	5	106	5	108	5	100	5	118
Canned Foods	8	130	8	134	7	111	7	138	8	120	8	123	8	120	8	117	8	103	5	127
Miscellaneous	25	131	23	122	23	126	23	125	24	116	24	125	21	113	25	113	11	102	11	124
General Index	51	130	49	123	49	129	47	128	50	116	50	123	45	111	51	112	33	102	33	126

Stores No.'s 1, 2, 3, and 4--Independently-owned, single unit, service.
Store No. 5--Independently-owned, single unit, non-service.
Store No. 6--Local chain, single unit, limited service.
Store No. 7--Kroger's.
Store No. 8--Karsell's Supermarket.
Store No. 9--Atlantic and Pacific Supermarket.
Store No. 10--Country General Store, Local Chain.

Chapter X

COMPARISON OF COSTS OF OPERATION OF CHAINS AND INDEPENDENTS

In this chapter an attempt will be made to compare the costs of operation of chain and independently-owned grocery stores in Indiana. The data were obtained through personal interviews as a part of the study made in 1938 by the School of Business at Indiana University.

Although this study[1] was conducted in sixteen selected counties representing the four classifications mentioned above (Industrial, Semi-Industrial, Semi-Rural, and Rural), conclusions will be drawn here only from the information obtained from the groceries located in Bloomington. The reason for this is that the number of stores studied in this city is a large enough proportion of the total to eliminate the necessity for using mathematical procedures

---

1. This Indiana study was primarily to obtain some facts about the relative tax loads of chains and independents. Concrete information about taxes paid could be obtained easily from the grocers' tax receipts, and this could be checked against the state and county records. Unfortunately the same cannot be said about other retailing costs. The absence of any adequate system of record-keeping in the grocery business, particularly in the smaller stores is appalling. Statistical methods are of little value. What, for example, is the average rent paid by two grocers, one of whom gets his rent "free" because his mother-in-law, who lives with his family, owns the building his store is in; the other pays $40 a month rent, with a business doing less than $10,000 a year on a 20 per cent gross margin?

for testing the reliability of the sample.[2]

The variations in costs of operation among grocery
stores, both chains and independents, are considerable.
For example, Table XII shows the dispersion in one group
of chain stores, all located in the same county, and all
owned and operated by the same company:[3]

Table XII

Variations in Costs of Operation

Range	Gross Margin*	Total Expense*	Net Profit*
Low	19.40%	16.81%	1.58%
Average	22.67	18.52	4.16
High	25.72	20.34	8.91

* In terms of percentage of sales.

2. "In the usual run of marketing investigations, there
    seldom is opportunity or need for the more advanced
    statistical technique often found useful in the exact
    sciences. Extreme refinements are usually unnecessary,
    too, for marketing data ordinarily contain unknown
    'loaded' errors greater than the theoretically probable
    error in a given statistical manipulation. This prin-
    ciple is sometimes overlooked by statisticians who
    place too great emphasis upon the technique of their
    craft. The higher flights in statistical analysis are
    very interesting to one who has mastered them and it is
    easy to become absorbed in the beauties of a brilliant
    technical exercise in statistical theory, while losing
    sight of the practical realities of a marketing situa-
    tion."

    "The Technique of Marketing Research." Prepared by the
    Committee on Marketing Research Technique of the American
    Marketing Soceity, p. 359. McGraw-Hill Book Company,
    Inc. New York. 1937.

3. These data were obtained by the author directly from the
    records of this organization.

Stores belonging to the same local chain in Bloomington
varied in the ratio of rent to sales from a low of 0.58 per
cent to a high of 1.78 per cent. (See Table   XV   )
Differences in operating costs of independently-owned grocers were even greater. To illustrate, two stores from
which rather detailed and apparently reliable information
about expenses was obtained, each with an annual sales
volume of approximately $40,000, showed ratios of wages to
sales to be 4.72 per cent and 13.71 per cent (absolute
amounts, $1832 and $5482 respectively). These variations
are due to a number of factors, such as inequalities in
rentals paid, differences in the merchandising abilities of
the proprietors, and so on. One important cause of such
variations is the fact that many grocers can obtain the
help of their wives and other members of their families
without cost. Their situations are very similar to that of
a farmer with several grown sons and daughters who are able
and willing to help him with his farming.

There are 58 grocery stores listed in the Bloomington
telephone book. Of these, eight belong to the local chain,
one is a unit of the Kroger Grocery and Baking Company, and
two are supermarkets (Atlantic and Pacific Tea Company and
Karsell's, the latter operated by an independent grocery

wholesaler.) There are, then, approximately 48 independently-owned, single-unit groceries. More or less detailed
information about expenses was obtained from 34 of these,
and a complete statement of operations for the year 1937
was supplied by the owner of the local chain. Although no
report on this particular Kroger store was procured, comparisons can be made by inference, based on complete statements of other Kroger stores operating in essentially the
same situations.

Not much is known about the operating expenses of the
supermarkets in Bloomington. The Atlantic and Pacific Tea
Company supplied detailed statements containing averages of
a number of stores in various localities throughout the
state of Indiana, but refused to divulge information about
individual units. The attempt to investigate the expenses
of Karsell's was unsuccessful. The investigator was fortunate, however, in being able to ascertain the costs of a
supermarket located in a larger city about 100 miles distant.

The reports supplied by A. and P., Kroger's, and the
local chain give considerable information about the costs
of wholesaling operations for these types of organizations.
Costs of independent wholesalers in this comparison are
judged by inferences based on material recently published
by the Indiana Tax Study Commission.

The data presented here concerning the operating expenses of grocers in Bloomington were obtained by an investigator who had more than ten years experience in the

grocery business. He called on the stores individually,
and secured the information by inspecting the grocer's
records, by questioning him about his expenses, and by
"sizing up" the store. The expense distributions obtained
were classified according to the annual volume of sales
reported in the following manner:

Table XIII
Classification of Stores Included in Bloomington Expense Study

	Annual Sales Volume	Number of Cases	% of Total Number of Cases	% of Total No. of 48 Independ.	% of Total No. of 58 Groceries
Class A	Over $50,000	4	10.5%	8.3	6.8%
Class B	$20,000 to $50,000	12	31.6	25.0	20.7
Class C	10,000 to 20,000	10	26.3	20.8	17.3
Class D	Less than $10,000	12	31.6	25.0	20.7
	Totals	38	100.0	79.1	65.5

Apparently there is little to be gained from a comparison that includes the Class D group.[5] An analysis of the
information obtained from these twelve stores and the
author's own experience in the field during the Indiana
survey warrant the following description of a typical
grocery in this class:

It is a "one-man store." The proprietor does most of

---

5. "It would be interesting to compare the chain store
    method of distribution with that of an efficient and up-
    to-date wholesaler-retailer combination, rather than
    with the group. We have so many inefficient wholesalers
    and retailers who tend to make any group study mislead-
    ing." Statement by Professor Malcolm D. Taylor, in a
    personal letter to the author.

the work, but is assisted by his wife and other members of
the family, who receive no pay. He is usually located in a
poor residential district, and draws most of his trade from
the lower income group. He makes a few deliveries in the
immediate neighborhood; probably carrying the groceries on
foot while his wife "watches the store." He has to "carry"
a number of his customers when they are not working, and
hope some day to collect from them. His stock inventories
at cost about $200, and his fixtures at $500. The latter
are old, however, and would bring little at a forced sale.
He keeps few records,[6] but his operations would be repre-

---

6. One proprietor of a small grocery, when the author asked
to see his books, reached up behind a can of beans for a
roll of invoices. He had no other records, so far as
could be determined. Reports of the other investigators
showed that this case was not unusual.

(See next page)

sented by the following statement:

Stock	$200	Annual Sales	$7000		100.00
Fixtures	500	Cost of Merchandise			
Total Capital		(80% of sales)	600		80.00
Investment	$700	Gross Margin	1400		20.00
		Total Expense	1393		19.86
		Net profit	7		0.14

Expenses
Owner's Salary (Estimated at $15 per week)[7] 11.1% $780.00
Wages Paid ------------------------------- None
Rent (Front room of dwelling--family lives in
    the rear--estimated[9] at $5 per month) 0.86 60.00
Light, heat, power, and water ------------ 1.43 100.00
Telephone (Pay station--estimated[9] minimum
    required by telephone company
    $3 per month) ---------------- 0.51 36.00
Supplies (estimated at $10 per month)---- 1.71 120.00
Taxes & Licenses
  Gross Income (1% on sales, less $3000
           exemption)-------------$40.00
  State license--------------------- 3.50
  License to sell oleomargarine-------- 6.00
  Local property tax (estimated)[8]------ 12.50
     (9)   Total----------- 62.00-0.89 62.00
Advertising (none)   (9)
Maintenance and Depreciation (estimated
      at $10 per month)------ 1.71 120.00
Dues and Donations (none)[9]
Insurance (estimated) --------------- 0.29 20.00
Interest on Investment at 5% --------- 0.50 35.00
Miscellaneous (estimated at $5 per month) 0.86 60.00

           Total Annual Expense   19.86 1393.00

---

7. Based on typical wage of $18 per week paid to grocery salespeople in the local chain in Bloomington. This man could not compete as a grocery clerk with younger and more active men.

8. Actual average of property tax paid for year 1937 by 13 grocery stores in Bloomington, all with annual sales volume of less than $10,000. Obtained from local tax records.

9. Other estimates based on information obtained by investigator.

In a sense, such stores as the one just described are more of the nature of outlets for the independent wholesaler than they are individual businesses. Considering the amount of labor obtained from the proprietors' families at not cost,[10] the wholesaler gets cheap distribution, compared, for example, to the owner of the local chain in Bloomington.[11]

Certainly some wholesalers solicit the trade of these small stores. One proprietor in this group reported that the number of salesman calling on him each week averaged about as follows:

Bread	4
Cakes	2
Candy and tobacco	3
Coffee	4
Cookies and crackers	2
Flour	3
Fruits and vegetables	4
Ice cream	1
Meatpacking houses	3
Milk	2
Soft drinks	6
Wholesale grocers	3
Total	37

This same proprietor also stated that 66 meatpacking houses send their representatives to Bloomington. The sales reported for this store were as follows:

1934	$3,750
1935	7,881
1936	5,818
1937	5,952
1938 (1st 3 mos. only)	1,635

10. Six out of the 12 proprietors in this group said their wives and other members of the family helped in the store without pay.

11. See p. 127.

In the Class C group one begins to find that more business-like methods are used. Six of the twelve cases studied were able to supply the investigator with fairly complete records of their operations. Five of the twelve, with an average annual sales volume of $12,998[12] reported that they had no paid employees. Not one of the twelve included in his report any salary paid to the owner. Three showed no rental charge, six apparently did no advertising, and none made any charge against the business for donations or association dues.[13]

The following typical operating statement was constructed from the reports of four stores in Class C, with an average

---

12.

	Annual Sales Volume
Case #13	$10,800
Case #14	11,060
Case #15	12,000
Case #17	14,303
Case #20	16,829
	$64,992

13. Just one of the 38 cases studied made any charge against his business for donations or dues. Reference to this fact will be made in a later chapter.

(See next page)

annual sales volume of $16,549.[14]

Capital Investment

Stock (Inventory at Cost)		$	800
Fixtures (Purchase Price)			1,700
Total ----		$	2,500

Total Sales (Based on 1937 Records)	$ 16,550	100.00
Cost of Merchandise Sold (Average Markup of 20%)	13,240	80.00
Gross Margin ----	$ 3,310	20.00
Total Operating Expense	$ 4,290	25.40
Gross Margin	3,310	20.00
Net Loss	$ 980	5.40

Stock Turnover (Times annually) --20

Expenses

	Amount	Per Cent of Sales
Proprietor's Salary[15]	$ 1,300.00	7.85
(Estimated at $25. a week)		
Other Salaries & Wages	1,300.00	7.85
Rent	300.00	1.81
Light, Heat, Power & Water	200.00	1.21
Telephone	50.00	0.30
Supplies	150.00	0.91
Delivery	250.00	1.21
Advertising	50.00	0.30
Maintenance & Depreciation	100.00	0.60
Insurance	50.00	6.30
Taxes & Licenses		
State License ---- $ 3.50		
Oleomargarine Permit 6.00		
Property Tax ----- 40.00		
Gross Income Tax 135.50		
Federal Old Age Pension 130.00		
	315.00	1.90
Interest on Investment at 5%	125.00	0.76
Miscellaneous	100.00	0.60
Total Expense	$4,290.00	25.40

14.
Case #19	$15,483
Case #20	16,829
Case #21	16,882
Case #22	17,000
	$66,194
Average	16,549

(1937 figures)

15. Comparable to the $25.00 per week paid to the managers of the units in the local chain at Bloomington.

It is obvious that the proprietor of a store of this
size, who must meet expenses such as listed, is not receiving an income equivalent to what he could earn as a grocery
clerk who has no investment and no responsibilities beyond
his daily routine.[16] On the other hand, a family of just a
man and wife, by working together, with perhaps some extra
help on Saturdays, could with such a store have a joint income of approximately $1500 a year. In addition, they would
be obtaining food supplies at wholesale prices. A man with
a large family and plenty of help at no cost, where the
savings obtained on grocery bills would be considerable,
could with his grocery store obtain at least an income at
subsistence level, with some degree of security and
independence.[17]

One gains from this typical record of operations an
inkling of why independent wholesalers have fought the chain
stores so bitterly. If the former can get outlets, each
with an annual volume of approximately $13,000 (at wholesale
prices) and requiring at least two persons to operate, at a
total annual labor cost of $1500, with no initial outlay be-
yond the credit granted, they are getting distribution with
lower wage costs than the chains can obtain. It leads one
to question the sincerity of their appeal to the community's

---

16. The proprietor of a grocery in Mishawaka, Indiana, who
    was formerly an employee in a bank that failed, told
    the author he would gladly give up his store for a
    permanent position at $40 a week.

17. There is also the feeling of satisfaction at "being in
    business for himself."

sympathy for the small merchant.

Fairly complete (and ostensibly accurate) records were obtained from eight of the twelve cases included in the Class B group (sales volume in 1937, $20,000 to $50,000). Wide variations appear in the amounts of the individual items. Cases #24, #27, #28, and #31 reported sales as $35,302, $40,000, $40,000, and $50,000 respectively, with corresponding wage bills of $5258, $5482, $5202, and $6032. These wage payments are very much higher than the $1820, $2070, $1832, and $1724 reported by Cases #23, #25, #26, and #29 (see Table XIV below). For $5482 a grocer could employ,

Table XIV

Showing Differences in Wage Payments Reported
Class B ($20,000 to $50,000 annually)

	High Reported Sales 1937	Reported Wage Costs		Low Reported Sales 1937	Reported Wage Costs
Case #24	$35,302	$5258	Case #23	$30,000	$1820
Case #27	40,000	5482	Case #25	36,400	2070
Case #28	40,000	5202	Case #26	38,968	1832
Case #31	50,000	6032	Case #29	48,189	1724
Averages	$41,326	$5494		$38,389	$1862

at the top prevailing wage for grocery clerks in Bloomington, 274 salespersons for one week, or more than 50 for the entire year. The author knows of no grocery in Bloomington of that size.[18]

Similar discrepancies appear among the other expense
items. There seem to be no definite correlations between
the amounts of these items and the reported sales volumes.
Rent ranges from a low of $300 per year to a high of
$1163;[19] advertising from $24 for a volume of $48,189 to a
high of $365 for a $40,000 volume;[20] delivery from $124,
volume $48,189, to $462, volume $38,968.

The expense distribution shown here for this group is
adapted from the one reported for Case #29. Only three
items were missing (owner's salary, supplies, and insurance), and the stated amounts appear reasonable, judging
from the reports of the entire group of 38. A sharp division appears in this group that seems to be explained only
by the quasi-monopolistic situation discussed in the previous chapter. Cases #24, #27, and #29 report average mark-
ups of 30.9 per cent, 23.2 per cent, and 33 1/3 per cent
respectively, and their records seem to bear out these
statements. The other cases agree on 20 per cent. Tabulated they appear as follows:

		Case #27	Case #28
Total Sales (1937)	$35,302	$40,000	$48,189
Cost of Mdse Sold	24,435	30,734	32,114
Gross Margin	$10,867	$ 9,266	$16,075
Ratio, Gross Margin to Sales	30.7%	23.2%	33.3%

18. The larger amounts stated may include a salary for the
    owner, although only one report, Case #25, made an addi-
    tional allowance, $900, for owner's salary.
19. Two cases reported ownership of location, no allowance
    for rent.
20. Reports of volume are not dependable, since the amount
    of sales determines the amount of gross income tax to
    be paid.

Expense Distribution of Independently-Owned Groceries
in Bloomington, Indiana
(Class B, Sales Volume $40,000 to $50,000)
(Adapted from Actual Report, Case #29)

Capital Investment—		Sales Volume (1937)[1]—$48,000	100.00
Stock (Inventory at Cost)[1]—$1,200		Cost of Mdse Sold	
Fixtures ——— [1]	2,000	(Markup 33 1/3% on	
Total ——	$3,200	cost, 25% on sales) 36,000	75.00
		Gross Margin —— $12,000	25.00
		Total Expense 6,390	13.34
		Net Profit —— $ 9,610	11.66

Expense Distribution

	Amount	Ratio (% of Sales)
Owner's Salary (at $40 per week[2]) ——$2,080		4.33
Other Salaries & Wages ———	1,800	3.75
Rent ——[3]	575	1.20
Light, Heat, Power & Water[1]	200	0.47
Telephone — [1]	50	0.10
Supplies ——[4]	275	0.57
Delivery ——[5]	285	0.58
Advertising [6]	140	0.29
Taxes, Permits & Licenses [7]	475	0.99
Maintenance & Depreciation[8]	250	0.52
Donations, Association Dues, etc (none)	——	——
Insurance [10] ——	100	0.21
Interest on Investment at 5% —	160	0.33
Credit Losses —— [11] —	-	-
Total Expense	$6,390	13.34

1. As reported.
2. Equivalent to highest salary paid to a manager of a unit in the local chain in Bloomington.
3. Average of 8 cases in this group. Case #29 reported a rental of $492.
4. Average of 5 cases.
5. Average of 6 cases. Case #29 reported $124.
6. Average of 6 cases. Case #29 reported $24, evidence that little advertising has been necessary to hold the established trade of this store. Proprietor stated that he used only handbills. The author has observed that apparently these are used, not to attract new trade, but to give the regular customers information about the weekend specials as a guide to their ordering; a service the main purpose of which is to hold the trade already established.
7. As reported. Gross income tax paid checks closely with sales figures given, and also with average of 6 reporting on this item of expense.
8. Most reports made little or no allowance for depreciation of fixtures. Ten per cent annually allowed here, plus $50 for maintenance. Probably too low.
9. Only one report contained information on this item.
10. Average of 8 cases. No agreement. Amounts reported range from $18 to $360. Proprietors apparently do not separate personal property insurance from the insurance that should be charged directly to the business.
11. No information. Case #26 reported a loss on bad debts in 1937 of $800, volume $38,968. Depends to large extent on agressiveness of proprietor in collecting unpaid accounts.

The Class A group of four stores, with sales volumes in
1937 ranging from $60,000 for Case #35 to $76,636 for Case
#25, show as wide variations in the individual expense items
as do the other groups. Examples are shown below:

	Low	High
Wages	$4,404	$5,807
Rent	500	900
Heat, Light, Power & Water	348	720
Telephone	66	114
Delivery	156	1,200
Advertising	60	360

When two groceries in the same city, with reported
sales as close as $69,091 and $75,000, show delivery costs
as widely different as $156 and $1,200 respectively, one
finds it difficult to arrive at a typical cost figure.
Credit and delivery costs have been identified as being one
cause of the price differential existing between chains and
independents.[21] Here are groceries large enough to make
accurate accounts an absolute necessity, but submitting reports showing a wide divergence in this important expense
item.[22] Even the largest delivery expense item reported is
less than 2 per cent of the reported annual sales volume.
And in the Class B group, the $800 loss reported by Case #26
on unpaid accounts in 1937 was only 2 per cent of his re-

---

21. An investigator reported to the author that Kroger's
    chain store and the two supermarkets in Bloomington
    are the only large food stores operating on a strictly
    cash-and-carry basis. The local chain and the inde-
    pendents all deliver without extra charge.

22. Nor is there any incentive to falsify figures, as with
    the sales volume.

123

ported sales volume of $38,968. This leaves unexplained
the difference between the price index (based on average
prices quoted) of 95 for Karsell's cash-and-carry supermarket, and 103 for the lowest-priced full-service independent. Tabulated, this comparison is as follows:

	Index
Lowest-Priced Full-Service Independent---	103
Highest-Priced Cash-and-carry Chain------	95
Difference--	8
Highest Reported Delivery Cost (% of Sales)	1.60
Highest Reported Credit Lose (% of Sales)	2.05
Total	3.65

An article costing 95¢ at Karsell's could profitably
be charged and delivered for 99¢ (assuming sufficient volume). The additional 4¢ differential indicated by the
indexes cannot be explained as a service charge. The difference is even more striking when the indexes are compared
that were computed with the lowest quoted prices as the
bases (see Chapter IX). Taking Kroger's as a typical chain
store, with an index of 111, the local chain, which delivers
and gives a very limited amount of credit to carefully
selected customers, has an index of 123 or a differential
of 12 points; the highest price, full-service independent's
index is 130 with a difference of 19 points.

In other words, a considerable differential exists between the prices of cash-and-carry chains and full-service
independents, even after allowance is made for the costs
of service. This differential apparently can be explained
only by the element of monopoly present, which was discussed
in the previous chapter.

The typical expense distribution presented here was constructed from the four reports obtained in the Class A group (1937 sales of more than $50,000). In this group the lowest sales reported were $60,000; the highest, $76,636. Definite information secured from these reports have made possible what appear to be rather accurate estimates of the actual amounts of the various expense items.[23]

Typical Expense Distribution of Groceries in Bloomington, Ind.
(Class A Group-1937 Sales More than $50,000)

Capital Investment-		Annual Sales (1937)	$73,500	100.0
Stock	$4,500	Cost of Mdse Sold-	60,000	87.6
(Inven. at cost)		Gross Margin-	$13,500	18.4
Fixtures-	10,000	Total Expense-	13,279	18.08
Total	$14,500	Net Profit	221	0.28

Expenses

	Amount	Ratio-% of Sales
Owner's Salary-[1]	$3,000	4.08
Other-Salaries & Wages	5,000	6.80
Rent	600	0.82
Light, Heat, Power & Water	400	0.54
Telephone	100	0.14
Supplies	350	0.48
Delivery	600	0.82
Advertising	200	0.27
Maintenance & Depreciation	1,200	1.63

Taxes, Permits, & Licenses

Store License	$3.50	
Oleo Permit	6.00	
Property Tax	64.50	
Gross Income Tax	705.00	
Federal Old Age Benefit	50.00	

	Amount	Ratio-% of Sales
Total	1,829	1.74
Insurance	175	0.24
Interest on Investment	725	0.98
Miscellaneous	100	0.14

1. Estimated wage as a manager.

---

23. For example:

(see next page)

The individual stores in the local chain show almost
as wide a variation in the expense items as the single-
unit, independently-owned stores. The local chain consists
of eight stores in Bloomington, and at the time the report
was obtained there were at least two in other locations. A
new one has just been opened up not far from the city limits
of Indianapolis. The site of the largest store is the downtown business district of Bloomington on the courthouse
square. The capital investment in this store in 1937 was
$31,186,51, and an annual rent of $3,925 is paid for the
location. The sales for this store for four years were reported as follows:

1934	$234,820.77
1935	263,647.17
1936	222,483.51
1937	219,259.41

1st 3 months, 1938--$43,784.97

---

23. (continued)

Case #35   Annual Sales   Actual Total of Expenses per
month in 1937 was $665.12,
including the following items:

	Annual Sales
1935	$58,000
1936	65,000
1937	60,000

Rent (@ $90 per month)
Salaries & Wages
Drawing Account
Light, Heat & Power
Advertising
Supplies
Delivery
Phone
Taxes & Insurance
   Total (annual) $9061.44

The total of these same items in the typical expense
account is $8,704.

Case #36--   Annual Sales

	Annual Sales
1935	$29,405
1936	49,613
1937	65,091

Net profit in 1937--$3,490.83, or 5.47% of sales.

The other stores show no such variation in volume, except No. 5 which went from $29,000 in 1934 to $45,000 in 1935; then dropped to $36,000 in 1936 and $32,000 in 1937. If the sales in the largest store continued at the same rate for 1938 as they were for the first three months, the expected volume for that year would have been $175,139.88. This very considerable drop from previous years may be due to the opening of other stores in this same chain or of the two supermarkets. The rent paid for the location of this downtown store is more than twenty times the $180 paid annually for No. 5. The ratio of rent to sales, based on 1937 figures, is 1.78 per cent as compared to 0.58 per cent for No. 5. Table XV shows the ratios, totals, averages, and means for all the individual expense items.

Stores No.'s 2, 3, 4, 6, 7, and 8 in this local chain show a considerable degree of uniformity in operation expense and sales volume. It is difficult, however, to determine from the records the amount of warehouse expense that should be charged to each store. An investigator reported that the firm engages in the wholesale business as well as supplying the stores. This firm reported sales at wholesale of more than $200,000.

The average markup, either at wholesale or retail, is not known, but from the price study made it appears that the retail markup is slightly less than those stores which reported a markup of 20 per cent. According to the report of this firm, the wholesale expense based on sales at wholesale prices is 6.45 per cent.

Table XV

Expense Ratios of 8 Stores of a Local Chain in Bloomington of 1937

	Store #1	Store #2	Store #3	Store #4	Store #5	Store #6	Store #7	Store #8	Average of Eight Stores	Median
Rent	1.78	1.07	1.12	0.93	0.58	1.17	1.12	1.58	1.17	1.12
Salaries & Wages	9.75	7.85	8.26	7.54	7.86	7.36	8.29	7.38	8.04	7.86
Light, Power & Water	0.66	0.83	1.19	0.88	0.83	0.80	0.78	1.16	0.89	0.83
Telephone	0.10	0.11	0.17	0.16	0.19	0.14	0.15	0.13	0.14	0.18
Advertising	0.85	0.28	0.49	0.43	0.51	0.40	0.42	0.38	0.47	0.43
Maintenance	0.25	0.12	0.14	0.35	0.26	0.12	0.28	0.42	0.24	0.26
Insurance	0.41	0.13	0.23	0.20	0.35	0.18	0.18	0.17	0.23	0.19
Federal Old Age Benefit	0.07	0.05	0.06	0.05	0.06	0.05	0.05	0.05	0.06	0.05
Unemployment Compensation	0.14	0.12	0.13	0.11	0.13	0.11	0.11	0.11	0.12	0.12
Supplies	0.38	0.25	0.40	0.29	0.24	0.25	0.27	0.39	0.31	0.28
Gross Income Tax	0.79	0.95	0.98	0.97	0.99	0.98	0.98	0.87	0.94	0.98
Other Tax & License	0.19	0.11	0.18	0.17	0.20	0.16	0.17	0.14	0.17	0.17
Service	1.12	0.47	0.81	0.65	0.71	0.64	0.68	0.65	0.71	0.67
Total	16.49	12.34	14.16	12.73	12.91	12.36	13.48	13.41	13.49	13.14

The operating statement for an orthodox chain, shown below, was constructed from the report for a chain store unit, located in a near-by town and operating under essentially similar conditions. This is done to avoid any chance of disclosing the operations of an individual unit.

Operating Statement of a Typical Kroger Chain Store Unit

		Amount	% of Sales
Capital Investment--	Sales (1937)	$50,000	100.00
Fixtures (not given)	Cost of Mdse	38,938	77.88
Inventory (at cost)----$2,000	Gross Margin	11,062	22.12
	Total Expense	9,850	19.69
	Net Profit	1,212	2.43

Expenses--Retailing	Amount	% of Sales
Salaries (1)	$4,182	8.37
Rent -----	792	1.58
Light, Heat, Power		
Water	565	1.13
Telephone	100	0.20
Supplies---	405	0.81
Advertising---	192	0.38
Maintenance & Deprec.--	233	0.49
Taxes		
Property Tax--(e)	125	0.25
Gross Income Tax--	500	1.00
Chain Store Tax--	145	0.29
Other Taxes & Licenses	10	0.02
Other Expense-- (2)	923	1.85
Total Retailing Exp.	$8,172	15.88
Expenses--Wholesaling-	992	1.98
Transp-Whlsng	686	1.37
	$1,678	3.35
Total Expense---------	$9,850	19.69

e. Estimated
x. Not given
1. Includes charge against store for supervision
2. Includes insurance, interest, and administration

The Atlantic and Pacific Tea Company's store, which was formerly located on the east side of the courthouse square, was closed when the supermarket was opened. It was in operation in 1937, however, the year for which costs were obtained, and the operating statement of this store for that year was obtained directly from the company.

Operating Expense Statement of A. & P. Store Formerly
Located in Bloomington--Now Closed

Capital Investment--		Amount	% of Sales
Fixtures (not given) (4)	Sales (1937)	$69,802	100.00
Stock--Inventory at Cost--$3,564 (1)	Cost of Mdse	55,018	78.82
	Gross Margin	$14,784	21.18
	Total Exp.	15,847	22.69
Expenses--Retailing (3)	Net Loss	$ 1,063	1.51

	Amount	% of Sales
Manager's Salary-----	$ 2,676	3.83
Other Salaries & Wages-	3,278	4.68
Total Salaries & Wages	$ 5,954	8.51
Rent--	2,700	3.86
General Branch Exp. incl (2)		
Depreciation & Deferred Exp	3,082	4.42
Advertising--Direct $ 94		
Indirect 296		
Total------	390	0.56
Taxes, Permits &		
Licenses		
Property Tax--------	196	0.28
Store	145	0.21
Gross Income Tax-----	681	0.98
Other Taxes & Licenses	23	0.03
	$13,171	18.85
Expenses--Wholesaling		
Delivery & Wholesaling	1,268	1.82
Supervision & Admin.	1,408	2.02
	2,676	3.84
Total Expense, Whls & Ret.	$17,583	22.69

1. The "cost of merchandise" ratio to sales used above, 78.82, was obtained from the report supplied by another national chain. Confidential.
2. Includes light, heat and power, telephone, supplies, insurance, maintenance and depreciation, interest on investment, and misc.
3. A business man in Bloomington, in casual conversation with the author, remarked that "the A. and P. store that used to be here didn't do so well."
4. Assessed valuation, $2,000.

130

No direct information could be obtained about the operating expenses of the supermarkets. The statement below is adapted from the report of another supermarket, located in a city less than 100 miles away, and operating under essentially the same conditions.

Expense Distribution of A Cash-and-Carry Supermarket
Located in Central Indiana

Capital Investment--		Amount	% of Sales
Fixtures---$ 8,000	Sales (1937)	$235,000	100.00
Stock-- 7,200	Cost of Mdse	185,000	78.72
$15,200	Gross Margin	50,000	21.28
	Total Expense	41,100	17.49
	Net Profit	8,900	3.79

Expense Distribution	Amount	% of Sales
Owner's Salary--------	$ 4,000	1.70
Other Salaries & Wages--	19,400	8.26
Total Salaries & Wages	23,400	9.96
Rent -------	3,600	1.53
Light, Heat, Power & Water	1,300	0.55
Telephone	360	0.15
Supplies--	1,860	0.79
Advertising---	3,000	1.28
Maintenance & Deprec.	2,840	1.21
Taxes--		
Property Tax-	400	0.17
Gross Income Tax--	2,350	1.00
Federal Old Age Benefit	190	0.08
Unemployment Compensation	380	0.16
Other Taxes & Licenses	390	0.17
Miscellaneous--	$ 41,100	17.49

The wholesaling ratio (total expenses, exclusive of profit, to sales at wholesale prices) is assumed for purposes of comparison to be 6.50 per cent for the independent wholesalers and 4.00 per cent for the chains. The net profit margin for the independents is taken as 1.00 per cent of sales at wholesale prices.

This figure of 6.50 per cent for the independent wholesalers is midway between the figure shown in the report of
the local chain doing a wholesale business, and the total
expense ratio for the wholesale grocery business published
in the report of the Indiana Tax Study Commission. (See
Table XVIII.) The ratio reported for the local chain can
be shaded downward, because the report shows no wholesaling
charge made against the retail stores in the chain. The
figure published by the Commission can be shaded upward,
since the item labeled "Cost of Goods and Other Services
Purchased" evidently includes some charge in addition to
the cost of the merchandise.

The ratio of net profit to sales for the profit group
is given by the Commission as 1.22 per cent. This can be
shaded downward, because approximately one-sixth of the
wholesale grocery business in Indiana is operated at a
loss. The wholesaling cost of an orthodox chain is shown
to be 3.35 per cent, but this is shaded upward to allow a
margin of safety for the variations in costs known to
exist. (See page 133 .)

The evidence presented here supports the following
conclusions concerning the grocery business in Bloomington,
Indiana:

1. In the independently-owned, single-unit, full-
service group, the ratio of expense to sales in those stores
with an annual volume of less than $5,000 is approximately
20 per cent (19.86). This size of business produces for the

owner an income of approximately $800 per year, assuming a
markup of 20 per cent. But in most cases he gets some unpaid labor from his family, and he has no margin of pure
profit.

2. When the independent grocer's business increases
to between $10,000 and $20,000, the expense ratio rises
sharply to more than 25 per cent (25.4). If the proprietor
can establish himself in a quasi-monopolistic position because of the convenient location of his store, his friendly
relationship with his trade, or for some other reason, and
can obtain an average markup of 25 per cent, his business
will produce an income of approximately $1,100 per year.
This is less than the $25 per week he would receive if he
held a position as manager of a local chain unit in Bloomington, but there are other values, such as a feeling of
permanence and independence, and a satisfaction from the
friendly respect of his customers and neighbors.

3. In the Class B group, with an annual volume of
sales between $20,000 and $50,000, a considerable margin of
net profit appears. If the proprietor of a grocery store
can build up his business to a volume of approximately
$50,000 annually, and at the same time keep his expense
ratio down to the 13.34 shown in the cases studied (mainly
by the judicious employment of a relatively small labor
force) he can pay himself a salary of approximately $2,000
a year and still show a profit. This will be partly a
merchandising profit resulting from his ability as a mer-

chant, and partly a monopoly profit, depending on his price policies and the presence or absence of a partial monopoly resulting, for example, from having obtained a fortunate location.

4. With a sales volume above $50,000, the expense ratio rises to about 18.5 per cent (18.68). At this volume and in a city the size of Bloomington,[24] the owner must be in competition with the chains and supermarkets if he is obtaining this large a volume. According to the price study, his markup cannot be much above 18 per cent, and if he pays himself a salary of $3,000 a year, he will show no profit in his business.[25]

5. Excluding the more extreme variations, the records of the local grocery chain in Bloomington show a typical operating ratio of 13 per cent. (See Table XV.) This is very close to the 13.34 per cent for the Class B group of independents. It does not include any charges for wholesaling, transportation, or supervision, such as are found in the statements of the larger chains. The statement of wholesaling operations of this firm show an expense ratio of 6.56 per cent, based on wholesale prices. An adjustment must be made, however, before this ratio of 13 per cent is compared with the highest prices independents, because it

---

24. Population 18,000, 1930 census, exclusive of students.

25. A junk dealer once said to a business man who had just failed, "Let me give you some advice. Stay small." (Incident related to the author by the man who failed.)

is figured at a lower price level. However, the lowest
priced independent included in the price study had a
general index identical with this local chain (103).

6. Distribution costs in Bloomington when the merchandise moves through the manufacturer-wholesaler-retailer
channel are approximately as follows:

```
              Customer price              $1.00
              Retailer's margin-            .20
              Wholesaler's price
                to retailer                 .80
              Whlar's cost -.05
                " Profit-- .01
                   Total
                                            .06
              Producers' price to
                Wholesaler                  .74
```

It must be remembered that this amount paid to the producer
is not the same for all types of producers. (See Table
XVI.) The markup in the grocery business varies from 10
per cent on such commodities as sugar, flour, lard, butter,
etc., to 33 1/3 per cent on fancy groceries and fresh
fruits and vegetables.

7. The markup in the independently-owned groceries
which hold a quasi-monopolistic position is figured at a
higher price level than for the chains and the supermarkets.
The highest-priced independent is 14 per cent above the
orthodox chain, and 22 per cent above the cash-and-carry
supermarket.

The following computations appear to establish the
fact that the supermarkets pay less for the goods they sell
than do the orthodox chains, while the latter in turn are
favored over the independent wholesalers.

Table XVI

The Profit Chart

| | | Margins at Which Some Chains Sell Groceries | | |
		Proportion of Sales	Margin	Sales	Gross Profit
Class 1	Fresh Vegetables, Fresh Fruits, Fancy Groceries Miscellaneous Items	25%	33 1/3%	$12,000	$4,000
Class 2	Canned Fruits, Canning Supplies, Nuts, Relishes, Candies, Gum, Pickles Olives, Insecticides	15	30	7,200	2,160
Class 3	Canned Vegetables (except tomatoes), Canned Fish Dried Fruits, Bottled Beverages, Cheese, Catsup and Table Sauces, Spreads for Bread, Tea & Coffee, Coffee Substitutes, Syrups & Molasses, Macaroni Products, Chocolate, Cocoa, Desserts, Spices & Extracts, Rice, Beans & Peas	15	25	7,200	1,800
Class 4	Cakes, Crackers, Bread, Salad Dressing, Laundry Supplies, Household Supplies, Cigarettes, Tobacco, Canned Tomatoes, Canned Beans, Canned Meats, Package Flour, Salmon	10	20	4,800	960
Class 5	Laundry Soap, Soap Chips, Soap Powder, Toilet Soap, Soups	5	15	2,400	360
Class 6	Cereals, Canned Milk	5	12 1/2	2,400	300
Class 7	Sugar, Flour, Meal, Butter Oleo, Lard, Compounds, Eggs, Fresh Milk	25	10	12,000	1,200

$10,780 Gross Profit Equals 22.45% of $48,000 Total Sales

Source: Grocers' Commercial Bulletin, May, 1933, Page 12. 324 Fourth Ave. S., Minneapolis, Minnesota.

Producer - Wholesaler - Independent Retailer Market Channel

	Price Index
Lowest-Priced Independent-------------------	103
Gross margin (20% markup)------------------	20.6
Amount paid Wholesaler----------------------	82.4
Wholesaler's Margin (Expense 6.5%, Profit 1% of Sales at Wholesale Price)-------	6.2
Amount Paid Producer-----------------------	76.2

Producer - Orthodox Chain Channel

	Price Index
Chain -------------------------------------	94
Gross Margin (22.12 Markup) (1)-----------	20.8
Amount Paid Producer----------------------	73.2

Producer - Supermarket Channel

	Price Index
Supermarket--------------------------------	86
Supermarket (21.28 Markup)----------------	18.3
Amount Paid Producer----------------------	67.7

1. Includes wholesaling costs

There may be either of two explanations given for the existence of these differences between the prices paid to the producer by the independent wholesalers, the orthodox chains, and the supermarkets of 76.2¢, 73.2¢, and 67.7¢, respectively; that is, in that ratio. The chain store organizations would contend that their methods of distribution enabled the producer to use large-scale methods of production, eliminate selling costs, and reduce overhead expenses. The independent wholesalers would consider such differences as irrefutable evidence of secret rebates or excessive allowances, and concessions; in other words, unfair competition.

Laws such as the Miller-Tydings Act are intended to prevent the producers from granting or distributors from receiving secret rebates by making the latter illegal.

If the prices paid to producers by the chain store are lower than the prices quoted by the former to the independent merchants, is the differential justified as a difference in cost of production because of a more efficient use of capital and labor resulting from chain store methods of distribution, or is such a difference the result of pressure exerted on producers by the large distributing organizations because the large-scale buying of the latter virtually amounts to a subsidization of the producer? This question suggests a consideration of the data presented in the report Federal Trade Commission.

Unfair competition should be distinguished from monopolistic competition. Independent wholesalers formerly occupied a monopolistic situation.[26] A monopolist will fight when his position is threatened. His anxiety is of little concern to the consumer, although the later would support

---

26. Formerly the manufacturer sold to the wholesaler on a basis of low prices and the wholesaler collected higher prices by his monopoly of market information and sometimes by emphasizing the quality guaranteed by his brand. Today the situation is often reversed. The manufacturer, controlling a certain brand, may charge a little extra for its supposed virtues. But this brand ordinarily may be had from any wholesaler. Buying it, the consumer does not care where he buys. In such cases wholesalers and retailers are placed in the cleft stick of price competition and are forced to accept minimum margins of profit. The retailer particularly feels himself a puppet subject to the rival tugs of competiting advertisements.

him if his business were suffering because of "unfair"
business practices.

"Monopolistic competition"[27] exists when there is a
"differentiation of the product". Differentiation may be
based upon certain characteristics of the product itself,
such as exclusive patented features; trade-marks; trade
names; peculiarities of the package or container, if any;
or singularity in quality, design, color, or style.[28] To
these characteristics must be added the ability of a firm
to spend large sums in advertising, and thus to complete
the process of differentiation by creating special values,
either real or fancied, in the mind of the consumer.

When this differentiation of the product has been ac-
complished, the curve of demand for the product is changed
from a horizontal line to a down sloping curve.[29] The
manufacturer has attained some degree of monopoly, and
with it, to some extent at least, a control over the price.
His next step is to adopt, in some form or other, a "price
policy."[30]

> Centering about price policies and bearing in
> many cases a close relationship to branded,

---

27. Willard E. Atkins and collaborators, _Economic Behavior_,
    p. 300. Houghton Mifflin Co. New York. 1933.

28. Chamberlin, _op. cit._, p. 56.

29. Chamberlin, _Ibid._, p. 17 ff.

30. See Lyon, "Advertising Allowances." The Brookings
    Institution. Washington, D. C. 1932.

identifiable, and widely advertised goods, there
has grown up a new set of practices and phrases
more familiar to the business man than to the
economist. Those practices have found expression in such terms as price maintenance, price
cutting, price structure, allowances, deals,
discounts, and guarantees against price decline.[31]

"An advertising allowance may be said to be a manufac-

turer's (or other seller's) contribution to the joint ex-

pense of his customer and himself for point-of-purchase

promotion, real or nominal."[32] The granting of such al-

lowances and other price concessions is one of the chief

causes of the chain store controversy.

The statement has frequently been made that
chain-store organizations hold an important
advantage over independent dealers because
of the large discounts and allowances obtained by them on many items, which independent competitors are not able to obtain. It
is claimed further that these special discounts and allowances enable chains to sell
many items as leaders at prices which independent dealers cannot meet without taking a loss. This situation, it is charged,
leads the consuming public to believe that
chains charge low prices on all merchandise
which, it is asserted, is contrary to fact.
Another complaint made, and sometimes by
chain organizations themselves, is that the
very large chains obtain allowances which
are higher than those available to smaller
chains and independent dealers or are not
available at all to the smaller distribu-
ters.[33]

---

31. Lyon, op. cit., p. 3.

32. Lyon, Ibid., p. 7.

33. Federal Trade Commission. "Chain Stores. Special
Discounts and Allowances to Chain and Independent
Distributors. Grocery Trade." Senate Document
No. 89. 73rd Congress, 2nd Session. United States
Government Printing Office. Washington. 1934.

Of the 15,602 accounts sold in 1930 and reported to
the Commission by 464 manufacturers, 81 per cent carried
no special discounts and allowances.[34] For sales of
$351,600,000 by these 464 manufacturers in 1930, the al-
lowances totaled $6,439,514, or only 1.83 per cent.

> The price concessions found by the Federal
> Trade Commission appear, in general, to be less
> than those indicated by the evidence obtained
> in Bloomington. Yet regardless of whether or
> not they are significant, if they exist they
> are certain to arouse the resentment of the
> buyers who are unable to obtain them. The re-
> port of the Federal Trade Commission states
> that:

> The sales of the manufacturers to the chains
> amounted to about 82 percent of the manufac-
> turers' total sales to the three types of
> distributors for both years, and the chains
> obtained over 90 percent of all discounts
> and allowances granted by these manufactur-
> ers to chains (1.89 percent in 1929 and 2.02
> percent in 1930) were over twice the rates
> granted to wholesalers (0.87 percent in 1929
> and 0.91 percent in 1930), and nearly twice
> those given to co-operative chains (1 percent
> in 1929 and 1.04 percent in 1930).[35]

Wholesalers are human beings and, therefore, have
human reactions. It is not surprising that such discrimination would arouse the ire of the wholesalers and cause
them to engage in acts of reprisal, such as the active
sponsorship of anti-chain legislation. The contention of
the chains, as was pointed out above,[36] is that they not
only permit the manufacturer economies obtained through

---

34. F. T. C. Report. S.D. 89. Op. cit., p. VIII.

35. Ibid.

36. See Chapter VI, p. 34.

off-season production and the elimination of selling and
collection costs, but that they do provide effective promotional assistance at the point of sale, e. g. window dis-
plays and local advertising. Manufacturers are also human,
in addition to being good business men.

> The wholesaler has been accused of indifference
> to the manufacturer's advertising and sales
> promotional work, sometimes bordering on hos-
> tility and antagonism. He is particularly
> charged with failure to co-operate with the ad-
> vertiser in the distribution of dealer-helps
> to the trade as well as with neglect to syn-
> chronize his sales effort with that of the
> manufacturer. Such an attitude on the part of
> the wholesaler may be explained by his desire
> for self-preservation. If the manufacturer's
> advertising and other sales promotional activi-
> ties result in an increased demand for his
> products, he may insist that his goods be
> handled on a smaller margin or else he may go
> around the wholesaler .... Another reason for
> the wholesaler's alleged unfriendly attitude
> toward the manufacturer's aggressive advertis-
> ing programs is that such promotional work con-
> verts the wholesaler into a mere machine which
> supplies his customers with articles in demand.
> It leaves him no room for initiative and judg-
> ment.[37]

Moreover, it is impossible for the wholesaler to co-operate
with each of several manufacturers who are not only competing with each other, but also with the wholesaler himself
and his own private brands.

The consumer is little concerned with any dispute
about advertising allowances and other price concessions,
but from the independent wholesaler's point of view they
have a very important effect on profits. Moreover, from a

---

37. Theodore N. Beckman and Nathanael H. Engle, "Wholesaling Principles and Practices." Pages 253 ff. The
Ronald Press Company. New York. 1937.

social viewpoint their effects are significant, because
they increase the ill-will and animosity of the independent
merchants toward the chain store organizations, and cause
controversies with undesirable economic, political, and
social consequences. These will be discussed in more
detail in the chapter dealing with anti-chain store legislation.

Table XVII

Retail--Groceries*

		Profit Group	% of Gross Income	Loss Group	% of Gross Income	Com-bined Group	% of Gross Income
1	Gross Income						
2	Salaries and Wages		9.71		9.06		9.67
3	Officers' Compensation		.79		3.87		.96
4	Interest		.09		.21		.10
	Taxes						
5	State		1.02		.83		1.01
6	Local		.24		.08		.23
7	Federal		.05		.01		.05
8	Total		1.31		.92		1.29
9	Depreciation and Depletion		.64		.69		.64
10	Cost of Goods and Other Services Purchased		85.76		86.67		85.81
11	Total Expenses		98.30		101.42		98.47
12	Net Income or Deficit		1.70		-1.42		1.53
13	Federal Income and Excess Profit Taxes		.42				.42
14	Total of all Taxes (line 8 plus line 13)		1.74		.92		1.69

* The Report of the Indiana Tax Study Commission. January 1, 1939, p. 180.

Table XVIII

Trade*

Wholesale--Groceries

		% of Gross Income	Loss Group	% of Gross Income	Com-bined Group	% of Gross Income
		Profit Group				
1	Gross Income					
2	Salaries & Wages	4.03		4.13		4.05
3	Officers' Compensation	1.30		2.52		1.54
4	Interest	.17		.14		.16
	Taxes					
5	State	.29		.26		.28
6	Local	.19		.28		.21
7	Federal	.02		.02		.02
8	Total	.50		.56		.51
9	Depreciation and Depletion	.29		.26		.28
10	Cost of Goods and Other Services Purchased	92.49		93.11		92.61
11	Total Expenses	98.78		100.72		99.15
12	Net Income or Deficit	1.22		-.72		.85
13	Federal Income & Excess Profits Taxes	.17				.14
14	Total of all Taxes (line 8 plus line 13)	.67		.56		.65

* The Report of the Indiana Tax Study Commission. January 1, 1939. p. 81.

PART III

SOCIAL ASPECTS

of the

CHAIN STORE MOVEMENT

Chapter XI

THE CHAIN STORE AND THE COMMUNITY
(Continued)

Social Effects

Does the presence of chain stores weaken the spirit of a community? Do the chain store organizations fail to support, by appropriate contributions and by participation in local activities, the interests of the towns in which they are located? Do they reduce the effectiveness and lessen the need for the activities of various social and economic groups, such as banks, newspapers, and chambers of commerce?

The relationship of the chain stores to such groups is a very important aspect in the chain store movement. A community large enough to offer a profitable volume of business to a chain store unit is usually highly organized. It has its banks, newspapers, lawyers, building contractors, chambers of commerce, service clubs, charity organizations, and so on. Each of these groups has certain duties and functions to perform, and everyone in the community benefits either directly or indirectly from their services. And whenever a business enterprise accepts these benefits but refuses to carry its share of the financial burdens, or to participate in the activities, it incurs the resentment and animosity of the individuals comprising the various groups.

To illustrate, at one time there was a feeling among country bankers that the chain stores brought no business

to the banks, but used them merely as convenient depositor-
ies. In addition to his resentment at losing the accounts
of independent merchants who were unable to meet the competition of the chains, the country banker had the following
complaints against the chain stores:

1) The average chain store, in a small community, does
not maintain an adequate bank balance.

2) Units of chain store organizations do not use a
bank's loan facilities, nor buy any of the other services
offered.

3) Chain stores abuse the privilege of using the
free services of a bank, such as supplying the stores with
small change, check books, and monthly statements.

Statements by bankers in interviews with the author
warrant the statement that at one time these complaints
were justified. Perhaps in some places they still are. It
cannot be denied that when chain store organizations use
the services of the local banks, they must expect to offer
adequate compensation. There are various ways by which
this can be done, such as agreeing to maintain a balance
large enough to make the account profitable, and the payment
of a monthly fee for the services used.

Another important business enterprise in any community
is the local newspaper. In the past the county editors
have been in a very difficult position, and in many places
they still are. They have had to maintain a neutral position in the controversy between the independent merchants

and the chain stores, keeping on friendly terms with the
former, and yet at the same time finding a considerable
part of their incomes the result of the advertising of the
chains. A study of advertising expenditures of chain food
stores, made by the National Association of Food Chains in
February, 1938, showed that 33 companies operating a total
of 30,640 retail food stores with a sales volume of
$16,905,404 for all types of advertising. Nineteen compan-
ies reported an expenditure in 1937 of $9,935,874 on news-
paper advertising, or over 60 per cent of the total expenditure.[1] And an editorial in a Mid-West newspaper stated that
"newspapers, periodicals, and printers divide two hundred
million dollars spent by the chains annually."[2]

Resolutions recently passed by editorial associations
indicate clearly that country newspapers have a very friendly attitude toward the chain store organizations.[3] Judging
from statements to the author by newspaper men in Indiana,
and by the movement now under way in some states through
the state press associations to obtain increased expenditures in country newspapers by national advertisers, the
latter are prone to overlook the need for advertising at
the point of sale. Chain stores and voluntary chains, however, do a tremendous amount of local advertising, as an

---

1. According to information obtained by the author from
   the Institute of Distribution, Inc., 570 Seventh Ave.,
   New York City.

2. Chicago Evening American, May 20, 1938.

3. See Appendix A, Supplement to Chapter XIV.

examination of the current issues of country newspapers
will show.

One of the most important groups in any community,
which performs both social and economic functions, is the
local chamber of commerce. The charge has been made that
chain store managers do not belong to this group or take
active part in its activities. Chain store executives
deny this charge. The author found in his investigations
during the progress of the Indiana University survey that,
on the basis of participation in community activities,
there is no clear differentiation of chain store managers
and independent merchants. In Bloomington where thirty-
eight independent grocers were interviewed, only three belonged to some sort of civic group. In this same community a study made by an association of chain stores showed
that both the chain store organizations and the managers as
individuals made substantial contributions and too active
interest in community enterprises. Nine out of eleven
managers in the largest city in this county belonged to the
Chamber of Commerce. One manager of a unit operated by a
large national grocery chain reported that he was a deacon
of one of the churches, chairman of one of the committees
of the Chamber of Commerce, member of the executive board
of the Community Chest, member of the advisory board of the
Y. M. C. A., and an officer of the Lions Club.[4]

---

4. Confidential information from the files of the secretary
    of the associated chain stores in Indiana.

Another manager of a local unit owned by a national
variety chain stated that he was a deacon in his church,
member of one of the lodges, president of the Retail Merchants' Association, president of the Lions Club, and a
director in the Chamber of Commerce. His wife was also
active in social and welfare work. In a large midwestern
city a division manager of a large grocery chain who had
held that position for ten years is a member of the board
of directors of the Chamber of Commerce and one of the
leaders in the annual Community Fund drive. In this same
city, the manager of the retail store of one of the big
mail order houses has just been elected head of the Merchants' Association.

The author has just taken an active part in a drive for
increased membership in the Chamber of Commerce in Bloomington, and has had an opportunity to observe at first hand
the reactions of independent merchants and chain store
managers to his personal solicitations. His own conclusion
is that participation in community activities depends more
on the interests and personalities of the individuals that
upon the forms of the organizations with which they are
associated. The association of chain stores in Indiana has
recently employed an assistant to the secretary whose sole
duty is to travel around the state organizing clubs of chain
store managers. At the present time[5] he has promoted these

---

5. May, 1939.

clubs in 69 cities and towns in this state. One of the
objectives of this plan is to create among the managers a
better understanding of the relation of the chain store
organizations to the communities in which they operate, a
keener interest in community activities, and an apprecia-
tion of the necessity for building good will among the
various community groups. In some localities and with some
individuals this organizer has had a considerable degree of
success, and in others he has not. Just as in any group of
individuals, the chain store managers have qualities of
leadership in varying degrees.

The significant thing about the plan described above
is that the executives of chain store organizations, or at
least some of them, are at last realizing the need for
building up cordial relationships with the communities in
which they operate. In the past, chain stores have used
poor salesmanship. They have relied upon price appeals,
and have overlooked or neglected to use those psychological
principles so essential to successful selling of any form.
They have depended too much on reason and have failed to
evaluate emotion as an economic force.

Chain stores should have their community relations
directed by men with high intellect and broad understanding, possessing both the type of personality which makes
friends easily, and the authority to take direct action with
regard to community projects, undiscouraged by delays of
routine procedures. Only in this way can the chains attain

the strong economic position formerly held by the independent merchants. When one considers that most of our legislators come from rural communities, and that they either formulate or act on the legislation with which chain stores are continually threatened, one can appreciate the importance of community relationships.

There are other factors involved in the relationships between business enterprises and the communities in which they are located that lend themselves better to objective measurements than does the question of participation in community activities.

The number of memberships held in civic organizations by an independent or a chain store manager does not necessarily measure the value of either to the community.[6]

The chain store method of distribution has been criticised by many on the grounds that chain stores are not permanent. They are only renters. This attitude may be a vestige of one that under past conditions quite commonly prevailed, and is still found in many localities, namely, that the "renter", the man who does not own a home or a farm is, so to speak, in a lower caste than one who does. It is natural for one who has, after a long struggle, attained the economic position of a landholder, to feel superior toward one who has not.

---

6. The first and most important consideration, of course, is how well the functions of merchandising are performed.

But with the growth of large corporations, many positions were created which do not permit their holders to
have permanent residences. Salesmen, district and branch-
office managers, hotel managers, and those in similar types
of occupations are subject to transfer at very short notice.
No one criticizes them for not buying homes. The question
of permanence or lack of it does not appear of first importance.

On the other hand, one important basis for judging the
efficiency of any retail organization, whether chain or independent, is the effect of its merchandising operations on
the real estate values of the district in which it is located. Every merchant must answer the question. On the
basis of my annual volume of business, what rent must I
pay? This question is as important to the one who owns as
to the one who rents, because the business of the merchant
who owns his location should earn as much for him in rent
as he could get by leasing his building to someone else.
Moreover, the owner of real estate who leases to a merchandising establishment is vitally concerned in obtaining the
maximum amount of rent the location is worth, because the
income from the property determines to a large extent its
value.

This relation of rental to value is based on the
principle of capitalization of income. Wealth in any form
is valued according to the benefits, that is, the income,
which it produces. If the going rate of interest is, say,

six per cent, than any property producing a net income of
$100 a month, or $1200 a year, is worth $20,000, because
$1200 is six per cent of $20,000. If the property is held
at a higher value than that amount, either it is overvalued,
or else the owner is holding it for a speculative profit,
expecting that a higher income will be received in the
future.

The retail merchant should know the factors affecting
the selection of a business location, as well as the economic principles involved. When he selects a site, cheap rent
is often his main consideration. But many times he over-
looks the fact that the fact that the relative highness or
lowness of rent is measured by the volume of business done.
In other words, he forgets to apply the theory of economic
rent. The chain store organizations contend that their more
scientific methods of merchandising produce a greater volume
of business, thus increasing the rentals that can be paid
and, consequently, the values of both their own and the adjoining locations. In other words, they claim that they
use the factors of production in a more efficient combination than do the independent merchants.

The large chain store organizations can afford to
employ men who are experts in judging the volume of business that any particular site should produce. They have a
rich store of experience in the records of their organizations. They check traffic carefully, and they are interested
only in the shoppers that buy in the type of store they are

representing. If the appeal of this store is to the woman
buyer, the expert counts the number of women passing the
location during the shopping hours. He, also, studies
rental values carefully, and collects information about
leases that have been made, the sales volume of the section,
interest and amortization costs of alterations and improvements, real estate taxes, insurance, maintenance, and any
other charges. After collecting all of this information,
he decided what rental can be offered for the property in
question, and his decision is strongly influenced by his
intuitive judgment -- which is acquired only after long
experience.

But regardless of any attempt by either an independent merchant or a chain to use the principles of economic
rent in determining the "right" rent to pay, the amount
that is finally agreed upon is the result of bargaining between the lessor and the lessee.[7]

The rather extreme variations in the amount of rental

---

7. "It would seem that the trial and error method is the
    real method used by most chains, but I do not believe
    that method need necessarily be accurate. I believe
    Chain Stores probably take a number of stores that are
    doing particularly well, where the rental, perhaps, is
    moderate, then figure the percentage and say that that
    is the proper percentage to pay.
    Inasmuch as most leases are a matter of barter, there is
    nothing very scientific about rentals except, perhaps,
    in the case of the highest type of down-town retail
    stores. From a strictly technical point of view, I still
    do not see why groceries should pay around $2\frac{1}{2}\%$ and 5 and
    10 cent stores from five to seven percent. In both cases
    the individual sales are small and the turn-over fairly
    rapid." (From a personal letter written to the author by
    the head of a real estate firm in a large western city.)

paid by both independents and chains is clearly shown in
Table XIX. That the law of economic rent does operate is
rather clearly indicated by the positive correlation between rentals paid and annual volume of business.

The comparison presented in Table XIX suggests, although it does not verify, the conclusion that the large
chain store organizations pay higher rents for the individual sites they select than do those independents with a
comparable volume of business. The chains might use this
as evidence that they have a higher degree of efficiency in
their operations. Their opponents would argue that the
chains will not lease a location until its business producing qualities have already been created by the community in
which it is located. No attempt will be made here to decide
which explanation is correct. The only thing that appears
certain is that after the site has been selected and the
store opened, whether chain or independent, the law of
economic rent will operate to determine whether or not the
transaction was profitable to either the lessor or the
lessee or both; or more profitable to one than to the other.

Table XX shows the absolute amounts[8] of taxes paid by

---

7. (continued)

One who has observed the difference in the class of
trade seen on the sidewalks of this block and on the
sidewalks of the block on the opposite side of the
Courthouse can understand why the Atlantic and Pacific
store did not get the volume of business that was expected. (See expense statement in Chapt. X, p. 129.

8. Relative tax loads are discussed in Chapter XII.

250 independents and 104 chains in 16 counties in Indiana.
About all this table shows is that this chain store organization does make a considerable contribution to the state
of Indiana. Another chain (Kroger's) advertises that it
spends annually in Indiana $754,000 for rent and taxes.

The conclusions that seem warranted are:

1. The chain stores in Indiana make heavy absolute
amounts of payments in rent and taxes.

2. In spite of these payments, their operations on
the whole are profitable.

3. The higher absolute amounts of rent are explained
by the fact that their stores do a large volume of business.
In the reports of the two largest chains in Indiana, no
units are shown with a volume of less than $50,000. The
combination groceries in one national chain in these 16
counties, with one exception, show volumes considerable in
excess of $100,000 annually.

4. The same explanation applies to taxes. Heavier inventories are carried. Gross income payments are higher,
and to these are added an average payment of $145.00 per
unit because of the store license tax.

Summary of Tax Payments Made in 1937 by Chain and Independent Grocery Stores in 16 Counties in Indiana

To Less Than	Below $5,000				$5,000 to 7,000				$7,000 to 10,000				$10,000 to 15,000				$15,000 to 20,000				$20,000 to 30,000				$30,000 to 50,000			
	Co.	A.	Ma.	Mo.	Co.	A.	Ma.	Mo.	Co.	A.	Ma.	Mo.	Co.	A.	Ma.	Mo.	Co.	A.	Ma.	Mo.	Co.	A.	Ma.	Mo.	Co.	A.	Ma.	Mo.
$ 0- 25	21	2	-	3	36	-	3	4	-	-	-	-	-	-	-	-	-	-	-	-	-	-	-	-	-	-	-	-
25- 50	7	-	-	1	15	2	-	-	-	-	-	-	10	2	-	1	1	-	-	-	-	-	-	-	-	-	-	-
50- 75	-	-	-	-	12	3	2	-	7	2	-	-	17	3	1	1	1	1	1	-	-	-	-	-	-	-	-	-
75-100	1	-	1	-	7	1	-	2	12	6	-	-	6	1	3	3	6	1	1	-	8	1	-	-	3	1	1	1
100-150	1	-	-	-	7	-	-	-	6	2	-	-	2	1	1	1	5	2	1	1	6	1	1	-	6	3	1	1
150-200	-	-	-	-	-	2	-	-	2	2	-	-	1	1	1	1	1	1	-	1	5	1	1	-	15	1	2	2
200-250	-	-	-	-	2	1	1	-	2	1	-	-	-	2	2	-	1	-	-	-	3	1	1	-	4	4	1	1
250-300	-	-	-	-	-	-	-	-	-	-	-	-	-	-	-	-	-	-	-	-	2	1	-	-	4	3	1	-
300-350	-	-	-	-	-	-	-	-	-	-	-	-	-	-	-	-	-	-	-	-	-	-	-	-	4	3	-	1
350-400	-	-	-	-	-	-	-	-	-	-	-	-	-	-	-	-	-	-	-	-	-	-	-	-	2	2	1	1
400-450	-	-	-	-	-	-	-	-	-	-	-	-	-	-	-	-	-	-	-	-	-	-	-	-	1	1	1	1
450-500	-	-	-	-	-	-	-	-	-	-	-	-	-	-	-	-	-	-	-	-	-	-	-	-	-	-	-	-
500-600	-	-	-	-	-	-	-	-	-	-	-	-	-	-	-	-	-	-	-	-	-	-	-	-	-	-	-	-
600-700	-	-	-	-	-	-	-	-	-	-	-	-	-	-	-	-	-	-	-	-	-	-	-	-	-	-	-	-
700-800	-	-	-	-	-	-	-	-	-	-	-	-	-	-	-	-	-	-	-	-	-	-	-	-	-	-	-	-
Totals	29	2	-	5	36	3	4	2	29	3	4	-	36	6	5	5	38	11	5	3	24	3	2	-	39	8	4	6

Classification of Counties:

To	Chain-Store Group							
	Industrial		Semi-Industrial		Semi-Rural		Rural	
	Str.	Comb.	Str.	Comb.	Str.	Comb.	Str.	Comb.
$600 to less than $700	-	-	-	-	4	-	1	-
700- 800	-	-	-	-	1	-	1	-
800- 900	2	-	5	-	-	-	-	-
900-1000	30	1	4	-	-	-	-	-
1000-1250	25	9	-	-	2	1 (3)	-	-
1250-1500	-	10	-	4	-	3	-	-
1500-2000	-	-	-	-	-	-	-	-
2000-2500	-	2	-	-	-	-	-	-

"Str." - Straight groceries (no meats) "Comb" - Combination—all over $100,000 volume in 1937 (with one exception noted)

3. Volume $72,000 in 1937.

Table XX

Summary of Actual Monthly Rentals Paid by Chain and Independent Grocers in 16 Counties in Indiana (1)

Rent Paid ($.00 per cm.)

Rent Paid	Below $5,000				$5,000 to $7,000				$7,000 to $10,000				$10,000 to $15,000				$15,000 to $25,000				$25,000 to $30,000
	Co.	A.	Mad.	Mo.	Co.	A.	Mad.	No.	Co.	A.	Mad.	No.	Co.	A.	Mad.	No.	Co.	A.	Mad.	No.	Mo.
Owns	14	2	–	5	9	1	–	2	12	3	–	3	13	2	1	3	10	2	1	–	–
0–$7.49	2	2	–	–	3	–	1	–	3	3	–	1	1	1	1	–	1	1	–	1	1
$7.50	5	–	–	–	6	1	1	–	3	–	1	1	4	1	–	–	2	–	1	–	1
12.50	5	–	–	–	6	1	1	–	4	–	2	–	3	–	2	1	6	1	1	–	1
17.50	–	–	–	–	8	–	2	–	5	1	–	–	9	1	–	1	4	1	1	–	1
22.50	3	–	–	–	1	–	–	–	1	–	1	–	2	2	1	–	5	3	–	–	–
27.50	–	–	–	–	1	–	–	–	–	–	–	–	4	–	1	–	4	4	–	–	–
32.50	–	–	–	–	2	2	–	–	1	–	1	1	1	1	–	–	5	1	–	–	–
37.50	–	–	–	–	–	–	–	–	–	–	–	–	2	–	–	–	2	–	–	–	–
42.50	–	–	–	–	–	–	–	–	–	–	–	–	1	–	1	–	–	–	–	–	–
47.50	–	–	–	–	–	–	–	–	–	–	–	–	–	–	–	–	–	–	–	–	–
52.50	–	–	–	–	–	–	–	–	–	–	–	–	–	–	–	–	–	–	–	–	–
57.50	–	–	–	–	–	–	–	–	–	–	–	–	–	–	–	–	1	–	1	–	–
62.50	–	–	–	–	–	–	–	–	–	–	–	–	–	–	–	–	1	–	–	–	–
67.50	–	–	–	–	–	–	–	–	–	–	–	–	–	–	–	–	–	–	–	–	–
72.50	–	–	–	–	–	–	–	–	–	–	–	–	–	–	–	–	–	–	–	–	–
77.50	–	–	–	–	–	–	–	–	–	–	–	–	–	–	–	–	1	–	–	–	–
Totals	29	2	0	5	36	5	4	2	29	3	5	4	42	6	5	5	42	11	5	1	4

"—" None

Column—All 16 Counties combined

Column "A"—Allen County—Classification, "Industrial."—From the sample taken in this county.

Column "Mad."—Madison County—"Semi-Industrial"

Column "Mo."—Monroe County. Not all the items were obtained from each of the 38 cases.

(1) Source: Original data from Indiana Survey. Compiled by the author, based on a study of 250 stores in the Independent Group and 104 Units in the Chain.

Table XX (continued)

Summary of Actual Monthly Rentals Paid by Chain and Independent Stores
in 16 Counties in Indiana

Rent Paid ($ per mo.)	Independently-Owned Group					Units of a National Chain (2) (3)								
	$20,000 to $30,000		$30,000 to $50,000		Over 50,000 Monroe Co. Only	Industrial			Semi-Ind.		Semi-Rural		Rural	
	Co. A.	Mad. Mo.	Co. A.	Mad. Mo.		Str.	Groc.	Comb.	Str.	Ob.	Str.	Ob.	Str.	Ob.
Owns	8	–	10	–	1	–	–	–	–	–	–	–	–	–
0 - $7.49	2	–	1	–	3	–	–	–	–	–	–	–	–	–
$ 7.50	1	2	2	–	1	–	–	–	–	–	–	–	–	–
12.50	–	1	1	1	1	–	–	–	–	–	–	–	–	–
17.50	2	–	2	1	1	–	–	–	–	–	–	–	–	–
22.50	4	–	7	1	1	–	–	–	–	–	–	–	–	–
27.50	3	1	5	1	2	–	–	–	–	–	–	–	–	–
32.50	1	–	4	1	1	–	–	–	–	–	–	–	–	–
37.50	3	1	1	–	–	1	–	–	–	–	–	–	–	–
42.50	3	1	5	–	1	–	–	–	–	–	1	–	1	–
47.50	–	–	1	–	1	–	–	1*	–	–	–	–	–	–
52.50	2	1	4	–	–	–	–	–	–	–	–	–	–	–
57.50	1	1	1	–	–	9(2)	–	–	–	–	–	–	–	–
62.50	1	1	3	–	–	–	–	–	–	5	–	3	–	–
67.50	–	–	1	–	1	–	–	–	–	–	–	–	–	–
72.50	–	–	–	–	–	–	–	–	–	–	–	–	–	–

* This store had a sales volume in 1937 of $72,000; rent, $50 per month.

2. Confidential information supplied by the company.

3. "Str." -- straight grocery (no meats). "Ob." -- Combination. All straight groceries included in this tabulation had sales in 1937 between $50,000 and $75,000. All combinations (with exception of one noted above) had sales volumes in 1937 in excess of $100,000.

Table XX (continued)

Rent Paid ($ per mo.)	Independently-Owned Group									Units of a National Chain							
	$20,000 to $30,000			$30,000 to $50,000			Over 50,000		Industrial		Semi-Ind.		Semi-Rural		Rural	
	Co. A.	Med.	Mo.	Co. A.	Med.	Mo.	Mo.	Monroe Co. Only	Str. Groc.	Comb.	Str.	Ob.	Str.	Ob.	Str.	Ob.
$77.50	–	–	–	–	–	–	–	–	–	–	–	–	1	–	–	–
82.50	–	–	–	–	–	–	–	1	–	–	–	–	2	–	–	–
87.50	–	–	–	1	1	–	1	–	–	–	–	–	–	–	–	–
92.50	–	–	–	1	1	–	–	–	–	–	–	–	–	–	–	–
97.50	–	–	–	–	–	–	–	–	18	–	–	2	–	–	–	–
107.50	–	–	–	–	–	–	–	–	–	–	–	–	–	–	–	–
117.50	–	–	–	–	2	–	–	1	28	9	–	–	–	–	–	–
127.50	–	–	–	–	–	–	1	–	1	–	4	–	–	1	–	–
137.50 to 167	–	–	–	–	–	–	–	–	–	–	–	–	–	–	–	–
167.50	–	–	–	–	–	–	–	–	–	2	–	–	–	–	–	1
177.50	–	–	–	–	–	–	–	–	–	7	–	–	–	1	–	–
187.50	–	–	–	–	–	–	–	–	–	–	–	–	–	–	–	–
197.50	–	–	–	–	–	–	–	–	–	–	–	–	–	–	–	–
207.50 to 227	–	–	–	–	–	–	–	–	–	3	–	2	–	2	–	–
227.50	–	–	–	–	–	–	–	–	–	–	–	–	–	–	–	–
247.50 to 250	1	–	–	–	–	–	–	–	–	–	–	–	–	–	–	–
Total	28	3	2	4	50	8	4	11	57	22	9	4	7	4	0	1

Chapter XII

THE CHAIN STORE AND THE EMPLOYEE

The charge has been made against the chain stores that
they pay lower wages and work their employees longer hours
than do the independently-owned stores. The report of the
Federal Trade Commission does show a lower wage paid by the
chain stores. It states:[1]

> Comparable data on chain store and "independent"
> dealer wages for full-time store selling employees
> are available for the following eight kinds of
> business: Grocery, grocery and meat, drug, tobac-
> co, ready-to-wear, shoes, hardware, and combined
> dry goods, dry goods and apparel, and general
> merchandise. The weighted average weekly wage of
> 3,933 independent store selling employees in
> these eight kinds of business for the week end-
> ing January 10, 1931, was $28.48, as compared
> with $21.61 for the 107,035 chain-store selling
> employees. A simple average of the eight lines
> of business shows a narrower spread between the
> two figures ($28.10) for independents and $23.82
> for chains, respectively) but leaves the same
> distinct conclusion, namely, that for the period
> studied, the independents paid their store em-
> ployees more than did the chains.

The weakness of such a conclusion is that it fails to
take into account the many differences in the type of labor
included in the averages. To illustrate, there is in a
chain store grocery a wide difference between the stock
room boy who helps to unload the trucks, and unpacks the
shipments, and the manager who must assume a considerable

---

1. "Chain Stores--Chain Store Wages"--Report of the Federal
    Commission, Senate Document No. 82, 73rd Congress, 2nd
    Session, p. xv, U. S. Government Printing Office, Wash-
    ington, 1933.

amount of responsibility. There is almost as wide a difference between the girl in the variety store whose main job is to wrap packages and make change, and the clerk in the independently-owned store who must make a real selling effort, or who is capable of taking care of the store while the owner is away. To understand how difficult it is to make any direct comparison between the wages paid by the independents and the chain stores as groups, we must start with certain economic principles.

"Wages are the price paid for labor, and, like other prices, they must be explained in terms of demand and supply."[2] The marginal productivity theory of wages states that the wage paid to any group of laborers doing the same kind of work tends to just equal the value added to the product by the last man employed. The latter's wage cannot be more than his productive value to the employer, else he will not be employed. The size of this group will be determined on the one hand by the supply, and on the other hand by the demand for this type of labor, which in turn is determined by the demand for its product. Each laborer in the group will receive the same wage because the laborers are interchangeable.

Another economic principle which applies to this cuestion of comparative wage levels in chain and independently-

2. F. B. Garver and A. H. Hansen, "Principles of Economics", p. 383. Revised edition, Ginn and Company, New York, 1937.

owned stores is that which Alfred Marshall called "the principle of substitution."[3] An alert merchandiser is constantly seeking the best combination of the agents he employs -- and the chain store organizations are alert merchandisers. Of course, the volume of business in any one unit must be of optimum size if this principle is to apply. When a store employes a sales-person with exceptional salesmanship ability -- that is, the ability to create a want for a product in the mind of the customer, and thus create possession utility, there is a loss to the employer when the latter's time is spent in less productive work, such as sweeping out the store or unpacking shipments of merchandise. This, of course, is due to lack of specialization. To the extent that merchants can employ help with special abilities, they can pay their labor exactly what it is worth.

From a social viewpoint, there is a gain to society from the use of cheaper labor in a cash-and-carry store. When a customer selects merchandise himself, he increases the amount of goods that can be marketed per hour of employee

---

3. "The alert business man is ever seeking for the most profitable application of his resources, and endeavoring to make use of each several agent of production up to that margin, or limit, at which he would gain by transferring a small part of his expenditure to some other agent; and .... he is thus, so far as his influence goes, the medium through which the principle of substitution so adjusts the employment of each agent that, in its marginal application, its cost is proportionate to the additional net product resulting from its use." Alfred Marshall, "Principles of Economics," Chapter VI, p. 514-515. The Macmillan Company, London. 1930.

labor. This enables the proprietor to employ a less
skilled type of laborer, and is one explanation of the low
wage paid in the self-serve stores. There is less human
waste if an individual can be placed in an occupation where
his ability is adequate, and where he is of value to
society. If he cannot qualify for an occupation or profession requiring greater ability, there is nothing to be
gained by trying to force him into such an occupation.

Many chain store organizations have elaborate training
programs for their employees.[4] But many of the latter do
not respond to such training. The author recently completed a study in Kokomo, Indiana,[5] to determine the attitudes of individuals engaged in distribution, both employers
and employees, toward a program of vocational training in
specialized phases of merchandising; to get an expression of
their needs; to seek correlations between attitudes and
significant individual characteristics; and to find motives
on which to base appeals for interest and attendance in
extension classes. These classes have been organized in
various cities in Indiana as a part of the program of business education provided for by the George-Deen Act, passed

---

4. Sears, Roebuck and Co., for example. Also Safeway
Stores, Inc., who state, "We are seriously attempting
to train our employees constantly day after day through
personal contacts and especially through our managers,
supervisors and higher executives. This is not done in
a school-room atmosphere, but rather in a day to day
program of practical instruction."

5. Bulletin No. 4. Distributive Education Series. Indiana
University, Bloomington, 1939.

by Congress in 1936. The information presented in the report on this survey was obtained by the author and his assistant through personal interviews with more than 500 employers and employees. The following summary of conclusions is quoted from the author's report:

1. That ambition, the feeling of need for further training, and willingness to sacrifice time and effort to obtain this training, is an innate characteristic, and is not related to other individual characteristics which can be measured objectively.

2. That in a city or town comparable to Kokomo, with similar characteristics, a working assumption is that not more than 50% of those in the distributive occupations can be actively interested in this program of business education. This assumption, of course, is based on the additional assumption that there will be no change in the attitudes of employees and employers.

3. That there must be definite incentives created to which strong appeals can be made if even this 50% is to be reached.

The replies to the questions about the feeling of need for specialized training in business and the willingness to attend classes regularly indicated clearly that there is little correlation between the attitudes of individuals and their conditions of employment.

A comparison of the wage rates paid by independent merchants and the local chain in Bloomington is shown in Table No. XXI. No significant differences appear.[6] Reliable

---

6. One dollar and forty-seven cents per week higher in independents on the average. But no account is taken of the part-time and unpaid help in the independent stores. See Appendix A, Supplement to Chapter XII.

data were not obtained in the Indiana survey concerning the wage rates prevailing in the large chains. Even if such data were available there, it would be difficult to make a comparison, because other rewards to chain store employees, such as bonuses or allowances for illness, which, although they may be included in the returns obtained from the central offices of the two large chains, are not identifiable in the records.

Do the chain store organizations stifle individual initiative and prevent individuals from becoming independent merchants, operating their own establishments? It is alleged by many that they do. Indeed, this is one of the charges most often made by the enemies of the chains. In a pamphlet issued by the Freedom of Opportunity Legion the following statement appears:[7]

> Instead of being doomed to slave for an absentee boss until disqualified by age, high school and college graduates can again start life in a locally owned enterprise with an equal opportunity some day to own and operate the business themselves, not in competition with ruthless absentee owned enterprises, but with other similarly situated enterprises having substantially the same purchasing power.

A more dispassionate and specific statement of this charge was made by the manager of a large independently-owned department store, during a personal interview with

---

7. "The Community vs Absentee Control." A booklet explaining the Aims and Purposes of the Freedom of Opportunity Legion. Published by C. T. Habegger at Berne, Indiana. 1938. See Chapter XVI for a more detailed discussion of this organization.

the author. This executive stated that the employees of
large chain department stores are uncertain of their tenure,
and cited a case in his city where, on orders from headquarters, the local unit of this department of chains, within a period of three weeks, unconditionally discharged
fifty-six employees, many of whom had been with that store
for years. He questions the ability of any firm to retain
the loyalty of its employees under such conditions. He
pointed out that in his own store such an emergency would
be met in a quite different manner, and that the manager
would make any effort possible to reduce the shock resulting
from a drastic reduction of labor costs lessened, by extending the period of curtailment over a considerable period
of time.

He stated further that the internal management of a
chain department store suffers from long-range control:

We are constantly encouraging our department
heads in the creation and development of merchandising plans and ideas. When a buyer comes
to me with some plan which he has evolved, with
his enthusiasm at white heat, he wants an immediate 'Yes' or 'No.' If I have to say 'No,'
then it's up to me to show him just why his
idea will not work, and encourage him to alter
it to conform with the conditions in other departments or in the store as a whole. But it
is also up to me to see that his enthusiasm is
not chilled nor his initiative deadened. On
the other hand, if I am manager of a chain
store, and am forced to put him off with ex-
cuses until I can take it up with the central
management at long range, where the enthusiasm
and energy of the buyer cannot be made evident,
then most of the motive force back of the idea
is lost.

168

The conclusion which the evidence presented here indicates, but does not verify, is that the chains are correct
in their contention that they pay the prevailing wage for
the type of labor they employ.[8] Other intangible considerations enter into a comparison between the chains and the
independents with respect to their employees which cannot
be measured objectively. The dispute between the chains and
their opponents about the relative opportunities offered to
employees for advancement does not take into account individual differences among the employees or their ability and
willingness to take advantage of these opportunities. An
ambitious person can _learn_ merchandising methods in either
a chain or an independently-owned store, assuming that both
are operated efficiently. His chances to become an executive or an independent are determined largely by his abilities and inclinations, and by whatever future falls to his
lot.

---

8. This checks with the analysis made by Professor Vaile
    of the data obtained in his study in Minneapolis.
    Roland S. Vaile, "Grocery Retailing with Special Ref-
    erence to the Effects of Competition," p. 27. _Univer-
    sity of Minnesota Studies in Economics and Business_,
    No. 1. 1932. See Appendix A, Supplement to Chapter
    XII.

Table XXI

Comparison of Wage Rates Paid by Independent
Grocers and by the Local Chain in Bloomington

Wages per Week	Salesperson Part-time		Salesperson Full Time				Meat Cutter	
	Indep.	Chain	Indep. W	Indep. M	Chain W	Chain M	Indep.	Chain.
$2 to less than $3	1							
4								
5	6							
9								
10								
11								
12						1		
13	1		1	2		1		
14								
15				5		1		
16				1				
17						2		
18				6				
19								
20				10		3	1	
21								
22					1			1
23					1			1
24								
25					1	2	3	
26						1	1	1
27								
28								
29								
30						1	1	1
Totals	8		1	24	3	12	6	4

Ten managers in the local chain each receive $25.00 per week.
W-Women   M-Men
Note: In a university town, student help is often used in the groceries.

Average Weekly Earnings for Full-time Salespeople

Indep.		Chain	
W.	M.	W.	M.
$13.00	$19.57	$12.60	$18.10

The average of all independents in the sample taken in Allen County
(Fort Wayne) was $18.94 for salespersons and $25.50 for meat cutters;
the latter checking closely with the average of $25.00 for both the
independents and the local chain in Bloomington.

Chapter XIII

ANTI-CHAIN STORE LEGISLATION

A study of the laws of the United States is essential to an understanding of its political and industrial history, and its economic development. A reading of the Constitution alone will take one through various phases of our nation's past life, including such epochal events as the freeing of the slaves, the granting of suffrage to women, and the passage (and repeal) of the Eighteenth Amendment. Wise laws, laws that are in conformity with the principles of economics and the needs of the people, serve to chart our course and direct us into those activities and endeavors which result in the greatest prosperity and happiness for the largest number. Such laws are usually the reflections of the universal experiences and crystallized sentiment of a thinking people, directed by able leaders. Bad laws, passed in haste to appease an angry populace, or through the efforts of a small, selfish, but powerful group, may retard the economic development of a nation or bring industrial disaster to a community.

Starting with the "Granger Laws" in the early seventies and extending through a long evolutionary period to the present time, a body of legislation has been developed by which we have governmental regulation of transportation. In the field of production, the trust movement was followed

closely by the passage of state and federal laws designed
to break up trusts and to prevent the existence of conditions favorable to the development of monopolies.

A truism of history, or science, or religion, or any
other branch of knowledge based on the thoughts or actions
of individuals is that the discovery of a new way of doing,
which forces people to reconstruct their beliefs, their
ways of thinking, or their modes of endeavor, meets with
violent opposition, often leading to savage conflict. It
is but natural, then, that such a radical change in the
method of distribution of merchandise as was occasioned by
the rapid development of chain stores since 1930, with its
attendant merger movement leading to unified control by a
comparatively limited number, should have aroused antagonism, and have led to a wide-spread and determined effort on
the part of those most affected -- the independent merchant
and his allies, the wholesaler and the jobber -- to preclude
the growth of the chain store method of merchandising. It
is also to be expected that those opposed to the chains
would take action in the direction that was most obvious
and that promised the quickest results. Through their state
legislatures, where their representatives could be most
easily influenced, they sought legislation designed to
strengthen their economic position by imposing financial
burdens upon the chain stores.[1]

---

1. The introductory paragraphs in this chapter are repeated from the author's thesis, "Anti-Chain Store
Legislation." University of Washington. 1930.

So much has been written on the subject of legislation
taxing chain stores and regulating prices that anything in
addition would be mere repetition.[2] Moreover, it is impossible to treat the subject adequately within the con-
fines of one chapter. The intention here is simply to indicate the various situations that have arisen, and, in
particular, to analyze briefly some of the propaganda that
has been carried on by organized groups of those who are
involved in the chain store controversy.

The constitutional validity of laws which levy taxes
on chain stores is derived from the decision of the United
States Supreme Court in the Jackson case.[3] Here the court
held that the differences between chain stores on the one
hand, and independently-owned stores, department stores,
and mail order houses on the other, warranted a separate
classification by the legislature for taxing purposes.
Some years later the same court sustained the Louisiana
law, which taxes chain store organizations on the basis of
the number of units operated, regardless of where they are
located.[4] The court held that the competitive advantages
of the chains extend beyond the boundaries of the state.
Also, municipalities may levy taxes in addition to those
levied by the state.[5]

---

2. See Bibliography, p. 167.

3. The State Board of Tax Commissioners of Indiana, et al
    v. Jackson, 1931, 283 U. S. 527.

4. Great Atlantic and Pacific v. Grosjean et al, 1937.
    301 U. S. 412.

5. Great Atlantic and Pacific v. City of Spartanburg, 1933.
    170 S. E. 273.

In support of its decisions upholding the principle
that chain store organizations and independent merchants
belong in different classifications, the supreme court has
listed many of those advantages which have been discussed
in the preceding chapters. But one can well raise these
questions:

Do all chain store organizations necessarily
possess these advantages?

Are all the units of a chain equally profitable?

Is relative size also a measure of the relative
ability to pay?

Evidence presented in preceding chapters indicates a
negative answer to each of these questions. If this is a
true answer, then many of the existing and proposed laws
taxing chain store organizations are not equitable.

Two different bases have been used for the purpose of
levying taxes on multiple-unit systems: one, the total
volume of gross sales and two, the number of units operated.
In Florida those two bases have been combined. The law
places a tax of 0.05 per cent on all gross receipts, and
also a license fee graduated on the basis of the number of
stores owned. Because a question has been raised as to the
constitutionality of a classification based on the volume
of sales,[6] most chain store tax laws use the number of
stores operated as the base.

Chain store organizations have been affected not only

---

6. See Steward Dry Goods Company et al v. Lewis et al,
    1935. 294 U. S. 550.

174

by legislation which levies taxes directly. This latter
group of laws includes the Robinson-Putnam Act, the Miller-
Tydings amendment, the minimum price laws, and the various
state resale price maintenance laws. Speaking of this type
of legislation, Professor Griffin says:[7]

> Ostensibly, these laws are aimed at differ-
> ent alleged evils. The Robinson-Patman Act
> purports to prevent unwarranted price favorit-
> ism in the purchase of goods. The state resale
> price maintenance laws give to a manufacturer
> the legal right to specify the price at which
> his branded goods will be resold, and the
> Miller-Tydings amendment is an attempt on the
> part of the national government to give effect
> to the purpose of the state laws. The laws
> against selling below cost are aimed at pre-
> venting some retailers from injuring others
> by an uneconomical retail price policy. The
> laws thus impinge upon prices in apparently
> different ways: the first deals with relative
> prices paid by retailers, the second with
> prices relative and absolute charged by re-
> tailers for identical branded goods, and the
> third group with prices charged by retailers
> on any and all goods relative to the costs of
> thos goods.
>
> The Robinson-Patman Act makes it[8]
>
> unlawful for any person engaged in commerce
> to discriminate in price or terms of sale
> between purchasers of commodities of like
> grade and quality, to prohibit the payment
> of brokerage or commission under certain
> conditions, to suppress pseudo-advertising
> allowances, to provide a presumptive meas-

---

7. C. E. Griffin, "The Economic Significance of Recent
Price Legislation." Paper read before the joint meeting of the American Marketing Association and the American Accounting Association at Detroit in December,
1938. Reported in the Journal of Marketing, Volume
III, No. 4, April, 1939, p. 367. Published by the
American Marketing Association.

8. As stated in the preamble of the bill when it was introduced in Congress. Public No. 692, 74th Congress,
approved June 19, 1936.

ure of damages in certain cases and to protect the independent merchant, the public
whom he serves, and the manufacturer from
whom he buys, from exploitation by unfair
competitors.

The Miller-Tydings Act, an amendment to the Sherman Anti-

Trust Act and the Federal Trade Commission Act, legalizes

(in interstate commerce) minimum price agreements for

branded or identified commodities sold in those states

where such agreements are valid under state laws.[9] At the

time the act was passed, forty-three states had such laws.

As Professor Griffin points out in his paper, the independent merchants, both wholesale and retail, who are
most affected by the competition of the chain stores, and
who are the real sponsors of the legislation described
above, have -- through the medium of legislation -- attacked
the chains on three fronts: first, with laws intended to
outlaw price concessions made to the chains by the manufacturers; second, with laws to prevent the lowering of profit
margins; and third, with punitive tax legislation openly
designed to destroy the national chain store organizations.

The identification of the groups sponsoring anti-chain
store legislation leads naturally to an analysis of the
methods of propaganda employed by them to secure the public's support, and by the chain store organizations to
combat these attacks. As is to be expected, each side
charges the other with the distortion of facts. In the

---

9. See John W. Norwood, "Trade Practice and Price Law.
Federal," p. 136 ff. Commerce Clearing House, Inc. New
York. 1938.

booklet published by the Freedom of Opportunity Legion appears the following statement:[10]

> Congressional investigation of the lobbying
> practices of the corporate chain stores shows
> beyond refutation that chains have spent
> millions of dollars to employ all manner of
> undercover propaganda to receive the American
> people, and to delude them into believing that
> their mass buying power is being used for the
> welfare of the people ..... Certain chain store
> interests financed for months a Farm to Market
> News, employed well-known members of the staff
> of the American Farm Bureau and get it out in
> a form similar to the Farm Bureau Publications,
> all to deceive and mislead the farmer into be-
> lieving that their own people recommended the
> chain store as a benefit to the farmer. This
> episode was styled by the chains as their
> "cornstalk Brigade."

The chain store organizations, in defending themselves

against such attacks, charge the independent merchants with

misrepresentation of the truth. At a meeting of the Ameri-

can Marketing Association, Mr. Ralph B. Sharbrough, research

statistician of the Great Atlantic and Pacific Tea Company,

made the following statements:[11]

> Of recent years, a new situation has arisen in
> American business. Organized pressure groups,
> representing selfish minorities, have instituted
> drives for legislation which would favor the
> operation of their own businesses or handicap
> that of their competitors. Recently, by way of
> illustration, the chain stores of the nation
> have been made the targets of punitive legisla-
> tion instigated by groups of wholesalers and
> jobbers. These minorities have agitated for

---

10. "The Community vs. Absentee Control," op. cit., p. 148.

11. Ralph B. Sharbrough, "Statistical Problems in Food Dis-
    tribution." Paper read before a joint meeting of the
    American Marketing Association and the American Statis-
    tical Association at Detroit in December, 1938. Re-
    ported in the Journal of Marketing, Volume III, No. 4,
    April, 1939, p. 383. Published by the American Market-
    ing Association at 450 Ahnaip St., Menasha, Wisconsin.

the adoption of taxes so prohibitive as to
assure the destruction of chain stores.
Statisticians enter the picture because the
proponents of chain store taxes have resorted
to the use of half-truth and distorted reports
and figures. Failing to obtain authentic facts
to substantiate their charges, they have mis-
represented the true state of affairs to the
public. In such cases it becomes the duty of
the statistician to detect the misleading use
of figures, and to acquaint the public with
the true facts.

Both the chain store organizations and the proponents

of anti-chain store legislation are well organized. The

former have their Institute of Distribution, Inc., located

at 570 Seventh Avenue, New York City, their National Asso-

ciation of Food Chains, with headquarters at Washington,

D. C., and other associations in various states. The in-

dependent merchants work through their retail associations

and are represented at Washington by the American Retail

Federation. Both groups, in their many trade papers and

other publications, flood the country with articles attack-

ing or defending the chain store systems, arrange for

speakers to present their cases at state and national con-

ventions of manufacturers, realtors, and other types of

businesses, and in every other way possible attempt to

create for themselves a favorable public opinion.

The Freedom of Opportunity Legion, mentioned above, in

a type of organization which is less common today than it was

some years ago. At one time it was estimated that anti-

chain organizations were actively operating in 260 cities

and towns, and that, in addition, eleven radio stations were

broadcasting anti-chain store propaganda and sixteen publi-

cations were engaged exclusively in its dissemination.[12]
Probably the most colorful of those crusaders who were most
active in the early part of this decade was W. K. Henderson,
of Shreveport, Louisiana, whose nightly vitriolic attacks
on "the foreign chain store menace," over Station KWKH,
were classics of invective diatribe. His organization, The
Merchants' Minute Men of America, collected "the modest
sum of $12.00 per calendar year" from the independent store
owners to carry on the fight against the chains.

A very recent and dramatic development has linked the
name of a congressman with a large wholesaling establishment which deals in drugs and sundries and which distributes
through a national organization of independent retailers.
It appears that this concern financed a series of lectures
and addresses which the congressmen made in various cities,
the purpose of which was "to consolidate the sentiment of
retailers, manufacturers and business men generally behind
the Robinson-Patman law for the elimination of discrimination between customers and the establishment of fair play
in business."[13] When newspapers were printing stories
about the defalcations of a former president of this firm,
statements were made indicating that the National Association of Retail Druggists was the chief sponsor of the

---

12. See Business Week, April 9, 1930.

13. Statement issued from Herald-Tribune Bureau, Washing-
    ton, December 17, 1938.

Robinson-Patman Act and the Miller-Tydings amendment.[14]

The largest national chain grocery store organization recently made an open bid for the public's support in its effort to defeat the attempted enactment of the Patman bill.[15] A startled public opened its newspaper one morning to read an advertisement in which "two elderly brothers broke a combined public silence of 108 years" to address the nation through the medium of "some 1400 newspapers over their own signatures, George L. Hartford and John A. Hartford. Even the A. and P.'s enemies admit, with admiring handshaking, that its lawyerlike organization and rhetorical persuasiveness made it a honey of a job."[16]

There is no way of knowing at this time just what will be the effects of these various state and federal acts. Manufacturers, merchants, market analysts, research agencies, and many others are watching developments closely. With regard to the laws taxing chains, the chain store organizations make much of the following statement in the final report of the Federal Trade Commission:[17]

> To tax out of existence the advantages
> of chain stores over competitors is to tax

---

14. See, for example, an article by Willard Edwards in the Chicago Tribune, for December 20, 1938.

15. See Appendix C.

16. J. C. Furnes, "Mr. George and Mr. John." Saturday Evening Post, Volume 221, No. 27, p. 8. December 31, 1938. The Curtis Publishing Company, Philadelphia. See Appendix A, Supplement to Chapter XVI, for a copy in full of this advertisement.

17. Federal Trade Commission. "Final Report on the Chain Store Investigation." Senate Document No. 4, 74th Congress, 1st Session, p. 91-2. U. S. Printing Office. Washington.

out of existence the advantages which the
communing public have found in patronizing
them, with a consequent addition to the cost
of living, for that section of the public.
That portion of the public which is able to
pay cash and is willing to forego delivery
service in return for the advantage of lower
prices will be deprived of that privilege,
generally speaking, although there are exceptions both ways.

It will also tend toward an arbitrary
frustration of whatever saving in cost of
production and distribution results from integration of the functions of producer, wholesaler, and retailer.

So, on the whole, the number of people
adversely affected by such a tax would constitute a very substantial percentage in comparison with the number adversely affected by
present conditions. The graduated tax on chain
stores cannot accomplish fully the social ends
aimed at by such legislation without producing
incidentally these results.

The practical effects of the price laws may or may not

be significant. But, as Professor Griffin points out,[18]

... The significance of these laws lies not so much
in their own effects as in the fact that they are
merely special manifestations in this field of retailing of a movement and an attitude of mind which
has become very general in recent years, ... the
increasing desire to protect existing institutions
and the old ways of doing things against the competition of new institutions and new ways ... They
represent in the retail field the growing forces of
conservation which are appearing in many other
fields. If the people of the country and our legislators in particular do not develop a willingness
and an ability to see such measures in terms of
the general welfare, rather than considering them
separately group by group, there is serious danger
that the system of free enterprise will be still
further impaired ..... The restrictions upon production, the standardization of wages, the limita-
tions of hours, the resale price maintenance laws,

---

18. Griffin, op. cit., p. 371 ff.

the minimum price laws, and the anti-chain store
legislation are all alike in that they are aimed
at conserving and protecting either groups or
the whole society against the disturbing effects
of change. It is a comfortable policy; it may
be a sane policy; it may even be an inevitable
policy; but it is not a progressive policy.

Very definite information concerning the relative
loads of chain stores and independents was obtained by the
Indiana Tax Study Commission. Table XIX in Chapter XI
presented one comparison in terms of absolute amounts. In
this chapter dealing with the effect of the chain store tax
on the tax loads, one is more interested in a comparison of
ratios of tax payments to sales. Tables XIX and XX show
the figures published in the report of this commission.[19]
Table XIX shows the figures obtained by the survey at
Indiana University, and Table XX shows the ratios obtained
by the commission, based on information supplied by the
state and federal tax collecting agencies. The two sets
of figures are in close agreement.[20] The commission's conclusion was[21] "that the higher average license tax payment
by chain grocery stores virtually accounted for the difference in taxes paid by independent and chain grocers." In

19. The report of the Indiana Tax Commission of January 1,
     1939, p. 161-162.

20. If the state averages arrived at by Professor Haas are
     weighted according to the relative amounts of total
     volume of business done -- which is roughly on the
     basis of three parts independent to one part for chains
     -- the average would be 1.24 per cent which is only .01
     below our average for all retailers.

21. Ibid., p. 161.

other words, the tax load of the chains is heavier then
that of the independents by almost exactly the amount imposed by the chain store tax.

Investigations by the author of tax records in a number
of county seats in Indiana discloses the fact that gross
inequalities exist in the amounts of the property tax payments made by grocers. However, for those stores with an
annual sales volume of $25,000 and over, the amount of the
gross income tax is large enough to completely overshadow,
in most cases, the payments for property taxes. (See
Tables XIX and XX).

As closely as the author can determine, the general
sentiment in Indiana at the present time among the legislators is against any upward revision of the Indiana chain
store tax. In other states, indications are that this wave
of anti-chain store legislation has subsided. Dr. Wilford
L. White, chief of the Marketing Research Division Bureau
of Foreign and Domestic Commerce, in a talk given before
the Indiana Sales Management Conference, Indiana University,
November 7, 1939 made the following statement:

> As to anti-chain store legislation, there
> have been at one time or another, 25 states with
> anti-chain store laws, although there have not
> been 25 such laws at the same time. Today,
> there are only 19 states, according to my latest
> information, with anti-chain store laws, and
> this number may be reduced to 18 because in
> recent weeks a lower court decision in Minnesota
> has invalidated the existing law. I am informed
> that anti-chain legislation was introduced dur-
> ing the last legislative year in 17 states, and
> that in no case was the act passed. You recog-
> nize and I recognize that both sides in this
> struggle are exerting all possible influence on
> the consuming public, but judging from the

trends in the last couple of years, there is
evidence to support the belief that the anti-
chain store legislation is not so acceptable
to the general public as it used to be.

The thing to keep in mind when you are
tempted to turn to legislation for trade regulation is: 'Will this legislation benefit or
hurt the ultimate consumer?' because in the
long run, law or no law, the matter will be
decided upon just that point.

There are also indications that proponents of anti-chain
store legislation will find themselves hoist on their own
petard. The recent newspaper dispatch by Mr. Roscoe Fleming
to the Indianapolis Times[22] states that in Colorado, pursuant to a recent court decision, the state treasurer will
file claims for the amount of the tax for the four years of
the law's existence against independent groceries bound up
in buying groups under the wing of a single wholesaler,
against the retail agencies of tire companies, against drug
stores financed by wholesale houses and many other such
groups. In this same dispatch it is stated that Safeways
Stores, largest grocery chain in the state, which had been
paying more than $100,000 a year of the tax, began building
supermarkets and cutting down the number of its retail outlets. It now has about 30 less outlets than during 1938.
This situation in Colorado supports a statement recently
made by Mr. Paul H. Nystrom

Using legislation and the help of politicians
to crush competitors who are themselves engaged in
legitimate methods of doing business is at any time
an exceedingly dangerous proposition. It is doubly
dangerous now, not only for its possible kick-back

---

22. November 13, 1939.

on those who attempt it, but also as an additional argument that will be used by those who urge
that business cannot conduct itself properly without government regulation and control. He who
seeks to destroy others by government regulation
is himself likely to be destroyed by government
regulation.[23]

Summarizing the conclusions suggested by the material
presented in this chapter:

1. With an increase of the knowledge on the part of
the public about absolute and relative costs in independently-owned and chain grocery stores, and with improved methods
of merchandising employed both by wholesalers and retailers,
existing opposition to the chains will decrease in strength.

2. Are the chains taxed fairly? This question cannot
be answered by an unequivocal "yes", or "no". In Indiana,
at least, the conversations the author has had with officials
of chain-store organizations lead him to believe that the
latter have accepted the Indiana chain-store tax and will
not attempt to have it removed, but will resist with every
means at their command any movement on the part of the
legislators to increase this tax.

3. In these conversations mentioned above, the officials
did not indicate that any definite steps had been taken in
Indiana to reduce the number of units operating. A tax of
$145.00 on a unit with a volume in excess of $100,000 is,

---

23. "On the Road to Economic Recovery", Paul H. Nystrom,
Pres. Limited Price Variety Stores Association, New
York. Past President, Sales Executive Club of New
York. An address delivered at the Fourth Annual Con-
vention of the National Federation of Sales Executives
at Philadelphia, June, 1939. Published in the report
of the Proceedings by the Secretary's Office of the
Nat. Fed. 630 Fifth Ave., New York, 1939, p. 34-35.

relatively speaking, not burdensome.

4. Increasing demands for revenues by state governments may cause voluntary chains and similar associations to be subjected to the chain-store tax.

Table XXII

Relative Tax Loads of Chains and Independents in 16 Counties in Indiana

Classification	County	City	Average Percentage Total Tax to Sales	
			Independent	Chain Store
Industrial	St. Joseph	South Bend	1.04	1.76
	Allen	Fort Wayne	1.23	1.77
	Vanderburgh	Evansville	1.57	1.56
	Vigo	Terre Haute	1.20	1.47
	Lake	Gary	0.85	1.64
Averages for Industrial Group			1.18	1.64
Semi-Industrial	Clark	Jeffersonville	1.21	1.40
	Elkhart	Goshen	Not Obtained	1.56
	Grant	Marion	1.13	1.34
	Madison	Anderson	1.24	1.47
Averages for Semi-Industrial Group			1.19	1.44
Semi-Rural	Henry	Newcastle	1.13	1.35
	Jay	Portland	0.91	1.48
	Knox	Vincennes	1.24	Not Obtained
	Monroe	Bloomington	1.03	1.50
	Shelby	Shelbyville	Not Obtained	1.43
Averages for Semi-Rural Group			1.08	1.44
Rural	Orange	Paoli	1.27	1.44
	Parke	Rockville	1.10	1.38
Averages for Rural Group			1.19	1.41
Averages for Entire State			1.16	1.48

BIBLIOGRAPHY

"Adjustment of Operations by Wholesale Grocers -- with Special
       Emphasis on the Budget." Policyholders Service
       Bureau, Metropolitan Life Insurance Company,
       New York City.

Alexander, R. S., "A Study in Retail Grocery Prices" -- being a com-
       parison of prices of fifty nationally advertised
       products in chain and individually owned grocery
       stores in ten neighborhoods of New York City.
       Published by N. Y. Journal of Commerce, 1929.

Beckman, T. N. and Engle, Nathanael H., "Wholesaling Principles and
       Practices." The Ronald Press Company, New York,
       1937.

Beckman, T. N. and Nolen, H. C., "The Chain Store Problem." McGraw-
       Hill Book Company, Inc., New York. 1938. Also see
       Appendix A, Supplement to Chapter IV, for the census
       classifications.

Bibliography: A List of Books, Pamphlets and Publications on Market-
       ing, Retailing, Salesmanship, and Merchandising.
       (Prepared by B. Frank Kyker, Special Agent, Research
       in Commercial Education. U. S. Department of the
       Interior, Office of Education. Vocational Division)
       June, 1938.

Bjorklund, Einar and Palmer, James, "A Study of the Prices of Chain
       and Independent Grocers in Chicago." Studies in
       Business and Administration. The University of
       Chicago, Vol. I, No. 4, 1930.

Boer, A. E., "Mortality Costs in Retail Trades." Journal of Marketing,
       Vol. 2, No. 1. July, 1937.

Brewster, Maurice Ray, "Price Differentials in Chain and Independent
       Grocery Stores of Atlanta, 1930." Georgia School of
       Technology. Bulletin No. 10, July 25, 1932.

Breyer, Ralph F., "The Marketing Institution." First edition, McGraw-
       Hill Book Company, New York, 1934.

Buehler, E. C., Chain Store Debate Manual. National Chain Store
       Association, New York City, 1931.

Census of Business: 1935. Retail Distribution, Vol. IV. "Types of
       Operation." p. 9. United States Department of Com-
       merce. Bureau of the Census. January, 1937.

"Chain vs. Independent Stores." Commonwealth Club of California. Vol.
       VII, No. 28, Part 2 of The Commonwealth. July 14,
       1931.

Chain Store Bibliography. Published by Institute of Distribution,
    Inc., New York City.

Chamber of Commerce of United States, "Mass Merchandising." Report of
    17th Annual Meeting, 1939, Washington, D. C.

Converse, Paul D., Prices and Services of Chain and Independent Stores
    in Champaign-Urbana, Illinois. University of
    Illinois. NATMA Bulletin No. 4, October, 1931.
    Published by National Association of Teachers of
    Marketing and Advertising, New York.

_____ "Analysis of Retail Trading Areas." The National
    Marketing Review, Vol. 1, No. 4, 1934.

_____ and Mitchell, Robert V., "The Movement of Retail
    Trade Within a Metropolitan Area." Journal of
    Marketing, Vol. 2, No. 1, July, 1937.

Cover, John H., "Dispersion of Retail Prices," p. 326. The National
    Marketing Review, Vol. 1, No. 4, 1934.

Cunningham, Frank S., "The Outlook for the Independent; How the Tonic
    of Competition has Invigorated the Small Store
    Owner." Article from Executive Service Bulletin,
    August, 1930.

Davison, Craig, "What About Supermarkets?" Saturday Evening Post.
    The Curtis Publishing Company, Philadelphia, Septem-
    ber 17, 1938.

Discriminatory Store Taxes, Institute of Distribution, Inc., 570-7th
    Ave., New York City.

Donald, W. J., "Mergers and Marketing."

Dovell, Ray, "Chain Stores can be Good Citizens."

Dowe, Dorothy, "A Comparison of Chain and Independent Store Prices."
    Journal of Business, University of Chicago, April,
    1932.

Edwards, Willard, The Chicago Tribune. December 20, 1938.

Engle, N. H., "Implications of the Robinson-Patman Act for Marketing."
    Journal of Marketing. Published by American Market-
    ing Association, 383 Madison Ave. October, 1936.

Epstein, Ralph C., "Industrial Profits in the United States." National
    Bureau of Economic Research, New York, 1934.

Expenses-Margins, Net Profits, Stock Turns in Retail and Wholesale
Business (with the Table "How Much a Salesperson
Should Sell") published by Merchants Service, The
National Cash Register Company, Dayton, Ohio.

Fairchild, F. R., Furniss, E. S. and Buck, N. S., Elementary Economics.
The Macmillan Company, New York, 1930.

Faville, David E., "Comparison of Chain and Independent Grocery Stores
in the San Francisco Area." Journal of Marketing,
Vol. 1, No. 2, October, 1936.

Fetter, Frank A., Economic Principles. The Century Company, New York,
1915.

"Financial Statement Ratios of General, Grocery, Hardware, and Drug
Stores, in 1923." Nebraska Studies in Business, No.
9. Published by Committee on Business Research,
College Business Administration, University of
Nebraska, Lincoln, Nebraska, May, 1924.

Furnas, J. C., "Mr. George and Mr. John." Saturday Evening Post, Vol.
221, No. 27. The Curtis Publishing Company,
Philadelphia, December 31, 1938.

Garver, F. B. and Hansen, A. H., Principles of Economics. Revised
edition, Ginn and Company, New York, 1937.

Gault, E. H., "Cooperation by Business Groups." Journal of Marketing,
Vol. 1, No. 4.

Gault, Edgar H. and Smith, Raymond F., "Wholesale Distribution of
Breakfast Cereals in Southern Michigan." Michigan
Business Studies, Vol. V, No. 4. University of
Michigan, School of B. A., Bureau of Business Re-
search, Ann Arbor, 1933.

Great Atlantic and Pacific v. Grosjean et al, 1937, 301 U. S. 412.

Great Atlantic and Pacific v. City of Spartanburg, 1933. 170 S. E. 273.

Grether, Ewald T., "Market Factors Limiting Chain-Store Growth."
Business Review, April, 1932.

Griffin, C. E., "The Economic Significance of Recent Price Legislation." Journal of Marketing, Vol. III, No. 4, April,
1939.

Haas, Harold M., "Anti-Chain Store Legislation." Master's thesis,
University of Washington, 1930.

Hall, T. E., Current, Conflicting Views on the Chain Store Controversy. Published by National Research Bureau.

Investment Bulletin, Vol. II, No. 2. School of Business, Indiana
University, November, 1938.

Kyrk, Hazel, A Theory of Consumption. Houghton Mifflin Company. The
Riverside Press, Cambridge.

Lutz, Harley L., Public Finance. D. Appleton-Century Company, New
York, 1936.

Lyon, Leverett S., Advertising Allowances. The Brookings Institution,
Washington, D. C., 1932.

Marshall, Alfred, Principles of Economics. Macmillan and Company,
London, 1935.

Maynard, H. H., Weidler, W. C., and Beckman, T. N., Principles of
Marketing. Third edition, The Ronald Press Company,
New York, 1939.

McNair, Malcolm P., Expenses and Profits in the Chain Grocery Business
in 1929. Bureau of Business Research, Harvard University, Bulletin No. 84. Published by Graduate School
of Business Administration, Harvard University, Vol.
XVIII, No. 1, June, 1931.

_____ "Chain Store Expenses and Profits." An Interim
Report for 1932. Harvard University School of
Business Administration, 1934.

_____ Chain Store Expenses and Profits, An Interim Report for 1932. Bureau of Bus. Res. Bulletin No. 94,
Harvard University, Graduate School of B. A., Bureau
of Bus. Res., Soldiers Field, Boston, Mass., Aug.,
1934. Publications of the Graduate School of B. A.,
Vol. XXI, No. 7.

Mueller, Harold, "Chains -- Menaces or Blessings?" Oklahoma City
Times staff writer. Oklahoma Publishing Company,
Oklahoma City, 1930.

Nichols, John P., Chain Store Manual. Published by the National
Chain Store Association, New York City, 1932.

_____ Chain Store Manual. Institute of Distribution, Inc.,
New York City, 1936.

Norwood, John W., Trade Practice and Price Law. Federal. Commerce
Clearing House, Inc., New York, 1938.

Nystrom, Paul H., Chain Stores. Domestic Distribution Department
Chamber of Commerce of the United States, Washington, D. C. Revised edition, April, 1930.

hio State University Bureau of Business Research, Bulletin No. 50.

"Operating Expenses of Retail Grocery Stores in Nebraska, 1929."
Nebraska Studies in Business, No. 27. College of
Business Administration, The University of Nebraska,
No. 77, November, 1930.

Operating Expenses of 110 Selected Food Stores. Published by The
Progressive Grocer (National Magazine of the Grocery
Trade) (by the Butterick Publishing Company) 161-6th
Ave., New York City, 1935.

Palmer, Edgar Z., Journal of Commerce, July 19, 1930, and August 2,
1930, and in Chain Store Progress, September, 1930.

Phillips, Charles F., "Colgate University." Reported in Chain Store
Progress, May, 1931.

_____ "Chain, Voluntary Chain, and Independent Grocery
Store Prices." Journal of Business, University of
Chicago, April, 1935.

"Preliminary Report on a Model System of State and Local Taxation."
Proceedings of the National Tax Association, 1919.

Preliminary Bibliography of ... in Business Education. Federal Security Agency, U. S. Office of Education, Washington,
June, 1939.

"Pro and Con, Shall We Curb the Chain Store?" Reader's Digest,
December, 1938.

Pyle, J. R., Marketing Principles. First edition. McGraw-Hill Book
Company, Inc., New York, 1931.

Refener, L. A., Principles of Economics. Houghton Mifflin Company,
New York, 1927.

Rush, Myrtle, "A Study of Chain Grocery Stores in Albuquerque, New
Mexico." University of New Mexico, 1931. Reported
in Chain Store Progress, Nov., 1931.

Sharbrough, Ralph B., "Statistical Problems in Food Distribution."
Journal of Marketing, Vol. III, No. 4, April, 1939,
Published by American Marketing Association, Menasha,
Wisconsin.

Slaton, William H., Cost of Doing Business Survey of Retail Grocery
Stores in Colorado. Business Bulletin No. 38,
Bureau of Business and Government Research Extension
Division, University of Colorado. Boulder, Colorado,
July, 1938.

192

Small Scale Retailing. Domestic Commerce Series No. 100. U. S. Department of Commerce, U. S. Government Printing Office, Washington, D. C., 1938.

Starr, George W., "Industrial Development of Indiana." Indiana Studies in Business, Bureau of Business Research, School of Business Administration, Indiana University, Bloomington, Indiana, September, 1937.

Stevens, W. H. S., "A Comparison of Special Discounts and Allowances in the Grocery, Drug, and Tobacco Trades, I." The Journal of Business of the University of Chicago. Vol. VII, No. 2, April, 1934.

_____ "A Comparison of Special Discounts and Allowances in the Grocery, Drug, and Tobacco Trades, II." The Journal of Business of the University of Chicago, Vol. VII, No. 3, Chicago, Illinois, July, 1934.

Steward Dry Goods Company et al v. Lewis et al, 1935. 294 U. S. 550.

Stockbridge, Frank Parker, "The Truth About The Robinson-Patman Act." Three articles reprinted from the magazine Today, issues of Nov. 7, 14 and 21, 1936. Issued by the Institute of Distribution, Inc., New York City.

Taylor, Malcolm D., "What Price Chain Groceries?" Harvard Business Review, Vol. VIII, July, 1930.

_____ "Prices of Branded Grocery Commodities During the Depression." Harvard Business Review, July, 1934.

The Chain Store, an Element of Revolution. Central Union Trust Company of New York.

The Community vs Absentee Control. A booklet explaining the aims and purposes of the Freedom of Opportunity Legion. Published by C. T. Habegger at Berne, Indiana, 1938.

The Report of the Indiana Tax Study Commission. (Authorized by Chapter 317 House Concurrent Resolution No. 7) 80th session Indiana General Assembly. Published January 1, 1939.

The State Board of Tax Commissioners of Indiana, et al v. Jackson, 1931, 283, U. S. 527.

"The Truth About the Robinson-Patman Act." Three articles reprinted from the magazine Today, issues of November 7, 14 and 21, 1936.

Thirty-three Questions; 33 Answers Important to Your Pocketbook. Institute of Distribution, Inc., 1936.

J. S. Department of Commerce, "The Retail Grocer's Problems", Distribution Cost Studies, No. 5. United States Government Printing Office, 1929.

J. S. Department of Commerce, "The Wholesale Grocer's Problems - Costs, Customers, and Commodities." Distribution Cost Studies, No. 4. United States Government Printing Office, 1928.

J. S. Department of Commerce, Bureau of Census, "Retail Distribution (Merchandising Series), Food Chains (Grocery-Store Chains, Meat-Market Chains, Combination-Store-Grocery and Meat-Chains, Other Food Chains." Fifteenth Census of the U. S., census of distribution (merchandising series), Distribution No. R-70, U. S. Government Printing Office, 1932.

J. S. Department of Commerce, Fifteenth Census of the U. S., "Retail Distribution in the United States." Census of Distribution, 1930.

Waile, Roland S., Grocery Retailing with Special Reference to the Effects of Competition. The University of Minnesota Press, No. 1, April, 1932, Minneapolis, Minnesota.

Waile, Roland S. and Child, Alice M., "Grocery Qualities and Prices." University of Minnesota Studies in Economics and Business. The University of Minnesota Press, No. 7, Minneapolis, April, 1933.

Webbink, Paul, "The Chain Store Problem in 1930." Commercial Law League Journal, Vol. II, No. 4, April 24, 1930.

LIST OF CHAIN-STORE REPORTS OF THE FEDERAL TRADE COMMISSION

Federal Trade Commission, "Cooperative Grocery Chains," Senate Document
No. 12, 72nd Congress, 1st session, U. S. Government
Printing Office, 1932.

F. T. C., "Wholesale Business of Retail Chains," Senate Document
No. 29, 72nd Congress, 1st session, U. S. Government
Printing Office, 1932.

F. T. C., "Sources of Chain-Store Merchandise," Senate Document No.
30, 72nd Congress, 1st session, U. S. Government
Printing Office, 1932.

F. T. C., "Scope of the Chain-Store Inquiry," Senate Document No. 31,
72nd Congress, 1st session, U. S. Government Print-
ing Office, 1932.

F. T. C., "Chain-Store Leaders and Loss Leaders," Senate Document
No. 51, 72nd Congress, 1st session, U. S. Government Printing Office, 1932.

F. T. C., "Growth and Development of Chain Stores," Senate Document
No. 100, 72nd Congress, 1st session, U. S. Govern-
ment Printing Office, 1932.

F. T. C., "Chain-Store Private Brands," Senate Document No. 142, 72nd
Congress, 2nd session, U. S. Government Printing
Office, 1933.

F. T. C., "Short Weighing and Over Weighing in Chain and Independent
Grocery Stores," Senate Document No. 153, 72nd
Congress, 2nd session, United States Government
Printing Office, 1933.

F. T. C., "Sizes of Stores of Retail Chains," Senate Document No. 156,
72nd Congress, 2nd session, United States Government
Printing Office, 1933.

F. T. C., "Quality of Canned Vegetables and Fruits (under Brands of
Manufacturers, Chains, and Other Distributors)",
Senate Document No. 170, 72nd Congress, 2nd session,
U. S. Government Printing Office, 1933.

F. T. C., "Gross Profit and Average Sale per Store of Retail Chains,"
Senate Document No. 178, 72nd Congress, 2nd session,
U. S. Government Printing Office, 1933.

F. T. C., "Chain-Store Manufacturing," Senate Document No. 13, 73rd
Congress, 1st session, U. S. Government Printing
Office, 1933.

F. T. C., "Sales, Costs, and Profits of Retail Chains," Senate Document No. 40, 73rd Congress, 1st session, U. S. Government Printing Office, 1933.

F. T. C., "Prices and Margins of Chain and Independent Distributors, Washington, D. C. -- Grocery," Senate Document No. 62, 73rd Congress, 1st session, United States Government Printing Office, 1933.

F. T. C., "Prices and Margins of Chain and Independent Distributors, Memphis, -- Grocery," Senate Document No. 69, 73rd Congress, 1st session, United States Government Printing Office, 1933.

F. T. C., "Prices and Margins of Chain and Independent Distributors, Detroit -- Grocery," Senate Document No. 81, 73rd Congress, 2nd session, United States Government Printing Office, 1933.

F. T. C., "Chain-Store Wages," Senate Document No. 82, 73rd Congress, 2nd session, United States Government Printing Office, 1933.

F. T. C., "Chain-Store Advertising," Senate Document No. 84, 73rd Congress, 2nd session, U. S. Government Printing Office, 1934.

F. T. C., "Chain-Store Price Policies," Senate Document No. 85, 73rd Congress, 2nd session, U. S. Government Printing Office, 1934.

F. T. C., "Special Discounts and Allowances to Chain and Independent Distributors -- Tobacco Trade," Senate Document No. 86, 73rd Congress, 2nd session, U. S. Government Printing Office, 1934.

F. T. C., "Invested Capital and Rates of Return of Retail Chains," Senate Document No. 87, 73rd Congress, 2nd session, U. S. Government Printing Office, 1934.

F. T. C., "Prices and Margins of Chain and Independent Distributors, Cincinnati -- Grocery," Senate Document No. 88, 73rd Congress, 2nd session, U. S. Government Printing Office, 1934.

F. T. C., "Special Discounts and Allowances to Chain and Independent Distributors -- Grocery Trade," Senate Document No. 89, 73rd Congress, 2nd session, U. S. Government Printing Office, 1934.

F. T. C., "Service Features in Chain Stores," Senate Document No. 91, 73rd Congress, 2nd session, U. S. Government Printing Office, 1934.

F. T. C., "The Chain Store in the Small Town," Senate Document No. 93,
73rd Congress, 2nd session, U. S. Government Printing
Office, 1934.

F. T. C., "Special Discounts and Allowances to Chain and Independent
Distributors -- Drug Trade," Senate Document No. 94,
73rd Congress, 2nd session, U. S. Government Printing Office, 1934.

F. T. C., "Prices and Margins of Chain and Independent Distributors,
Cincinnati-Drug," Senate Document No. 95, 73rd
Congress, 2nd session, United States Government
Printing Office, 1934.

F. T. C., "Prices and Margins of Chain and Independent Distributors,
Detroit-Drug," Senate Document No. 96, 73rd Congress,
2nd session, United States Government Printing
Office, 1934.

F. T. C., "Prices and Margins of Chain and Independent Distributors,
Memphis-Drugs," Senate Document No. 97, 73rd
Congress, 2nd session, United States Government
Printing Office, 1934.

F. T. C., "Prices and Margins of Chain and Independent Distributors,
Washington, D. C. -Drug," Senate Document No. 98,
73rd Congress, 2nd session, U. S. Government Printing Office, 1934.

F. T. C., "Miscellaneous Financial Results of Retail Chains," Senate
Document No. 99, 73rd Congress, 2nd session, U. S.
Government Printing Office, 1934.

F. T. C., "State Distribution of Chain Stores," Senate Document No.
130, 73rd Congress, 2nd session. U. S. Government
Printing Office, 1934.

F. T. C., "Final Report on the Chain Store Investigation," Senate
Document No. 4, 74th Congress, 1st session. U. S.
Government Printing Office, 1935.

APPENDIX A

APPENDIX A

Supplement to Chapter I.

1. "In Hanseatic history two great stages can be distinguished, the period when it was dominated by the drive
to expansion and that of stagnation and decline. The
first may be dated from approximately 1150 until the
treaty of Stralsund. During the first century of this
early Hanseatic period, while the merchants were still
carrying their wares from port to port and sharing the
risks of foreign travel with a group, or hanse, of
their comrades, their enterprise was motivated by a
cooperative spirit. But after about 1250 the compul-
sion became individualistic and for the next hundred
and twenty years there was manifested an unrestrained
quest for private gain far surpassing that evidenced
at any period in Hanseatic history. The new stimulus
of commercial activity was provided by the changes accompanying the introduction of writing which enabled
the merchant to operate on an efficient basis. Instead
of being forced to undertake trading voyages in person
the merchant from 1250 onward could and did establish
a central office, the skrivekamere or Kontor, from
which he conducted business with all the towns in the
sphere of his interests by means of written documents.
At the central office he maintained a bookkeeping system; remarkable examples of these early books have
been preserved. The employment of assistants, partnership contracts and agreements with commission agencies
were introduced and grew constantly more common, widen-
ing the potentialities of commercial activity at the
same time that they made it more complex."
Frist Rorig. Encyclopedia of the Social Sciences.
Vol. VII, p. 266. MacMillan Co., New York, 1932.

2. Senate Resolution 224, Seventieth Congress, first session:
      Whereas it is estimated that from 1921 to 1927 the
retail sales of all chain stores have increased from approximately 4 per centum to 16 per centum of all retail
sales; and
      Whereas there are estimated to be less than four
thousand chain-store systems with over one hundred
thousand stores; and
      Whereas many of these chains operate from one hun-
dred to several thousand stores; and
      Whereas there have been numerous consolidations of
chain stores throughout the history of the movement, and
particularly in the last few years; and
      Whereas these chain stores now control a substan-
tial proportion of the distribution of certain commodities in certain cities, are rapidly increasing this pro-

portion of control in these and other cities, and are
beginning to extend this system of merchandising into
country districts as well; and

Whereas the continuance of the growth of chain-
store distribution and the consolidation of such chain
stores may result in the development of monopolistic
organizations in certain lines of retail distribution;
and

Whereas many of these concerns, though engaged in
interstate commerce in buying, may not be engaged in
interstate commerce in selling; and

Whereas, in consequence, the extent to which such
consolidations are now, or should be made, amenable to
the jurisdiction of the Federal antitrust laws is a matter of serious concern to the public; Now, therefore,
be it

RESOLVED, That the Federal Trade Commission is
hereby directed to undertake an inquiry into the chain-
store system of marketing and distribution as conducted
by manufacturing, wholesaling, retailing, or other types
of chain stores and to ascertain and report to the
Senate (1) the extent to which such consolidations have
been effected in violation of the antitrust laws, if at
all; (2) the extent to which consolidations or combinations of such organizations are susceptible to regulation under the Federal Trade Commission Act or the antitrust laws, if at all; and (3) what legislation, if any,
should be enacted for the purpose of regulating and controlling chain-store distribution.

And for the information of the Senate in connection
with the aforesaid subdivisions (1), (2), and (3) of
this resolution the commission is directed to inquire
into and report in full to the Senate (a) the extent to
which the chain-store movement has tended to create a
monopoly or concentration of control in the distribution
of any commodity either locally or nationally; (b) evidences indicating the existence of unfair methods of
competition in commerce or of agreements, conspiracies,
or combinations in restraint of trade involving chain-
store distribution; (c) the advantages or disadvantages
of chain-store distribution in comparison with those of
other types of distribution as shown by prices, costs,
profits, and margins, quality of goods and services rendered by chain stores and other distributors or resulting
from integration, managerial efficiency, low overhead,
or other similar causes; (d) how far the rapid increase
in the chain-store system of distribution is based upon
actual savings in costs of management and operation and
how far upon quantity prices available only to chain-
store distributors or any class of them; (e) whether or
not such quantity prices constitute a violation of either
the Federal Trade Commission Act, the Clayton Act, or any
other statute; and (f) what legislation, if any, should
be enacted with reference to such quantity prices.

Appendix A.

Supplement to Chapter II.

1-- "Chain stores are in the United States a relatively recent development, whose growth has been short of the
spectacular. From 1900 to 1929, a period of 28 years,
chain stores have multiplied 2,800 per cent, and the
growth has been consistent throughout the period. At
the present time, chain stores take a substantial proportion of the total volume of the retail business of
the country. Anywhere from 25 to more than 30 per cent
of all retail store business is now being absorbed by
the chain systems, depending upon how a chain is defined and on what basis the statistics were gathered.
Not only that, but in certain lines of business, chain
stores claim even a larger share of the business volume.
For example, in the grocery trade, they claim more than
40 cents of the consumer's dollar; in the shoe business
they do approximately 50 per cent of the total retail
volume; and in the variety store field chain stores
have over 90 per cent of the business."
     Beckman, T. N. and Nolen, H.C. The Chain Store
Problem. Pages 11, 12. McGraw-Hill Book Company.
New York. 1938.

6--   The comparatively recent growth of many of the
large chains is apparent from the Federal Trade Commission's report. It says:

    "For a considerable number of the larger chains
the record reaches back for a sufficient period of
time to cover the greater part of the development of
these chains. The store-detail record for the Kroger-
Grocery & Baking Company begins with 40 stores in 1903;
for the Sanitary Grocery Company, Inc., 23 stores in
1910; for H. G. Hill Company, 26 stores in 1913; for
Daniel Reeves, Inc. 41 stores in 1913; and for Mutual
Grocery Company, 9 stores in 1917. In the drug group
The Owl Drug Store's first report was in 1907 with 7
stores; Peoples Drug Stores, Inc. in 1921 with 8 stores;
Walgreen Company in 1924 with 44 stores; and Whelan Drug
Company, Inc. in 1925 with 23 stores. In the variety
group, S. S. Kresge, first reports in 1911 with 64 stores;
McCrory Stores Corporation, 1902 with 20 stores; the
present F. & W. Grand-Silver Stores, Inc., in 1916 with
13 stores; G. C. Murphy Company in 1912 with 12 stores;
and McLellan Stores, Inc. in 1916 with 9 stores. In the
shoe business, W. L. Douglas Shoe Company reports store
details beginning with 17 stores in 1895; Beck Hazzard,
Inc. with 14 stores in 1914; G. R. Kinney Co., Inc. and
Melville Shoe Corporation, both in 1917; with 54 and
14 stores, respectively; The Schiff Company, with 6
stores in 1921; and the Wohl Shoe Company, with 10
stores in 1924. In the millinery and hat and cap chains,

Appendix A.

Supplement to Chapter II.

Consolidated Millinery Company reports store retail beginning with 6 stores in 1914. Gross Millinery Company
reports 7 stores in 1923, and Sarnoff Irving Hat Stores,
Inc. reports 50 stores in 1918.
"The figures for Louis K. Liggett Company and F. W.
Woolworth Company begin with the dates of consolidations
creating the existing chains, 1916 and 1912 respectively,
the former having 144 stores and the latter 596. The
Great Atlantic & Pacific Tea Co. record begins midway
between these two in 1914 with 585 stores."
Federal Trade Commission. Growth and Development
of Chain Stores. S. D. 100. Page 4. U.S. Govt.
Printing Office. Washington. 1932.

Appendix A

Supplement to Chapter III.

2-- "The transition from the status of a single or multi-
unit independent to that of a chain occurs in fact when
the method of supplying the stores with merchandise changes. So long as merchandise is bought for each store separately, or for a single large store from whose stocks
the smaller branches draw their merchandise, the stores
constitute a multi-unit independent operation, differing
in no essential from the growing retailer who expands
into the building next door or into additional floor
space above.

"But with more multiple units there soon comes a time
when the owner finds it expedient to standardize his
stocks, buy in larger quantities and supply the stores
from a central source. Thereupon the stores become links
in a chain, which not infrequently develops into a chain
of 'outlets' for central-office purchases instead of distributors of goods selected primarily to meet the varying needs of each individual store's customers. The
change is intangible but significant, in that it is the
underlying cause of much of the criticism directed at
some chains in recent years. Buying tends to become the
controlling interest of management to the neglect of a
retailer's primary function, which is to supply the customer with what he wants in the way he wants to buy it.

"The method of merchandising being the main line of demarkation between an independent and a chain, the Census
would base its classification upon the degree of centralization of buying if such data were available. As
a workable substitute, all retailers with two or three
stores are classified as multi-unit independents and
all with four or more stores in the same general line
of business are classified as chains, except where evidence to the contrary is conclusive."

Census of Business, 1935.

Appendix A.

Supplement to Chapter III

3-- (Continued)

"The term "chain" obviously implies more than one
unit. The only characteristic common to practically
all organizations of multiple establishments reporting
to the commission is the ownership of a controlling
interest in each unit. This general characteristic
of common control applies equally to those chain organizations with 2 establishments and to those with 10,000.
From the standpoint of the number of units involved,
therefore, it seems logical to define a chain in terms
of two or more units rather than to restrict its application to a more arbitrary basis beginning at some point
above two. The great bulk of the chain-store business
treated in this report, however, is conducted by organizations with numerous units.

"Similarly, the term "chain' is defined without
reference to the extent of centralization in management.
The returns to the commission's chain-store schedule,
which will be considered in subsequent reports, show
that, from an operating standpoint, chains as above defined may vest one, some, or all of the principal features
of management either exclusively or partially in the hands
of the headquarters organization, in those of the unit
managers or in some form of managerial organization intermediate between the two. The character and extent of
operating control exercised depend on such factors as the
commodities handled, the size of the chain, the location
of the units, and the policies of the particular management.
Moreover, the extent of management centralization or de-
centralization is obviously dependent entirely upon those
who are in control. Overnight a highly centralized organization may become highly decentralized, and vice versa,
at the will of the controlling interest. The term 'chain'
therefore has been defined without reference to the readily changeable factor of internal organization. In most
of the chain-store business considered in this report,
however, centralized management of the individual units
is important."

Federal Trade Commission. Chain Stores--Scope of the
Chain-Store Inquiry. Senate Document No. 31, 72nd Con-
gress, 1st Session. Page 2. U.S. Government Printing
Office. Washington. 1932.

Appendix A.

<u>Supplement to Chapter III.</u>

3-- There have been many attempts to define a chain store.
The following are examples:

"As used in the reports on this inquiry, the term
'chain' or 'chain store' is applied to organizations
owning a controlling interest in two or more establishments which sell substantially similar merchandise at retail. In a broad sense, a chain or chain system may be
defined as two or more agricultural, commercial, financial, industrial, or other business establishments in
which a controlling interest is owned by a single individual, partnership, corporation, or other organization."
Federal Trade Commission. <u>Chain Stores--Scope of
the Chain Store Inquiry.</u> Senate Document No. 31, 72nd
Congress, 1st Session. Page 2. U.S. Government Printing
Office. Washington. 1932.

"Chains are groups of 4 or more stores in the same
general kind of business, owned and operated jointly,
with central buying, usually supplied from one or more
central warehouses."
Official definition used by the Bureau of the Census.
Census of Business: 1935, Retail Distribution, Vol.
IV, Types of Operation, p. 11, U.S. Department of Commerce, Washington, January, 1937.

"A chain store organization may be said to consist
of two or more units centrally owned, handling on the
same plane of distribution, substantially similar lines
of merchandise."
Maynard, H. H., Weidler, W. C., and Beckman, T. N.
<u>Principles of Marketing.</u> Revised edition, Page 146.
The Ronald Press Company. New York. 1923.

"A chain store is one of a group of retail stores
of essentially the same type, centrally owned and with
some degree of uniformity of operation."
Report of the Committee on Definitions. Bulletin
No. 4, page, 4, November, 1933 series, National Association of Teachers of Marketing and Advertising.

"The chain store is a corporation engaged primarily
in retailing of merchandise through a fairly large number of store units which are owned and controlled by the
corporation."
Palmer, James L. "Economic and Social Aspects of
Chain Stores." Journal of Business. Vol. II, July,
1929. Page 273. The University of Chicago Press.

205

Supplement to Chapter III.

4-- "A cooperative chain is an association of independent
retailers acting cooperatively either by themselves or
with a wholesaler to obtain advantages in buying, advertising, or in the performance of other merchandising
functions or activities. According to the control of
the organization there are two types, the retailer cooperative chain and the wholesaler-retailer cooperative
chain.
"The retailer cooperative chain is an organization
of independent retailers which advertises, functions as
a wholesaler, or performs other merchandising activities
cooperatively, and which is not connected with any particular wholesaler in such activities. The wholesaler-
retailer cooperative chain is a group of independent
retailers affiliated with a wholesaler for buying, advertising, or other merchandising activities.
"The term cooperative is used in this report partly
because of its convenience but primarily because in its
broad sense, members of these groups, whether wholesalers or retailers or both, are cooperating in numerous
ways with a more or less common end in view. In a few
cases it is technically correct to refer to retailer cooperative organizations as cooperatives since they have
all three of the following characteristics:
"(1) They sell only to members, or if to non-members,
only at higher prices.
"(2) Profits, if any, are returned to the members
in the form of patronage dividends.
"(3) Control of the organization is vested in the
hands of the members, each member having only one vote.
"In most cases, however, the retailer groups have
only one or two of the foregoing characteristics."

Federal Trade Commission. Chain Stores--Cooperatives
Grocery Chains. Senate Document No. 12, 72nd Congress,
1st session. Page xvi. U.S. Government Printing Office.
Washington. 1932.

"Buying groups ... have existed in all parts of the
country, particularly since about 1925. Because in many
cases common store fronts, centralized supervision, cooperative advertising, and to some extent common prices
have been used, the term 'voluntary chain' has been
coined to describe such buying groups . . . One (type)
is the cooperatively owned wholesale house; the other is
the wholesaler-sponsored voluntary chain."

Maynard, H. H., Weidler, W. C., and Beckman, T. N.
Principles of Marketing. Revised edition. Page 171.
The Ronald Press Company. New York. 1932.

Appendix A

Size and Extent of Chain Store Systems

Supplement to Chapter IV.

Beckman draws the following conclusions from the
census data on chain stores:

"1. In the United States, the chain store has become
a retailing institution of great importance, absorbing
31 cents of the consumer's dollar spent in retail stores.
While the number of chain stores seems to be decreasing,
the tendency is for the proportion of business taken to
increase.

"2. A correct measurement of the significance of
chain stores cannot be obtained by dealing in totals. The
analysis must be made by lines of retail trade in which
chains actually operate. It seems that chain stores prefer
to concentrate in a few kinds of retailing where operations
can be fairly standardized. In those lines of business in
which they concentrate, the proportion of business attracted
by chains runs very high and results in keen competition
with independents. In some of those fields, notably in
the variety store business, they have attained a virtual
monopoly.

"3. Chain stores gravitate to sections of the country
which are densely populated, over 50 per cent of them being
located in the Middle Atlantic and East North Central states,
although they are now spreading into the more sparsely populated areas. In those lines of retailing in which chains
prefer to function, they seem to have approached a point of
saturation in the more heavily populated states, when judged
by the relative changes that took place since 1929.

"4. Chains are largely urban institutions. Their
affinity for the larger cities aggravates the competitive
situation and tends to cause much alarm and antagonism
toward them. In the largest cities of the country, chains
absorb the bulk of the business in the few fields of retailing in which they specialize.

"5. The trend is for chains to become larger and
sectional or national in character. The concentration of
the chain business in the hands of large organizations has
been proceeding apace and the end is not yet."

Beckman, T. N. and Nolen, H. C.-- The Chain store Problem.
Pages 40, 41. McGraw-Hill Book Company, Inc. New York. 1938.

Appendix A

Supplement to Chapter IV.

2-- "Heretofore there has been almost no attempt to
classify stores as to type of operation except to
distinguish between so-called independents and
so-called chains. However no such simple demarkation
coincides with known facts and the attempts in that
direction have led to confusion.

"Much of the confusion arises from lack of uniform
definition of terms. What one person may mean by
the term "chain" is not conveyed to others with the
same clarity, and local stores often are classed as
chains which are not chains at all and have none of
the characteristics of chains.

"A chain is a group of reasonably similar stores in
the same kind or field of business, under one ownership and management, merchandised wholly or largely
from central merchandising headquarters and supplied
from one or more distributing warehouses or directly
from the manufacturer on orders placed by the central
buyers. Mere ownership is not the distinguishing
feature, and there are many financial mergers of
stores without central merchandising or buying which
are not chains. Change of ownership does not necessarily change the method of operation, and as long as
stores continue to plan and buy independently they are
independents as far as type is concerned.

"Nor does an independent proprietor become a chain
operator if, in lieu of adding to the size of his
store, he adds one or two branch stores and continues
to manage and merchandise them as if they were all
under one roof. The stores become a chain only when
merchandise planning and buying are centralized apart
from the stores, and a warehouse or other central
point or points are employed to accumulate and distribute merchandise to the stores.

"For the retail census it has been necessary to set
an arbitrary limit of three stores beyond which an
independent proprietor is classified as a chain operator, simply for the reason that the individual returns
on which the census is based do not reveal whether
multiunit stores are centrally merchandised or not. If
data on this point were fully and uniformly reported,
it would be possible to distinguish between chains and
multiunit independents even beyond the arbitrary

independent limit of three stores. In the census,
however, all groups of four stores or more are classified as chains except a few local branch systems,
which are groups of small suburban and neighborhood
branches which have been developed around a dominant
downtown parent store and which are merchandised from,
and largely supplied from the stocks of, the parent
store.

"The principal types of operation shown in the census
are: (1) single store independents; (2) two-store and
three-store independents; (3) local branch systems;
(4) local chains (four or more local stores centrally
merchandised); (5) sectional chains, and (6) national
chains."
Fifteenth Census of the United States, 1930.
Distribution, Vol. I--Retail Distribution, Part 1.
Page 17. U. S. Department of Commerce. Bureau of the
Census. U. S. Government Printing Office. Washington.
1933.

Table 1

Distribution of Chains and Independents in United States

	Population 1	Density per Square Mile 2	Number of Independents 3	Number of Chains 4	No. Chains per 100 Miles (Approximately) 5	Ratio Independents to Chains 6
New England	8,166,341	131.8	98,485	12,671	155	8
Maine	797,423	26.7	11,451	898	112	13
New Hampshire	465,293	51.5	6,401	593	127	11
Vermont	359,611	39.4	4,432	463	129	10
Massachusetts	4,249,614	528.6	46,599	7,239	171	6
Rhode Island	687,497	644.3	8,003	926	135	9
Connecticut	1,606,903	333.4	21,299	2,552	158	8
Middle Atlantic	26,260,750	262.6	352,202	34,318	130	10
New York	12,588,066	264.2	178,874	17,050	136	11
New Jersey	4,041,334	537.8	59,481	6,060	150	10
Pennsylvania	9,631,350	214.8	113,847	11,208	117	10
East North Central	25,297,185	103.0	301,877	28,696	113	11
Ohio	6,646,697	163.1	80,446	8,263	124	10
Indiana	3,238,503	89.8	38,142	3,241	100	12
Illinois	7,630,654	136.2	88,151	8,873	116	10
Michigan	4,842,325	84.2	54,711	5,600	116	10
Wisconsin	2,939,006	53.2	40,427	2,719	92	15

Sources: 1930 Census of Population
Census of Business, 1935, Vol. IV, Retail Distribution.

Table 1 (continued)

	Population 1	Density Per Square Mile 2	Number of Independents 3	Number of Chains 4	No. Chains per 100 Miles (Approximately) 5	Ratio Independents to Chains 6
West North Central	13,296,915	26.0	174,319	12,679	96	14
Minnesota	2,563,953	31.7	34,153	2,463	96	14
Iowa	2,470,939	44.5	35,134	2,234	90	16
Missouri	3,629,367	52.8	45,895	3,595	99	13
North Dakota	680,845	9.7	8,218	575	85	14
South Dakota	692,849	9.0	8,659	637	92	14
Nebraska	1,377,963	17.9	17,393	1,245	91	14
Kansas	1,880,999	23.0	24,867	1,930	102	13
South Atlantic	15,793,589	58.7	163,628	12,049	76	14
Delaware	238,380	121.3	3,659	292	123	13
Maryland	1,631,526	164.1	20,773	1,656	102	13
District of Columbia	486,869	7,852.7	5,080	1,150	234	4
Virginia	2,421,851	60.2	24,027	1,776	74	13
West Virginia	1,729,205	72.0	16,765	1,195	69	14
North Carolina	3,170,276	65.0	27,044	1,740	55	16
South Carolina	1,738,765	57.0	15,493	883	52	18
Georgia	2,908,506	49.5	28,444	1,946	67	15
Florida	1,468,211	26.8	22,343	1,411	96	16
East South Central	9,887,214	55.1	86,159	4,752	48	18
Kentucky	2,614,589	65.1	26,826	1,529	59	18
Tennessee	2,616,556	62.8	24,885	1,625	62	15
Alabama	2,646,248	51.6	20,253	1,187	45	17

Table 1 (continued)

	Population 1	Density per Square Mile 2	Number of Independents 3	Number of Chains 4	No. Chains per 100 Miles (Approximately) 5	Ratio Independents to Chains 6
Mississippi	2,009,821	43.4	14,195	411	20	35
West South Central	12,176,830	28.3	127,791	7,719	64	17
Arkansas	1,854,482	35.3	17,170	686	37	25
Louisiana	2,101,593	46.3	21,569	1,052	50	21
Oklahoma	2,396,040	34.5	23,985	1,647	69	15
Texas	5,824,715	22.2	65,067	4,334	74	15
Mountain	3,701,789	4.3	44,776	2,925	79	15
Montana	537,606	3.7	7,175	466	87	15
Idaho	445,032	5.7	5,187	407	91	13
Wyoming	225,565	5.3	3,217	180	80	18
Colorado	1,035,791	10.0	13,169	795	77	17
New Mexico	423,317	3.5	4,542	224	53	20
Arizona	435,573	3.8	4,766	378	87	13
Utah	507,847	6.2	5,126	387	76	13
Nevada	91,058	0.8	1,594	88	98	18
Pacific	8,194,433	25.8	125,085	11,780	144	11
Washington	1,563,396	23.4	22,563	1,622	104	14
Oregon	953,786	10.0	13,675	986	102	14
California	5,677,251	36.5	88,847	9,172	161	10

Comparison of Retail Sales Ratios by Types of Operation, 1935, 1933, and 1929

	Independents			Chains		
	1935	1933	1929	1935	1933	1929
All stores	73.1	71.3	77.5	22.0	25.4	20.0
Grocery stores (without meats)	60.8	54.3	53.6	38.2	45.0	45.7
Combination stores (grocery and meats)	60.5	56.1	67.6	39.1	43.7	32.2
Beer and liquor stores (packaged)	48.0	x	x	1.6	x	x
Motor-vehicle dealers	95.6	94.6	x	4.4	5.3	x
Accessories-tire-battery dealers	50.0	x	x	50.0	x	x
Filling stations	77.8	64.3	66.0	21.5	35.5	33.8
Department stores	61.4	67.3	72.1	26.7	23.9	16.7
Variety stores	9.2	8.8	9.8	90.8	91.2	90.1
Men's clothing and furnishings stores	78.0	76.5	77.9	21.0	22.0	21.2
Family clothing stores	78.9	79.2	71.5	20.6	20.3	27.3
Women's ready-to-wear stores	72.3	74.5	74.3	25.2	23.3	22.7
Shoe stores	43.3	46.5	53.5	50.0	46.2	38.0
Furniture stores	86.0	84.6	83.9	13.5	14.2	14.2
Household appliance-radio stores	48.1	33.2	x	12.6	21.5	x
Radio dealers	75.6	82.7	79.0	23.1	15.6	19.1
Lumber and building material dealers	75.6	x	x	23.8	x	x
Hardware stores and implement dealers	95.4	95.6	x	4.3	4.1	x
Restaurants and eating places	84.0	84.8	86.1	14.5	14.9	13.6
Drinking places	99.2	x	x	0.1	x	x
Cigar stores and cigar stands	61.1	65.1	73.5	35.8	33.9	25.1
Fuel and ice dealers	82.7	x	x	16.5	x	x
Drug stores with fountain	71.1	74.0	81.2	28.8	25.1	18.5
Drug stores without fountain	84.1	x	x	15.4	x	x
Hay, grain and feed stores	71.6	x	x	16.0	x	x
Farm and garden supply stores	75.0	x	x	4.7	x	x
Jewelry stores	90.3	93.6	93.0	8.9	5.9	6.4
All other stores	78.8	79.6	x	14.3	15.0	x

Source: Census of Business: 1935. Retail Distribution, Volume IV. Types of Operation, p. 9.
         United States Department of Commerce. Bureau of the Census. January, 1937.

Supplement to Chapter VIII

Table 3

Comparison of Number of Grocery Chain-Store Units, Retailer-Members of
Voluntary Grocery Chains, and Populations in Various States
(Arranged in Rank According to Ratio Members to Population)

State	Population in Thousands 1930 Census[1]	Number of Chain-store Units Grocery and Combination[2]	Voluntary Chains[3]	Retailer Members[3]	Relatives Chains to Population[3]	Relatives Retailer-Mbrs. to Population
Minnesota	2,564	249	14	3,915	9	152
Oregon	954	325	5	1,347	35	141
Vermont	360	174	6	485	48	135
Maine	798	436	9	973	55	122
Washington	1,563	406	15	1,887	26	121
New York	12,588	8,205	76	14,166	65	112
California	5,677	2,350	21	6,356	41	112
Maryland	1,631	759	12	1,725	47	105
Delaware	238	121	2	237	51	100
Pennsylvania	9,651	5,351	79	9,545	56	99
Massachusetts	4,250	3,728	40	4,024	88	95
Missouri	3,629	990	17	3,409	27	95
New Hampshire	465	121	8	431	26	93
Dist. of Columbia	487	492	3	441	101	89
Rhode Island	687	717	8	524	104	76
Colorado	1,036	279	6	735	27	71
Connecticut	1,607	1,449	16	1,141	90	71
Illinois	7,631	3,364	56	5,226	44	69
Wisconsin	2,939	713	21	1,982	24	68
Michigan	4,842	2,594	38	3,250	54	67
New Jersey	4,041	3,782	16	2,726	94	67

1. Source: Statistical abstract of the United States.

2. Source: Census of American Business-Retail Distribution, 1933.

3. Source: "The Voluntary Chains" - Table I, p. 18. American Institute of Food Distribution, Inc.
   New York, 1933.

215

Table 3 (continued)

State	Population in Thousands 1970 Census	Number of Chain-store Units Grocery and Combination	Voluntary Chains	Retailer Members	Relatives Chains to Population	Relatives Retailer-Mbrs. to Population
Indiana	3,238	1,213	28	2,095	37	65
Iowa	2,471	454	22	2,238	18	65
Ohio	6,647	3,280	38	4,062	50	61
Virginia	2,422	767	20	1,448	32	60
Utah	508	96	1	300	19	59
Nebraska	1,378	229	7	751	17	53
South Dakota	693	76	3	345	11	50
Kansas	1,881	341	9	816	18	43
West Virginia	1,729	424	12	618	25	36
Kentucky	2,615	650	5	859	25	33
Texas	5,825	853	14	1,793	15	31
Florida	1,468	535	6	374	36	25
Montana	537	60	3	124	11	23
Tennessee	2,617	654	10	579	25	22
Georgia	2,909	742	7	515	26	18
North Carolina	3,170	623	8	509	20	16
Mississippi	2,010	141	4	284	7	14
Alabama	2,646	523	4	297	20	11
Arkansas	1,854	155	6	205	8	11
Idaho	445	89	1	37	20	8
Oklahoma	2,396	267	5	186	11	8
Louisiana	2,102	292	3	146	14	7

Supplement to Chapter IX

Table 4

Prices Quoted in Bloomington Groceries During September, 1939

	Store #1	#2	#3	#4	#5	#6	#7	#8	#9	#10	Average	Median	Low
Breakfast Foods													
Kellogg's Cornflakes	$0.13	.13	.085	.085	.11	.13	.085	.085	.085	.15	.108	.098	.085
Quaker puffed wheat	.10	.10	.10	.10	.10	.10	.075	.075	.075	.10	.095	.10	.075
Ralston cereal	.25	.25	.25	.25	.25	.25	.22	.23	.25	.25	.245	.25	.22
wheatena	.25	.25	.25	.23	.25	.25	.22	.23	.25	.25	.243	.25	.22
Wheaties	.13	.10	.11	.10	.12	.125	.105	.105	.11	.13	.114	.11	.10
Canned Foods													
Apricots #2½ 1st Grade	.25	.25	.23	.23	.25	.25	.175	.20	.23	.25	.232	.24	.175
Fruit Cocktail, Grade A	.15	.15	.15	.15	.18	.15	.115	.15	.15	.15	.15	.15	.115
Pears, 1st Grade (Fancy)	.29	.25	.23	.23	.25	.30	.20	.20	.23	.22	.240	.24	.20
Pears, 2nd " (Standard)	.20	.20	.20	.19	.20	.20	.185	.15	.20	*	.192	.20	.15
Peas, Tiny Green, #2	.18	.20	.18	.15	.13	.18	.12	.14	.135	*	.163	.18	.12
Peas, Green Giant	.15	.19	.15	.15	.18	*	.15	.15	.15	*	.159	.15	.12
Tomatoes, 1st Gr. #2½	.19	.19	.17	.17	.20	.20	.16	.17	.19	.19	.183	.19	.16
Pineapple, 1st Gr. #2½	.23	.23	.23	.27	.25	.25	.19	.23	.23	.25	.234	.23	.19
Flours													
Aunt Jemima Pancake #1	.15	.125	.13	.13	.13	.13	.10	.12	.10	.10	.122	.125	.10
Bisquick	.33	.33	.33	.32	.32	.35	.27	.29	.29	*	.314	.32	.27
Pillsbury or Gold Medal - 24 lbs.	.89	.89	.89	.85	.89	.98	.87	.89	.89	*	.884	.89	.85
Swansdown	.25	.25	.25	.23	.29	.25	.21	.23	.23	.25	.244	.25	.21

Table 4 ____ (continued)

Prices Quoted in Bloomington Groceries During September, 1939

	Store 1	#2	#3	#4	#5	#6	#7	#8	#9	#10	Average	Median	Low
Toilet Papers													
Scott's Tissue	(0.063	.035	.063	*	.063	.063	.058	*	.063	*	.077	.083	.058
Waldorf	.063	*	.063	*	*	*	.038	*	.038	.042	.055	.053	.033
Northern	.063	*	*	*	.063	*	.048	*	.048	*	.056	.056	.048
Soups													
Campbell's Tomato	.10	.063	.10	.063	.063	.063	.067	.07	.063	*	.084	.083	.067
Campbell's (Others)	.10	.10	.10	.10	.10	.10	.063	.063	.10	.10	.097	.10	.083
Heinz's	.15	.15	.15	.15	.15	.15	.125	.125	.15	*	.13	.15	.125
Soaps													
Camay	.067	.065	.063	.053	.075	.063	.042	.057	.053	.067	.06	.063	.042
Crystal White	.05	.05	.05	.042	.042	*	.035	*	.031	*	.043	.042	.031
Ivory (large)	.10	.063	.063	.063	.10	.10	.063	.077	.063	.10	.089	.063	.077
Lifebuoy	.063	.063	.06	.050	.075	.067	.055	.057	.055	.067	.062	.062	.055
Lux	.067	.063	.067	.067	.075	.067	.055	.055	.055	.067	.064	.067	.055
Palmolive	.067	.063	.067	.06	.075	.067	.057	.057	.055	.067	.063	.067	.055
P. & G. (Small)	.05	.04	.043	.075	.042	.042	.031	.048	.031	.04	.041	.041	.031
Woodbury's	.063	.077	.063	.077	.083	.083	.067	*	.077	.083	.071	.083	.067
Laundry Supplies													
Chipso	.20	.19	.19	.19	.23	.21	.19	.20	.19	.21	.20	.195	.19
Clorox (pt)	.15	.15	.15	.15	.15	.15	.125	.15	.15	.15	.143	.15	.125
Old Dutch Cleanser	.063	.067	.075	.075	.083	.083	.067	.075	.075	.09	.077	.075	.067
Oxydol	.23	.19	.21	.19	.23	.23	.185	.185	.185	.21	.205	.200	.185
Rinso	.25	.19	.19	.19	.23	.23	.185	.195	.185	.21	.206	.196	.185

Table 4 (continued)

Prices Quoted in Bloomington Groceries During September, 1939

Miscellaneous	Store #1	#2	#3	#4	#5	#6	#7	#8	#9	#10	Average	Median	Low
Maxwell House Coffee	0.26	.26	.27	.25	.26	.28	.26	.26	.26	.29	.265	.26	.25
Kraft's Vel. Cheese	.18	.15	.15	.13	.18	.17	.125	.15	.125	.17	.153	.15	.125
Kraft's Am. Treng.	.17	.13	.14	.15	.15	.15	.13	.15	.14	*	.144	.15	.13
Miracle Whip	.35	.33	.35	.33	.35	.35	.32	.35	.32	*	.34	.35	.32
Jello	.06	.05	.05	.045	.06	.06	.053	.058	.047	.05	.051	.05	.033
Royal Gelatin	.06	.06	.05	.05	.06	.06	.047		.047	*	.197	.05	.17
Royal Baking Powder	.23	.20	.19	.20	.20	.19	.17	.19	.20		.197	.20	.17
Crisco (1½ Can)	.55	.57	.49	.49	.55	.55	.49	.49	.49	.55	.522	.52	.49
Vanilla (2 oz. best)	.25	.25	.21	.25	.25	.25	.17	(4)	.25	.25	.234	.25	.17
Ritz Crackers	.25	.24	.21	.23	.20	.23	.21	.21	.21		.22	.23	.21
Morton's Iodized Salt	.10	.10	.10	.075	.10	.10	.085	.09	.09	.10	.094	.10	.075
Tuna (best Grade)	.18	.18	.18	.15	.13	.17	.13	.17	.15	.17	.171	.175	.15
Spam	.29	.29	.29	.29	.29	.29	.29	.29	*	*	.29	.29	.29
Olives, stuffed 3z.	.25	.25	.25	.19	.22	.25	.20	.23	.25	*	.209	.25	.19
Best Grade													
Pickles, sliced (pt)	.15	.15	.15	.15	.15	.15	.10	.15	.15	*	.144	.15	.10

4 - Poor Grade
* - Not Carried

Supplement to Chapter X

Table 5

Monroe County

Annual Sales	Inventory	Sales	Property Tax	Gross Income Tax	Other Tax	Total Tax	Gross Margin	Tax % Sales	Tax % Gross Margin
Below 10,000	400.00	3009.35	7.31	23.68	3.50	34.49	540.00	1.15	6.39
	650.00	6805.00	25.97	50.40	19.00	95.37	1020.00	1.40	9.35
	200.00	2669.00	1.83	1.69	3.50	7.02	533.80	0.26	1.32
	200.00	3316.36	4.50	8.16	9.50	22.16	663.26	0.67	3.34
	600.00	3811.00	14.60	26.28	9.50	50.38	762.20	1.32	6.61
	200.00	2600.00	5.48	x	9.50	14.98	520.00	0.58	2.88
	800.00	5952.00	16.24	34.52	9.50	60.26	1071.36	1.01	5.62
	400.00	7000.00	18.45	60.00	10.80	89.25	1400.00	1.28	6.40
	200.00	7717.00	14.60	42.17	3.50	60.27	1929.25	0.78	3.12
	500.00	6336.12	11.99	38.36	9.50	59.85	1267.24	0.94	4.72
	500.00	7347.64	22.32	67.04	9.50	98.86	1468.52	1.35	6.73
	500.00	850.00	1.29	x	3.50	4.79	170.00	0.56	2.82
	600.00	9338.00	15.76	68.38	3.50	87.64	1867.60	0.94	4.69
10,000-20,000	1500.00	16882.19	38.33	107.75	9.50	155.58	3376.43	0.92	4.61
	800.00	17000.00	25.55	80.00	9.50	115.05	3400.00	0.68	3.38
	800.00	12000.00	21.90	95.00	9.50	126.40	2400.00	1.05	5.25
	816.59	12218.28	35.06	97.18	9.50	141.74	2443.65	1.16	5.80
	800.00	11059.95	21.77	83.29	16.25	121.31	2211.99	1.10	5.48
	500.00	10800.00	109.50	34.32	9.50	153.32	2160.00	1.42	7.10
	700.00	16829.22	216.49	141.33	9.50	197.32	3365.84	1.17	5.86
	900.00	15482.97	36.87	129.02	23.02	189.71	3096.59	1.23	6.13
	500.00	14303.48	45.81	118.03	9.50	173.34	2363.91	1.21	7.33
	1100.00	14899.00	56.83	148.99	17.30	223.12	2979.80	1.50	7.49
20,000-30,000	1300.00	22364.03	40.19	191.28	16.00	247.47	4472.80	1.11	5.53
	3000.00	30000.00	22.81	250.00	23.30	296.11	3780.00	0.99	7.83
	700.00	25931.00	27.68	229.31	9.50	266.49	4586.20	1.03	5.81

Table 5 (continued)

Annual Sales	Inventory	Sales	Property Tax	Gross Income Tax	Other Tax	Total Tax	Gross Margin	Tax % Sales	Tax % Gross Margin
30,000-40,000	700.00	30000.00	10.95	250.00	9.50	270.45	6000.00	0.90	4.50
	4000.00	38966.31	75.28	364.68	9.50	449.46	7793.66	1.15	5.77
Over 40,000	5000.00	60000.00	64.76	562.47	x	627.23	12000.00	1.05	5.25
	4000.00	75000.00	77.75	822.93	67.57	968.25	15000.00	1.29	6.45
	4178.00	76635.91	61.69	738.16	88.20	888.05	15327.18	1.16	5.79
	1000.00	41000.00	14.42	x	6.20	20.62	x	x	x
	2500.00	50000.00	77.86	475.00	9.50	562.36	10000.00	1.12	5.60
	1200.00	50000.00	65.34	475.00	69.82	609.16	10000.00	1.22	6.10
	3000.00	50000.00	38.00	475.00	x	513.00	10000.00	1.03	5.13
	1200.00	48139.06	56.58	344.00	34.74	435.32	9637.88	0.90	4.52
	3000.00	40000.00	53.29	375.00	9.50	437.79	8000.00	1.09	5.45
	1484.00	65000.00	34.13	186.97	53.54	274.64	13018.00	0.42	2.11
Drugs									
	6000.00	35302.45	152.21	324.75	52.52	529.48	10590.73	1.50	5.00
	12500.00	80180.00	212.18	775.34	199.28	1186.80	21648.00	1.48	5.48
	5000.00	36400.00	52.38	250.00	90.00	392.38	10920.00	1.08	3.60
	25000.00	79154.19	236.68	735.32	888.74	1860.74	21746.00	2.35	8.56
	13500.00	57073.50	245.39	570.00	97.93	913.32	17122.03	1.60	5.33
	8000.00	40000.00	238.56	375.00	x	613.56	13333.00	1.53	4.60

Table 6

Allen County

Total Annual Sales	Gross Margin	% of Gross Margin to Sales	Stated Inventory	% of Stated Inventory to Sales	Assessed Inventory	% of Assessed Inventory to Stated Inv.	Property Tax	Gross Income Tax	Other Tax	% of Tax to Sales	% of Tax to Gross Margin
Sales under 10,000.00											
9513.09	1902.62	20.00	1000.00	10.51	925.00	92.50	25.20	70.13	23.35	1.25	6.24
7000.00	1400.00	20.00	750.00	10.71	200.00	26.67	6.72	45.00	8.50	.86	4.30
6356.64	1271.33	20.00	400.00	6.29	300.00	75.00	4.48	38.57	14.50	.91	4.53
6500.00	1300.00	20.00	300.00	4.62			x	45.00	14.50	.92	4.58
8977.62	1795.52	20.00	1200.00	13.37	1074.00	89.50	26.86	64.78	27.50	1.33	6.64
3300.00	660.00	20.00	600.00	18.18	420.00	70.00	13.26	18.00	9.50	1.24	6.18
7200.00	1440.00	20.00	900.00	12.50	x	x	x	47.00	9.50	.78	3.92
8250.00	1650.00	20.00	800.00	9.70	x	x	x	55.70	23.00	.95	4.77
Annual Sales 10,000 to 20,000											
20000.00	4000.00	20.00	1500.00	7.50	1150.00	76.66	49.28	175.00	27.75	1.26	6.30
10000.00	2000.00	20.00	350.00	3.50	365.00	104.29	17.81	75.00	14.50	1.07	5.35
19000.00	3800.00	20.00	2500.00	13.16	1400.00	56.00	45.92	165.00	66.50	1.46	7.30
18500.00	3700.00	20.00	1200.00	6.49	1200.00	100.00	72.24	160.00	20.75	1.37	6.84
14500.00	3625.00	25.00	3000.00	20.69	1160.00	38.66	33.49	120.00	27.78	1.25	5.00
14413.16	1161.32	5.98	944.56	4.87	x	x	26.88	152.12	8.50	.97	16.15
14462.35	2892.46	20.00	960.30	6.64	1000.00	104.13	22.40	139.62	40.50	1.26	6.31
19841.56	3897.49	19.64	870.00	4.38	750.00	86.20	18.37	173.42	20.50	1.07	5.44
18500.00	3700.00	20.00	700.00	3.78	x	x	x	160.00	14.50	.94	4.72
18000.00	3600.00	20.00	700.00	3.89	600.00	85.71	20.54	152.00	52.10	1.25	6.24
11260.40	2252.08	20.00	600.00	5.33	500.00	83.33	20.61	87.60	14.50	1.09	5.45
17129.00	3425.80	20.00	700.00	4.09	550.00	78.57	22.40	146.29	45.61	1.25	6.26
19918.00	3983.64	20.00	1963.88	9.86	764.00	38.59	22.27	174.18	14.50	1.06	5.30
18000.00	3600.00	20.00	900.00	5.00	949.00	105.44	35.50	150.00	25.42	1.17	5.86
17108.19	3421.64	20.00	700.00	4.09	x	x	31.70	146.00	20.40	1.16	5.79
12663.00	2532.60	20.06	627.94	4.96	350.00	55.73	10.30	101.63	14.50	1.00	4.99
14000.00	2860.00	20.00	1800.00	12.86	300.00	16.66	9.41	115.00	14.50	1.00	5.00

Table 6 (continued)

	Total Annual Sales	Gross Margin	% of Gross Margin to Sales	Stated Inventory	% of Stated Inventory to Sales	Assessed Inventory	% of Assessed Inventory to Stated Inv.	Property Tax	Gross Income Tax	Other Tax	% of Tax to Sales	% of Tax to Gross Margin
Annual Sales 20,000 to 30,000	23932.42	4786.48	20.00	1413.18	5.90	1235.00	87.39	42.02	214.32	23.50	1.17	5.85
	21152.40	4653.52	22.00	1000.00	4.73	500.00	50.00	18.82	181.52	39.72	1.13	5.16
	23873.22	4774.64	20.00	1308.26	5.48	1056.19	80.73	34.97	213.74	8.00	1.08	5.38
	22560.83	4512.16	20.00	1125.00	4.99	370.00	32.88	17.36	205.60	23.25	1.06	5.32
	25273.37	5054.67	20.00	1500.00	5.94	x	x	x	218.08	14.50	.92	4.60
	25619.53	5123.91	20.00	3500.00	13.66	x	x	x	250.18	78.68	1.28	6.42
	21679.31	5419.83	25.00	1778.71	8.20	862.00	48.46	34.61	196.78	21.50	1.17	4.67
	32248.17	6449.63	20.00	1342.51	4.16	1225.30	91.12	36.47	333.53	308.24	2.10	10.52
Annual Sales 30,000 to 40,000	40000.00	8000.00	20.00	2000.00	5.00	700.00	35.00	19.37	375.00	50.31	1.11	5.55
	38424.87	7684.97	20.00	6372.62	16.58	1013.73	15.90	48.04	359.24	48.22	1.19	5.93
	35107.06	10532.18	30.00	336.41	9.58	318.00	91.45	68.14	322.61	16.37	1.16	3.87
	35000.00	7000.00	20.00	1000.00	2.86	250.00	25.00	12.54	320.00	29.00	1.03	5.16
	32636.80	6527.36	20.00	11091.82	33.99	x	x	41.44	312.97	80.58	1.33	6.66
	35083.00	7016.60	20.00	2785.00	7.94	2190.00	182.50	43.68	339.00	241.50	1.78	8.90
	30480.09	7620.00	25.00	1200.00	39.37	5000.00	185.18	53.40	304.70	20.50	1.24	4.97
	37020.96	7404.19	20.00	2700.00	7.29	1020.00	69.86	112.00	345.21	121.42	1.56	7.81
	33791.54	6758.31	20.00	1460.00	4.32	700.00	20.00	29.57	342.91	35.30	1.12	5.59
	33000.00	6600.00	20.00	3500.00	10.61			26.32	315.00	312.50	1.98	9.91
Annual Sales over 40,000	75000.00	1161.30	20.00	6200.00	8.27	350.00	5.65	24.30	750.00	317.00	1.55	7.74
	45380.70	507.34	20.00	2200.00	4.85	1709.00	77.68	52.84	424.00	30.50	1.12	5.59
	68240.09	1247.31	18.73	3100.00	4.54	2810.00	90.65	96.54	678.67	472.10	1.83	9.76
	41193.90	493.96	20.00	2000.00	4.86	1075.00	53.75	39.46	396.00	58.50	1.20	6.00
	156000.00	1875.29	14.95	13800.00	8.85	4698.00	3.40	146.38	1560.00	168.91	1.20	8.04
	51000.00	722.70	25.00	4250.00	8.33	3000.00	70.59	95.20	500.00	239.50	1.42	6.02
	90245.00	1372.71	23.00	6500.00	7.20	2243.00	34.51	67.03	1110.38	195.30	1.52	6.62
	61883.54	812.74	25.00	3225.55	5.21	1900.00	58.90	37.20	571.02	204.52	1.31	5.25
	56000.00	681.42	25.00	3000.00	5.36	1400.00	46.67	52.42	560.00	69.00	1.22	4.87

Table 7

Reported and Assessed Inventories of Chain and Independently-Owned
Grocery Stores in Madison County (Anderson), Indiana

				Annual Sales Volume ($1000)					
Reported	Assessed	Reported	Assessed	Reported	Assessed	Reported	Assessed	Reported	Assessed
$ 500.00	$ 300.00	$1200.00	$ 800.00	$1450.00	$ 800.00	$ 800.00	$ 400.00	$ 7253.00	$ 300.00
650.00	250.00	1500.00	300.00	2000.00	700.00	800.00	800.00	4600.00	1200.00
500.00	515.00	800.00	300.00	750.00	600.00	3846.00	1500.00	2500.00	720.00
500.00	250.00	323.00	200.00	850.00	300.00			5424.00	1600.00
300.00	250.00	1000.00	400.00					16000.00	4000.00
1100.00	475.00	900.00	300.00					4000.00	2500.00
500.00	300.00	625.00	250.00						
550.00	700.00	603.00	550.00						
800.00	400.00	3500.00	500.00						

Compiled by the author from original data.

Table 8

Reported and Assessed Inventories of Chain and Independently-Owned
Grocery Stores in Monroe County (Bloomington), Indiana

Annual Sales Volume ($1000)

Below 10		10-20		20-30		30-40		Above 40	
Reported	Assessed	Reported	Assessed	Reported	Assessed	Reported	Assessed	Reported	Assessed
$ 400.00	$ 250.00	$1500.00	$ 900.00	$ 700.00	$ 500.00	$1000.00	$ 350.00	$ 3000.00	$4000.00
650.00	400.00	800.00	300.00	700.00	300.00	2300.00	1050.00	13500.00	5000.00
200.00	50.00	800.00	400.00	1300.00	1000.00	5000.00	1250.00	12500.00	5000.00
200.00	100.00	816.00	900.00	3000.00	600.00	6000.00	2100.00	5000.00	1200.00
600.00	400.00	800.00	400.00					400.00	1400.00
200.00	150.00	500.00	275.00					4118.00	1200.00
800.00	250.00	700.00	400.00					2500.00	1350.00
400.00	300.00	900.00	600.00					1200.00	1200.00
200.00	100.00	500.00	500.00					3000.00	700.00
500.00	250.00	1100.00	1000.00					1200.00	800.00
500.00	500.00							3000.00	1150.00
50.00	35.00							1484.02	750.00
600.00	400.00							24276.00	5750.00
150.00	0.00								

Compiled by the author from original data.

Table 9

Comparative Tax Loads of Chain and Independently-Owned Groceries
in Two Counties in Indiana

	Number of Cases	Average % Assessed Inventory To Stated	Average % Total Tax to Sales	Average % Total Tax to Gross Margin
Grant County (Marion)				
(Total Food Stores in Marion, 148)				
Independents:				
Annual Sales under $10,000	5	64.18	0.91	5.12
$10,001–$20,000	6	48.03	1.22	5.82
$20,001–$30,000	1	60.00	1.13	4.92
$30,001–$40,000	5	71.38	1.19	6.20
Over $40,000	2	66.36	1.22	7.08
Chain Organizations:				
Average of 2 stores (combination)			1.34	
Average of 4 stores			1.20	
Henry County (Newcastle)				
(Total Food Stores in Newcastle, 68)				
Independent:				
Annual Sales under $10,000	1	120.00	1.22	6.11
$10,000–$20,000	2	90.00	1.20	6.00
$20,001–$30,000	2	127.23	1.09	4.88
$30,001–$40,000	3	46.26	1.01	5.55
Over $40,000	3	56.78	1.13	6.20
Chain Organizations:				
Average of 3 groceries (without meat)			1.45	
Average of 2 combination stores			1.25	

Table 10

Inventories, Sales, and Tax Payments Reported by Independent Grocers
Interviewed in Monroe County, Indiana

Annual Sales ($1000)	Inventory	Sales	Property Tax	Gross Income Tax	Other Tax	Total Tax	Gross Margin	Tax % Sales	Tax % Gross Margin
	$ 400.00	$ 3009.35	$ 7.31	$ 23.68	$ 3.50	$ 34.49	$ 540.00	1.15	6.39
	650.00	6805.00	25.97	50.40	19.00	95.37	1020.00	1.40	9.35
	200.00	2669.00	1.83	1.69	3.50	7.02	533.80	0.26	1.32
	200.00	3316.36	4.50	8.16	9.50	22.16	663.26	0.67	3.34
	600.00	3811.00	14.60	26.28	9.50	50.38	762.20	1.32	6.61
Below	200.00	2600.00	5.48	*	9.50	14.98	520.00	0.58	2.88
10	800.00	5952.00	16.24	34.52	9.50	60.26	1071.36	1.01	5.62
	400.00	7000.00	18.45	60.00	10.80	89.25	1400.00	1.28	6.40
	200.00	7717.00	14.60	42.17	3.50	60.27	1929.25	0.78	3.12
	500.00	6336.12	11.99	38.36	9.50	59.85	1267.24	0.94	4.72
	500.00	7347.64	22.32	67.04	9.50	98.86	1468.52	1.35	6.73
	600.00	850.00	1.29	*	3.50	4.79	170.00	0.56	2.82
	600.00	9338.00	15.76	68.38	3.50	87.64	1867.60	0.94	4.69
	1500.00	16882.19	38.33	107.75	9.50	155.58	3376.43	0.92	4.61
	800.00	17000.00	25.55	80.00	9.50	115.05	3400.00	0.68	3.38
	800.00	12000.00	21.90	95.00	9.50	126.40	2400.00	1.05	5.25
	816.59	12218.28	35.06	97.18	9.50	141.74	2443.65	1.16	5.80
10-20	800.00	11059.95	21.77	83.29	16.25	121.31	2211.99	1.10	5.48
	500.00	10800.00	109.50	34.32	9.50	153.32	2160.00	1.42	7.10
	700.00	16829.22	216.49	141.33	9.50	197.32	3365.84	1.17	5.86
	900.00	15482.97	36.87	129.82	23.02	189.71	3096.59	1.23	6.13
	500.00	14303.48	45.81	118.03	9.50	173.34	2363.91	1.21	7.33
	1100.00	14899.00	56.83	148.99	17.30	223.12	2979.80	1.50	7.49

* $3000 exemption.

Table 10 (continued)

Annual Sales ($1000)	Inventory	Sales	Property Tax	Gross Income Tax	Other Tax	Total Tax	Gross Margin	Tax % Sales	Tax % Gross Margin
20-30	$1300.00	$22364.03	$40.19	$191.28	$16.00	$247.47	$4472.80	1.11	5.53
	3000.00	30000.00	22.81	250.00	23.30	296.11	3780.00	0.99	7.83
	700.00	25931.00	27.68	229.31	9.50	266.49	4586.20	1.03	5.81
30-40	700.00	30000.00	10.95	250.00	9.50	270.45	6000.00	0.90	4.50
	4000.00	3896.31	75.28	364.68	9.50	449.46	7793.66	1.15	5.77
Over 40	5000.00	6000.00	64.76	562.47	x	627.23	12000.00	1.05	5.25
	4000.00	75000.00	77.75	822.93	67.57	968.25	15000.00	1.29	6.45
	4178.00	76635.91	61.69	738.16*	88.20	888.05	15327.18*	1.16	5.79
	1000.00	41000.00	14.42		6.20	20.62		*	*
	2500.00	50000.00	77.86	475.00	9.50	562.36	10000.00	1.12	5.60
	1200.00	50000.00	65.34	475.00	69.82	609.16	10000.00	1.22	6.10
	3000.00	50000.00	38.00	475.00	x	513.00	10000.00	1.03	5.13
	1200.00	48189.06	56.58	344.00	34.74	435.32	9637.88	0.90	4.52
	3000.00	40000.00	53.29	375.00	9.50	437.79	8000.00	1.09	5.45
	1484.00	65000.00	34.13	186.97	53.54	274.64	13018.00	0.42	2.11
Drugs	6000.00	35302.45	152.21	324.75	52.52	529.48	10590.73	1.50	5.00
	12500.00	80130.00	212.13	775.34	199.28	1186.80	21648.00	1.48	5.48
	5000.00	36400.00	52.38	250.00	90.00	392.38	10920.00	1.08	3.60
	25000.00	79154.19	236.68	735.32	888.74	1860.74	21746.00	2.35	8.56
	13500.00	57073.50	245.39	570.00	97.93	913.32	17122.03	1.60	5.33
	8000.00	40000.00	238.56	375.00	x	613.56	13333.00	1.53	4.60

* Not given.

Supplement to Chapter XI

APPENDIX A

SUPPLEMENT TO CHAPTER XI

RESOLUTION

"After a thorough and exhaustive study of the measure pending before Congress, known as HR 9464, introduced by Representative Wright Patman of Texas, and having given consideration to the results that would follow the enactment of such a law, the Board of Directors of the Hoosier State Press Association, Inc., representing a majority of the newspapers of the State of Indiana, does hereby announce its conclusions from that survey and states its position with respect to the said proposed Patman law:

"That the motive for such a law as proposed is apparently born of personal animosity toward a merchandising group that has become an important factor in improvement of the economic life of the nation.

"That the reasons assigned by the author for such a law are without sound basis and are not substantiated in the statistics prepared by governmental departments, these statistics showing there has been an increase of independently owned retail establishments.

"That elimination of the chain store organizations would cause serious economic disintegration, if not a crisis, in every community which has benefited by the advanced merchandising and forward business processes of this group.

"That local units of government would be adversely affected by the operation of such law through the loss of tax revenue, and that general community life would suffer through a heavy increase of vacated business rooms and in the lowering of values of business properties.

"That agriculture would undergo reverses through depletion of adequate distribution of farm products now being promoted co-operatively between the farmers and the chain organizations.

"that if there is a 'chain store problem' it can be solved by the promotion of a better understanding of the community life where it operates on the part of the chain organization, which is now under way, and that such a problem would not be solved by the enactment of a law which is discriminatory, punitive, unfair and would not even accomplish the theoretical aims of its chief proponent.

"Therefore, it is hereby resolved by the Board of Directors of the Hoosier State Press Association that enactment of HR 9464 be opposed by this Association and by its individual members and that a copy of this resolution be provided to every member of this organization.

"Be it further resolved that a copy of this resolution be mailed to all members of Congress in the United States Senate and the House of Representatives from the State of Indiana.

"Passed this 23rd day of July, 1938".

NATIONAL EDITORIAL ASSOCIATION
ANTI-DISCRIMINATORY RESOLUTION
White Sulphur Springs, June 22, 1938
Annual convention of National Editorial Association

This Association, representing 5,00 weekly and small city daily newspapers in the United States unanimously adopted the following resolution:

"WHEREAS, there has been a tendency both at Washington and at the capitals of many states for legislative measures to be introduced and sponsored which are discriminatory and punitive in their application, and

"WHEREAS, there is considerable fear and hesitation among business men because of the uncertainties arising from such a tendency, and

"WHEREAS, we belive it is the duty of the Congress of the United States and our state legislatures, in view of unemployment and other depressed conditions and uncertainty among business leaders, to encourage, aid and assist business rather than take any action through discriminatory and punitive taxes which, in our opinion, would further retard commerce an would tend to increase living costs, therefore be it

"RESOLVED THAT the National Editorial Association goes on record in its Fifty-Third Annual Convention as opposing such legislative enactments and

"We further recommend that the Board of Directors be requested to dispatch a copy of the above action duly signed by its officers to the members of any legislative committee at Washington or at a State Capitol at such times when united action by the non-metropolitan weekly and daily papers of America is deemed, in the Board's judgment, to be prudent."

Supplement to Chapter XII

APPENDIX A

SUPPLEMENT TO CHAPTER XII

"Responsibilities to Employees"

"Your Company has for years endeavored to promote the well-being of its employees, not by any paternalistic influence over their private lives, but by paying adequate wages and salaries with provision for proper working conditions, vacations, group insurance, recognition of ability and security for old age through its Profit Sharing Fund. You may obtain an idea of the magnitude of this responsibility from the fact that the average total number of regular and extra employees on the payroll of the Company and its subsidiaries during the year ending January 31, 1937, was 56,095.

"Now, as always, your management will maintain its policy of keeping wage rates equal to or better than the rates being paid by other industries in the community for comparable work, and of advancing wages ahead of advancing cost of living.

"There has been much publicity recently regarding companies which are granting employees vacations and allowances for absences due to sickness. You as stockholders of Sears, Roebuck and Co. will be glad to know that your Company has been giving liberal illness allowances to all regular employees for the last 18 years, and for 14 years has had a vacation policy in effect which provides all regular employees of more than two years of service with two weeks paid vacation each year and those of from one to two years of service a one-week paid vacation.

"Provision of proper working conditions has always occupied your management's attention, and the standards are being raised constantly. Compensation standards are considered liberal. After six months of service, the safeguard of a group insurance policy is at the disposition of every employee who wishes to pay the small premium. The Company maintains first aid medical service in all its mail order and many of its smaller units which facilities are available without cost. A central personnel director reporting directly to the president of the Company working through a staff and through field representatives constantly keeps in touch with employees problems and assists in making prompt and considerate adjustment. For some years the Company's expressed policy has been to increase its personnel by taking on beginners and developing its executives from its own men, and to this end the Personnel Department representatives, working with the Company's senior and junior executives watch intently the work of the Company's personnel with a view to promoting from within. It is rare indeed when an individual is selected from outside the Company to fill one of the better positions. Courses of study are provided for such employees as wish to learn more about their specialties, although attendance is voluntary.

"From its 1936 profits, the Company has contributed $1,699,647 to the Employee's Savings and Profit Sharing Pension Fund. The benefits to an individual employee vary with length of membership and amount of the employee's annual deposits. (Deposits are limited to 5% of wages or salary, with a maximum of $250 a year in order to limit the portion of the proceeds of the Fund going to higher-salaried employees). Out of this $1,699,647, members of the Fund having ten or more years of service have been credited with, in addition to their own savings, $1.77 per dollar of their 1936 savings, those of five to ten years of service $1.18 per dollar of savings, those under five years 59¢ per dollar of savings.

"This Fund has been in existence in Sears since July, 1916. Its inception was due to Mr. Julius Rosenwald, who had the vision of Social Security for the employees of this Company twenty years before federal laws were enacted. During these twenty years, 65,000 employees, who have died, retired or otherwise left the employ of the Company or who have made partial withdrawals and who had deposited $10,042,304 have drawn out cash and stock valued (at the time of withdrawal) at $45,203,989 or $35,161,685 more than they themselves deposited. There are 19,000 members now in the Fund. They have deposited $8,267,141 in the Fund, and there is to their credit assets amounting to $44,205,568 as of the market of this date. To sum up, employees, past and present, have deposit $18,309,445, the Company has contributed $26,402,00 to the Fund and the assets, drawn out by employees and remaining in the Fund amount to $89,409,557. As previously mentioned, the Fund is the largest single stockholder in the Company and as such received the largest amount of dividends in 1936, a total of $2,891,333.

"As an example, a member who earned $1,200 a year for twenty and one-half years would today have credited to his account cash and securities worth $17,819, for which he, himself, would have deposited $1,230. All regular employees of the Company have been eligible to become members after three years of continuous services. Hereafter, employees with one year's continuous service will be eligible to become members."

"Stores Announce Yule Bonus Checks"

Christmas bonus checks amounting to several thousand dollars are being distributed to employees of two grocery firms and a department store here, officials of the stores announced yesterday.

"Checks totaling $8,000 were presented 800 employees of the Kroger Grocery and Baking Company in the Indianapolis area, J. F. Hugenberg, sales manager, announced. The average bonus to each employee amounted to $10, Mr. Hugenberg said.

"Bonuses amounting to $4,000 will be distributed to full-time employees of the Atlantic and Pacific Tea Company, John A. Lindgren, Jr., vice-president, announced. Besides the bonus, approximately 250 office, warehouse, and bakery employees of the company will be guests of Mr. Lindgren at a turkey dinner and Christmas party.

"Following the annual practice, the J. C. Penney store here will give Christmas bonuses equivalent to two weeks' salary to all regular employees, O. E. Campbell, manager of the Indianapolis store, announced.

"The Kroger Company bonuses will be distributed on the basis of $25 to junior keymen, $12.50 to store managers, $7.50 to full-time clerks with more than two years' service, warehouse transportation, bakery, dairy and branch office-employees, and $5 to clerks in the company's employment one to two years. The company's Indianapolis area consists of 40 counties in which 177 stores are located. A total of 15,000 Kroger employees in the entire country will receive bonuses amounting to $200,000."

"The Indianapolis Star." Volume 36, No. 202. Page 10. December 24, 1938.

"(The A. & P. has) what the company calls its 'retired pay roll', which has expanded into a system of employees' insurance and pensions, which, with wage increases over the past three years, has given the Company's full-time employees more than ten million dollars additional income."

Furnas, J. C. "Mr. George and Mr. John." "Saturday Evening Post." Volume 211, No. 27. Page 54. December 31, 1938.

QUESTIONNAIRE FOR STUDY OF ATTITUDES TOWARD DISTRIBUTIVE EDUCATION

Name _____ Business Address _____ Position _____

Please check:

Sex		Native-born	Education
Male _____	Married _____	or	Left school below 6th grade _____
or	or	Foreign-born _____	Finished 8th grade only _____
Female _____	Single _____		Completed in high school:
			1 yr. _____ 2 Yr. _____ 3yr. _____ 4yr. _____
			Completed in college:
			1 yr. _____ 2yr. _____ 3yr. _____ 4yr. _____

Age
Under 20 _____
20---29 _____
30---39 _____
40 & over _____

1. In your present position or occupation, have you ever felt the need for specialized training? Yes _____ No _____. If your answer is "Yes," please state briefly the type of training you need.

2. Would you attend regularly a class organized for those employed in retail stores? Yes _____ No _____.
   If your answer is "No," please state reason.
   If your answer is "Yes," please check one preference in each of the following columns.

Preference as to Time	Preference as to Number of Classes per Week:	Preference as to Class Personnel
Morning --8:00 to 9:00 _____	One _____ Two _____ Three _____ No Pref. _____	Employers and Employees Meeting Together _____
Afternoon--1:00 to 2:00 _____	Preference as to Season	Employers and Employees Meeting Separately _____
Evening ---6:00 to 7:00 _____	Fall _____ Winter _____ Spring _____	No preference _____
7:00 to 8:00 _____	Summer _____ Continuous _____ No Pref. _____	
8:00 to 9:00 _____		
No preference _____		

Please mark "1" for first choice of subjects, "2" for second choice, "3" for third choice:
Advertising _____ Salesmanship _____ Accounting _____ Credits and Collections _____ Window Display _____
Buying Methods _____ Stock Control Methods _____ Personnel Work _____ Problems of Management _____

3. Would you be willing to pay a small class registration fee (not over $2) Yes _____ No _____

Table 11

Classification of Replies on Basis of Educational Background

Educational Background	Total in Group		Feel Need of Specialized Training				Would Attend Classes						Would be Willing to Pay For Training					
	Number	% Total	Yes	% Total	No	% Total	Yes	% Total	No	% Total	Indefinite	% Total	Yes	% Total	No	% Total	Unanswered	% Total
Below Grade 8 Completed	14	2.8	7	1.4	7	1.4	4	0.8	10	2.0	--	--	1	0.2	1	0.2		
Grade 8 only	60	12.0	34	6.8	26	5.2	23	4.6	35	7.0	2	0.4	17	3.4	6	1.2		
High school																		
1 yr.	19	3.8	11	2.2	8	1.6	9	1.8	10	2.0	--	--	10	2.0	2	0.4		
2 yr.	55	11.0	39	7.8	16	3.2	29	5.8	26	5.2	--	--	16	3.2	4	0.8		
3 yr.	49	9.8	27	5.4	22	4.4	23	4.6	24	4.8	2	0.4	22	4.4	4	0.8		
4 yr.	240	48.0	128	25.6	112	22.4	112	22.4	119	23.8	9	1.8	101	20.2	13	2.6		
College																		
1 yr.	28	5.6	19	3.8	9	1.8	18	3.6	10	2.0	--	--	14	2.8	1	0.2		
2 yr.	12	2.4	9	1.8	3	0.6	7	1.4	5	1.0	--	--	6	1.2	1	0.2		
3 yr.	9	1.8	4	0.8	5	1.0	3	0.6	6	1.2	--	--	2	0.4	2	0.4		
4 yr.	14	2.8	9	1.8	5	1.0	8	1.6	6	1.2	--	--	5	1.0	2	0.4		
Totals	500	100.0	287	57.4	213	42.6	236	47.2	251	50.2	13	2.6	194	38.8	35	7.0	271	54.2

Compiled by the author from original data.

Table 12

Classification of Replies on Basis of Position

Position	Total in Group Number	% Total	Feel Need of Specialized Training Yes	% Total	No	% Total	Would Attend Classes Yes	% Total	No	% Total	Indefinite	% Total	Would be Willing to Pay For Training Yes	% Total	No	% Total	Unanswered	% Total
First Sample of 250																		
Owners	39	15.6	21	8.4	18	7.2	14	5.6	25	10.0	--	--	11	4.4	2	0.8	26	10.4
Executives	47	18.8	31	12.4	16	6.4	25	10.0	21	8.4	1	0.4	23	9.2	1	0.4	23	9.2
Employees	164	65.6	91	36.4	73	29.2	77	30.8	83	33.2	4	1.6	60	24.0	23	9.2	81	32.4
Totals	250	100.0	143	57.2	107	42.8	116	46.4	129	51.6	5	2.0	94	37.6	26	10.4	130	52.0
Second Sample of 250																		
Owners	69	27.6	35	14.0	34	13.6	24	9.6	42	16.8	3	1.2	21	8.4	2	0.8	46	18.4
Executives	24	9.6	16	6.4	8	3.2	15	6.0	9	3.6	--	--	18	7.2	0	--	6	2.4
Employees	157	62.8	93	37.2	64	25.6	81	32.4	71	28.4	5	2.0	61	24.4	7	2.8	89	35.6
Totals	250	100.0	144	57.6	106	42.4	120	48.0	122	48.8	8	3.2	100	40.0	9	3.6	141	56.4
Combined Sample																		
Owners	108	21.6	56	11.2	52	10.4	38	7.6	67	13.4	3	0.6	32	6.4	4	0.8	72	14.4
Executives	71	14.2	47	9.4	24	4.8	40	8.0	30	6.0	1	0.2	41	8.2	1	0.2	29	5.8
Employees	321	64.2	184	36.8	137	27.4	158	31.6	154	30.8	9	1.8	121	24.2	30	6.0	170	34.0
Totals	500	100.0	287	57.4	213	42.6	236	47.2	251	50.2	13	2.6	194	38.8	35	7.0	271	54.2

Compiled by the author from original data.

Appendix A. Supplement to Chapter XII

"The present study shows, for Minneapolis in 1930, average
sales per retail-grocery employee of $14,500, and $82,000 for wholesale-
grocery employee. This is the average for all employees, selling and
non-selling. These figures mean that the average sales per employee in
the combined wholesale-retail system are $12,300. The combined cost
of wages in wholesaling and retailing is 15.71 per cent of sales.
.... Thus the average wage is $1,935 ($12,300 x 15.71 per cent).

"In comparison, the chain-store sales per employee in
Minneapolis, as shown by the census of distribution, are $19,500.
This is a substantial increase over the $12,300 sold in the other
system. On the other hand, the payroll costs are only 9.1 per cent
of sales. .... This makes the average wage $1,775 per year, which
is $160 less than in the wholesale-retail system. The chain-store
method is more effective in its use of human energy, as shown by the
sales per employee. That method also uses lower-salaried employees
on the average. That is probably due to the greater centralization
of the activities requiring judgment and managerial ability. The
few highly paid executives, accountants, and buyers handle the
functions of assembly and control more economically than they are
handled in the older system."

Vaile, Roland S., "Grocery Retailing."p. 27.

Supplement to Chapter XIII

A STATEMENT OF PUBLIC POLICY
by
THE GREAT ATLANTIC & PACIFIC TEA COMPANY

The Honorable Wright Patman, representative in Congress of the first district of Texas, has announced that he will introduce in the next Congress a punitive and discriminatory tax bill frankly designed to put chain stores out of business. In the past, Mr. Patman has been very successful in securing enactment of legislation which he has sponsored. He has demonstrated that he is a very able lobbyist and propagandist for his own bills. The management of The Great Atlantic & Pacific Tea Company is therefore faced with the necessity of deciding upon a course of action in relation to this proposed legislation -- whether to do nothing and risk the possibility of the passage of the bill and the resulting forced dissolution of this business, or to engage in an active campaign in opposition to the bill.

In arriving at a decision, the interests of several groups of people deserve consideration -- the management, the 85,600 employees of the company, the consuming public, the millions of farmers producing the country's food, and labor.

1. The Interests of the Management

The interests of the management can be dismissed as of very little importance.

The Great Atlantic & Pacific Tea Company is managed by George L. Hartford and John A. Hartford under an arrangement made by their father, George Huntington Hartford, the founder of the business. George L. Hartford has been actively engaged in the grocery business for 58 years, working generally six days a week, 52 weeks a year during that entire period. John A. Hartford has been actively engaged in the grocery business for 50 years, working generally six days a week, 52 weeks a year during that period. Both of these men could, of course, retire without personal or financial inconvenience and live very comfortably if chain stores were put out of business. The record of the last calendar year shows that out of any money earned annually from the business, in the case of George L. Hartford 82 percent is paid to government in taxes; in the case of John A. Hartford, 83 percent is paid to government in taxes. As neither of the brothers has any children, any monies left out of their earnings would accrue to their estates, and in the event of their death, inheritance taxes would probably amount to two-thirds of such accrued earnings, leaving approximately 6 cents on the dollar as a motive for continued personal service.

It is therefore apparent that the interests of management need hardly be taken into consideration in arriving at a decision.

2. The Interests of the Employees

The interests of the employees of the company are, however, a matter of very grave concern.

It is simply a statement of fact to say that the employees of The Great Atlantic & Pacific Tea Company generally throughout the United States receive the highest wages and have the shortest working hours of any workers in the grocery business, whether chain store or individual grocer. Many of them have devoted all of their working lives to the interests of the company.

The management, therefore, has a definite obligation and duty to defend the interests of these 85,600 employees against legislation intended to throw all of them out of work.

3. The Interests of the Consumer

Since this business has been built by the voluntary patronage of millions of American families, we believe that we must give consideration to their interests in this matter. Millions of women know how acute is the present problem of providing food, clothing and shelter for themselves, their husbands and their children out of their present income. When food prices go up it is not a question of paying more for the same food. They do not have the additional money with which to pay. Therefore, they must buy less and eat less. A & P Food Stores last year distributed at retail $881,700,000 worth of food at a net profit of 1%.

This food was sold to the public at prices averaging from eight to ten percent lower than the prices of the average individual grocer. Literally, millions of sales were made at prices twenty-five percent lower than those of the average individual grocer. This saving of eight to twenty-five cents on each dollar is of vital importance to these millions of families. If they were denied the opportunities to buy at these lower prices it would simply mean that in millions of homes they would have to leave meat off the table another day a week, eat less fresh fruits and vegetables, give the growing child one bottle of milk less every week or stint on butter, cheese, poultry, eggs and many other of the most nourishing foods.

In the last 10 years during the greatest period of chain store growth, the number of individual dealers has increased rather than decreased. We maintain that there is nothing wrong when these dealers charge more than we charge. They must charge these prices in order to make a fair profit. The average grocer will, upon request, deliver the groceries to the customer's door and in many cases extends credit to some of his customers. Delivery service costs money. The grocer must put this added cost in the prices to his customers. In the same way the extension of credit involves the expense of bookkeeping, the tying up of capital, and credit losses. There is nothing wrong in the higher mark up of the individual grocer, because he is rendering a service that justifies his prices.

If some customers can afford and voluntarily elect to pay a
higher price for groceries and meats because they want credit or because they want delivery to their homes it is quite proper that they
should pay an additional price for such service. However, the
millions of families in this country whose income is limited and who
can have more and better food because they are willing to pay cash and
carry home their purchases, should not be denied this opportunity.
Millions of families of limited incomes can only enjoy their present
standard of living through these economies and savings. These millions
of American families have helped us build a great business because
they believe we have rendered them a great service. The company,
therefore, has an obligation and a duty to protect the interests of
these customers.

4. The Interests of the Farmer

Eight million farm families are engaged in producing the food
consumed by the American people. All of the farm homes in America,
therefore, comprising one-fourth of all of the population of the United
States, have a direct interest in the methods of distribution by which
the products of their labor and of the soil are marketed.

Approximately 30% of their production is marketed through the
chain food stores; about 70% through individual grocers. Their fruits,
vegetables and other foodstuffs are sold through the chain stores at
prices averaging 8% to 10% cheaper than the prices at which they are
sold by many grocers. If the farmer sells a given product to both at
the same price, the individual grocer must charge the public more to
take care of his higher costs. Thus 30% of the farmer's products
reach the public at low prices and 70% of his products reach the
public at higher prices.

If the public cannot consume a given crop of apples, potatoes,
berries or any other product, at the prices at which they are offered,
these goods do not move from the grocer's shelves; a surplus accumu-
lates and the farmer finds that he either cannot sell the balance of
his crop or must sell it at a substantial loss. Only too often a
situation arises when it is literally cheaper for the farmer to let his
apples or his peaches rot on the ground than to expend the labor costs
necessary to pack and ship them. Every farm economist knows that a
10% surplus does not mean 10% less return to the farmer but often more
than 20% less return.

In other words, the farmer's problem is to sell his products at
the cost of production plus a fair profit and to get them to the public
with as few intermediate costs and profits as possible. It is therefore obviously unfair to the farmer to propose legislation which would,
at a single blow, wipe out 30% of his distributing machinery -- and
that 30% the part which maintains the price to the farmer yet reaches
the public at low cost because of economical distribution. It would
be just as unfair to the farmer to propose putting out of business all
of the individual grocers of the country who distribute 70% of his

produce. Both chain food stores and individual grocers perform a distributive function vital to the interests of the farmer. If either failed to function the farmer would be faced with tremendous surpluses and heartbreaking losses.

For years the A & P has dealt with the farmers both as producers and consumers. We feel that we have a definite obligation and duty to oppose any legislative attack upon their best interests.

5. The Interests of Labor

Every business in this country has a vital interest in the purchasing power of labor. When labor has high wages and great purchasing power, everyone is prosperous. When labor's purchasing power is curtailed, all business suffers and the American standard of living is impaired. For many years it has been the wise policy of the national government to protect real wages and the purchasing power of the worker's dollar. Combinations or agreements to raise prices, thus reducing real wages, have been declared illegal.

It certainly seems strange that it should now be proposed to destroy a group of businesses for the frankly admitted reason that they furnish the necessities of life to the wage earner and his family at low prices. There are approximately 900,000 workers directly employed in the chain store industry. What course is open to us but to oppose the action of a man who, at a time when more than 11,000,000 wage earners are already out of work and 3,000,000 families on relief, proposes a bill that would add almost another million to the roll of unemployed, wipe out 30% of the distributing machinery of all of the farmers of the United States, and raise the cost of living of the wage earners of the United States.

We believe that our organization has rendered a great service to the American people and that it is as a result of that service that we have prospered. If we consulted our own interest it would be very easy to stop and enjoy whatever leisure we have earned. No one is dependent upon us except our fellow workers. However, after the fullest consideration of all interests, we have arrived at the decision that we would be doing less than our full duty if we failed to oppose, by every fair means, legislation proposed by the Honorable Wright Patman.

As we have said, Mr. Patman is an able politician, an able lobbyist and an able propagandist. In that field he is an expert. We are experts only in the grocery business. We believe the chain stores have a right to present their case to the American people. We will not go into politics, nor will we establish a lobby in Washington for the purpose of attempting to influence the vote of any member of the Congress. We expect only a full and fair opportunity to present the case for the chain stores as a great service organization for the American people.

Since the task we have set before us is one involving the widest dissemination of complete information to all of the American people, and since this is a profession in which we are not expert, we have engaged Carl Byoir & Associates, public relations counsel, to do this work. We realize that our views are seldom news. We know, therefore, that we must be prepared to spend a substantial sum of money in telling our story to all of the American people. We declare now that this money will be spent in the dissemination of information through paid advertising and every medium available to us, and in cooperating in the work or formation of study groups among consumers, farmers and workers, which provide open forums for a discussion of all measures affecting the cost of living.

We believe that when the American people have all of the facts they will make their decision known to their representatives in Congress. As Americans we will be content with that decision.

George L. Hartford   John Hartford

Appendix A

Supplement to Chapter XIII.

RESOLUTION

Adopted by the
National Association of Real Estate Boards,
Milwaukee, November 12th, 1938

WHEREAS it is probable that a bill will be introduced in the next Congress which will impose upon chain store organizations operating in more than one state punitive taxes which would compel their dissolution or their reorganization;

WHEREAS, skilled management of chain store organizations has tended to improve the character of retail districts to stabilize land values and thus has contributed directly to the stability of real estate and local governmental revenue;

WHEREAS disruption of this method of merchandising would occur if legislation of the character proposed were enacted by Congress and would entail a widespread disorganization of commercial property use and a consequent dislocation of real estate values in the business centers and subcenters of every American city, Involving for municipal government a direct loss of taxable values and adversely affecting business recovery;

NOW, THEREFORE, BE IT RESOLVED that this Association express to members of Congress its conviction that the enactment of Federal legislation of the kind contemplated by the proposed Patman Act is not in the public interest and would, if enacted, be harmful to normal development of our economic and community life.

Appendix A

Supplement to Chapter XIII

To insist upon evolving habit as the significant source of
economic behavior does not require complete denial of the role of
self-interest in human affairs. We readily admit that both formal
social structures and widespread habits are twisted variously according to the interest of various groups. Thus, although the
Constitution enables the American Government to restrain and control
certain activities, the use of these powers derives, not from the
fact that the Constitution says that certain activities must be controlled, but from the fact that dominant groups in society feel that
certain restrictions should be imposed, and then hire lawyers and
elect judges who will ingeniously interpret the Constitution to support their case. Calhoun insisted that the Constitution was founded
on the liberal principles of Jefferson. It followed by easy consequence that the Bank, subsidies to shipping, protection for industries, and encouragement of business enterprise by public assistance
were unconstitutional. On the other hand, Webster insisted that
"the main reason for the adoption of the Constitution was to give the
general government the power to regulate commerce and trade." Consequently, a protective tariff and a national bank were constitutional. These men were speaking for groups with different activities
and different points of view. Each group was attempting to make an
unrestricted field for its own way of doing things. They were merely
using the Constitution as a convenient weapon to subdue the opposition. One group left to itself would have had little difficulty in
reconciling the Constitution to its own particular desires.

Atkins, Willard E., and collaborators. Economic Behavior. p. vi.
Houghton Mifflin Company, New York. 1933.

Table 13

Inventories, Sales, and Tax Payments Reported by Independent Grocers Interviewed in Allen County, Indiana

Annual Sales ($1000)	Inventory	Sales	Property Tax	Gross Income Tax	Other Tax	Total Tax	Gross Margin	Tax % Sales	Tax % Gross Margin
Below 10	$1000.00	$ 9513.09	$ 25.20	$ 70.13	$ 23.35	$ 118.68	$1902.62	1.25	6.24
	750.00	7000.00	6.72	25.00	8.50	60.22	1400.00	0.86	4.30
	400.00	6356.64	4.48	38.57	14.50	57.55	1271.33	0.91	4.53
	300.00	6500.00	x	45.00	14.50	59.50	1300.00	0.92	4.58
	1200.00	8977.62	26.86	64.78	27.50	119.14	1795.52	1.33	6.44
	600.00	3300.00	13.26	18.00	9.50	70.76	660.00	1.24	6.18
	900.00	7200.00	x	47.00	9.50	56.50	1440.00	0.78	3.92
	800.00	8250.00	x	55.70	23.00	78.79	1650.00	0.95	4.77
10-20	1500.00	20000.00	49.28	175.00	27.75	252.03	4000.00	1.26	6.30
	350.00	10000.00	17.81	75.00	14.50	107.31	2000.00	1.07	5.35
	2500.00	19000.00	45.92	165.00	66.50	277.42	3800.00	1.46	7.30
	1200.00	18500.00	72.24	160.00	20.75	252.29	2700.00	1.37	6.84
	3000.00	14500.00	33.49	120.00	27.78	181.27	3624.00	1.25	5.00
	944.56	19413.16	26.86	152.21	8.50	187.50	1161.32	0.97	16.15
	960.50	14462.35	22.40	119.62	40.50	182.52	2892.46	1.26	6.31
	870.00	19841.56	18.37	173.42	20.50	212.21	3897.49	1.07	5.44
	700.00	18500.00	x	160.00	14.50	174.50	3700.00	0.94	4.72
	700.00	18000.00	20.54	152.00	52.10	224.64	3600.00	1.25	6.24
	600.00	11260.00	20.61	87.60	14.50	122.71	2252.08	1.09	5.45
	700.00	17129.00	22.40	146.29	45.61	214.30	3425.80	1.25	6.26
	1963.88	19918.00	22.27	174.18	14.50	210.95	3983.64	1.06	5.30
	900.00	18000.00	35.50	150.00	25.42	210.92	3600.00	1.17	5.86
	700.00	17108.19	31.70	146.00	20.40	198.10	3421.64	1.16	5.79
	627.94	12773.00	10.30	101.63	14.50	126.43	2532.60	1.00	4.99
	1800.00	14000.00	9.41	115.00	14.50	139.91	2800.00	1.00	5.00

Table 13 (continued)

Annual Sales ($1000)	Inventory	Sales	Property Tax	Gross Income Tax	Other Tax	Total Tax	Gross Margin	Tax % Sales	Tax % Gross Margin
	$1413.18	$23932.42	$42.02	$214.32	$23.50	$279.84	$4786.48	1.17	5.85
	1000.00	21152.40	18.82	181.52	39.72	240.06	4653.52	1.13	5.16
20-30	1308.26	23873.22	34.97	213.74	8.00	256.71	4774.64	1.08	5.38
	1125.00	22560.83	17.36	205.60	23.25	240.21	4512.16	1.06	5.32
	1500.00	25273.37	x	218.08	14.50	232.58	5054.67	0.92	4.60
	3500.00	25619.55	x	250.18	78.68	328.86	5123.91	1.28	6.42
	1778.71	21679.31	34.61	196.78	21.50	252.89	5419.83	1.17	4.67
	1342.51	32248.17	36.47	333.53	308.24	678.24	6449.63	2.10	10.52
	2000.00	40000.00	19.37	375.00	50.31	444.68	8000.00	1.11	5.55
	6372.62	38424.87	48.04	359.24	48.22	455.50	7684.97	1.19	5.93
	336.41	35107.06	68.14	322.61	16.37	407.12	10532.18	1.16	3.87
	1000.00	35000.00	12.54	320.00	29.00	361.54	7000.00	1.03	5.16
30-40	11091.82	32656.00	41.44	312.97	80.58	434.99	6527.36	1.33	6.66
	2785.00	35083.00	43.68	339.00	241.50	624.18	7016.60	1.78	8.90
	1200.00	30480.09	53.40	304.70	20.50	378.60	7620.00	1.24	4.97
	2700.00	37020.96	112.00	345.21	121.42	578.42	7404.19	1.56	7.81
	1460.00	33791.54	29.57	312.91	35.30	377.78	6758.31	1.12	5.59
	3500.00	33000.00	26.32	315.00	312.50	653.82	6600.00	1.98	9.91
	6200.00	75000.00	94.30	750.00	317.00	1161.30	15000.00	1.55	7.74
	2200.00	45380.70	52.84	424.00	30.50	507.34	9076.14	1.12	5.59
	3100.00	68240.09	96.54	678.67	472.10	1247.31	12783.05	1.83	9.76
	2000.00	41193.90	39.46	396.00	58.50	493.96	8238.79	1.20	6.00
Over 40	13000.00	156000.00	146.38	1560.00	168.91	1875.29	23320.00	1.20	8.04
	4250.00	51000.00	95.20	500.00	239.50	722.70	12750.00	1.42	6.02
	6500.00	90245.00	67.03	1010.38	145.30	1372.71	20756.43	1.52	6.62
	3225.55	61883.54	37.20	571.02	204.52	812.74	15470.88	1.31	5.25
	3000.00	56000.00	52.42	560.00	69.00	681.42	14000.00	1.22	4.87

APPENDIX B

Table 14

Chain Store Taxes Now in Effect
(As of August 10, 1938)

State	Kind of Tax	Rates	Period Effective	Miscellaneous
ALABAMA (Act approved	Store License Tax	a) Graduated License Tax. 1st store $1.00 2nd-5th stores 15.00 each 6th-10th stores 22.50 each 11th-20th stores 37.50 each All over 20 stores 112.50 each b) Filing fee of 50¢ for each store.	Jan. 1, 1936 and thereafter.	Administration - State Tax Commission. Licenses - To be renewed annually, not later than Jan. 31; licenses issued after July 1 to be paid at half rate. Applications and Payments. - To be made annually not later than January 31. Period Covered By Tax - Calendar year. Exemptions - (1) Stores selling petroleum products principally. (2) Stores selling ice where amount kept on hand is less than 4,000 lbs. Litigation - None.
COLORADO (Act approved Nov. 6, 1934 by referendum.)	Store License Tax	a) Graduated License Tax. 1st store $2.00 2nd-4th stores 10.00 each 5th-8th stores 50.00 each 9th-15th stores 150.00 each 16th-24th stores 200.00 each all over 24 stores 300.00 each b) Filing fee of 50¢ for each store.	Jan. 1, 1935 and thereafter.	Administration - State Treasurer. Licenses - To be renewed annually not later than Jan. 31; licenses issued after July 1 to be paid at half rate. Applications and Payments - Annually not later than January 31. Period Covered by Tax - Calendar year. Exemptions - None. Litigation - None. This act applies to wholesale stores as well as to retail stores.

From data compiled by the Institute of Distribution, Inc., 570 Seventh Avenue, New York City.

Table 14 (continued)

State	Kind of Tax	Rates	Period Effective	Miscellaneous
FLORIDA (Act approved June 1, 1935, superseding 1933 & 1931 laws.	Store License Tax	a) Graduated "Retroactive" License Tax. Class No. of Stores Tax in chain 1 1 $ 10 2 2-3 50 each 3 4-6 100 each 4 7-10 200 each 5 11-15 300 each 6 Over 15 400 each This tax is "Retroactive" in that the total number of stores operated in the state is first determined and then the tax for the class in which the total falls is applied to every store. b) Gross Receipts Tax. A tax of 2% of the gross receipts of all retailers, regardless of the number of stores operated, also is imposed c) Permit Fee. 50¢ per store, payable only once.	July 1, 1935 and thereafter.	Administration - State Comptroller. Licenses - Permits to do business to be obtained by July 31, 1935 or thereafter, before starting business. Payments - (1) License tax, annually July 1, (2) 2% gross receipts tax; monthly by the 15th together with return. (3) If additional store opened after July 1, thereby changing classification, tax is recomputed based on new classification and credit given for amount paid under original classification. Period Covered by Taxes - July 1 to June 30 Exemptions - Filling stations engaged exclusively in the sale of petroleum products. Litigation - Undertaken via the Institute of Distribution by 19 companies, namely: 1) A&P; 2) Sears; 3) Goodyear; 4) Goodrich; 5) Cannon; 6)Grant;7)Green;8)Kinney; 9)Lane; 10)Liggett; 11)McCrory; 12) Melville; 13)Kress; 14)Newberry; 15) J. C. Penney; 16)United Cigar; 17)Walgreen; 18)Woolworth; 19)Firestone. Counsel: (1) Thomas B. Adams, Esq. 1006 Bisbee Bldg. Jacksonville, Florida (2) H. P. Adair, Cooper & Osborne Barnett National Bank Bldg. Jacksonville, Florida

Table 14 (continued)

State	Kind of Tax	Rates	Period Effective	Miscellaneous
FLORIDA (Cont'd)				History and Result - As originally enacted, the law imposed both the graduated license tax and a graduated gross receipts tax ranging from 2% up to 5% on total receipts of chains of more then 15 units. On Nov. 26, 1935, the Florida Supreme Court upheld the per store tax, but voided all of the graduated gross receipts tax except first brackets imposing 2% tax on all retailers. Pursuant to Attorney General's petition for rehearing, State Supreme Court, on Feb. 25, 1936 entered order readopting opinion of Nov. 26, 1935. The effective date of the taxes later was determined by State lower court opinion holding "per store" taxes operative as of July 1, 1935, but 2% sales tax operative as of Feb. 25, 1936 only. State's appeal from Florida Supreme Court's decisions denied by U.S. Supreme Court. Provisions for "doubling" of per store tax, should gross receipts tax be invalidated, inoperative because 2% gross receipts bracket upheld. Applicability of 2% tax to gross receipts derived from liquor and restaurant sales upheld by State Supreme Court. Sale of bakery products.

Table 14 (continued)

State	Kind of Tax	Rates	Period Effective	Miscellaneous
FLORIDA (Cont'd)				dairy products, insecticides, agricultural products or implements, etc., are exempt from 2% sales tax only when sold by actual producer at retail outlet owned by said producer. (See State ex rel. Adams v. Lee and State ex rel. Lane Drug Stores v. Simpson 122 Fla. 639, 166 So. 227.) The Florida Supreme Court, on Dec. 22, 1937, held the Act inapplicable to hotels and restaurants not operated in connection with another business in Cloverleaf, Inc., v. State.
GEORGIA (Act approved March 27, 1937.)	a) Store License Tax	a) Graduated License Tax. 1st store $ 2.00 2nd store 10.00 3rd store 15.00 4th store 20.00 5th store 25.00 6th store 30.00 7th store 35.00 8th store 40.00 9th store 45.00 10th store 50.00 11th store 55.00 12th store 60.00 13th store 65.00 14th store 70.00 15th store 75.00 16th store 80.00	July 1, 1937 and thereafter.	Administration - State Revenue Commission. Licenses - Issued on payment of tax. Applications and Payments - Annually, not later than Dec. 31, for ensuing year. Payments for licenses issued after Jan. 1, will be diminished by 1/12 for every full month expired. Period Covered by Tax - Calendar year. Exemptions - Any place of business engaged principally in the sale of petroleum products. This Act applies to wholesale as well as to retail stores, whether stationary or traveling by motor, with certain specified exemptions, i. e.:

Table 14 (continued)

State	Kind of Tax	Rates	Period Effective	Miscellaneous
GEORGIA (Cont'd)	Graduated License Tax.			a) Manufacturers' plants, or manufacturers' trucks, distributing products of their own manufacture at wholesale only, or vehicles of manufacturers selling and distributing to wholesalers or retailers products of their own manufacture or processing exclusively.
	17th store	85.00		
	18th store	90.00		
	19th store	95.00		
	20th store	100.00		b) Factories, depots, warehouses, stores or other places where only fertilizer and cottonseed products, or where meat or meat products are sold by the persons, firms or corporations slaughtering the animals from which said meat or meat products are obtained and prepared for sale, and selling at least 90% of volume at wholesale.
	21st store	105.00		
	22nd store	110.00		
	23rd store	115.00		
	24th store	120.00		
	25th store	125.00		
	26th store	130.00		
	27th store	135.00		
	28th store	140.00		
	29th store	145.00		c) Depots, warehouses, or platforms, where ice is manufactured, stored or sold, or vehicles used for the delivery or sale of ice.
	30th store	150.00		
	31st store	155.00		
	32nd store	160.00		
	33rd store	165.00		
	34th store	170.00		
	35th store	175.00		d) Depots, dairies and vehicles used only in the delivery or sale of milk, butter, cheese, or ice cream, or other dairy products or malt beverages.
	36th store	180.00		
	37th store	185.00		
	38th store	190.00		
	39th store	195.00		
	40th store	200.00		
	All stores in excess of 40	$200.00 each.		

Table 14 (continued)

State	Kind of Tax	Rates	Period Effective	Miscellaneous
GEORGIA (Cont'd)	b) Mail order Stores (engaged in selling by mail from catalogs and order lists.	b) Graduated License Tax. 1 store $2000.00 2 stores 4000.00 3 stores 6000.00 4 stores 8000.00 In excess of 4 stores $10,000 for each addition- al stores. All retail stores operated by mail order houses are exempt from (b) but are sub- ject to the store license tax (a) Tax imposed under (b) does not apply to mail order store whose catalog covers only horticultural or agricultural products.		e) Depots and warehouses and other places where only soft drinks are man- ufactured, bottled or stored, or sold, including vehicles used in the delivery or sale of such soft drinks. f) Vehicles used only in the delivery or sale of bread and other bakery prod- ucts, salted nuts, potato chips, sand- wiches and candy. g) Stores, yards, warehouses, plants or vehicles used for the purpose of stor- ing, manufacturing, selling of deliver- ing only building materials, coal, charcoal, wood or coke. Litigation - None In an opinion of the Attorney General's office rendered on June 23, 1938, vol- untary or cooperative organizations are held not subject to the Act.

Table 14 (continued)

State	Kind of Tax	Rates	Period Effective	Miscellaneous
IDAHO (Act approved March 1, 1933)	Store License Tax	a) Graduated "Retroactive" License Tax. 1 store $5.00 each 2 stores 10.00 each 3 stores 20.00 each 4 stores 35.00 each 5 stores 55.00 each 6 stores 80.00 each 7 stores 110.00 each 8 stores 140.00 each 9 stores 170.00 each 10 stores 200.00 each 11 stores 230.00 each 12 stores 260.00 each 13 stores 290.00 each 14 stores 320.00 each 15 stores 350.00 each 16 stores 380.00 each 17 stores 410.00 each 18 stores 440.00 each 19 stores 470.00 each in excess of 19 stores $500 for each such store. (Note: The fees are retro-active. The total number of stores is first determined and then the fee for the bracket in which the total falls is applied to every store) b) Filing Fee-50¢ for each such store.	July 1, 1933 and there-after.	Administration - Commissioner of Finance. Licenses - To be renewed annually not later than Jan. 31; licenses issued after July 1, to be paid at half rate. Applications and Payments - Annually not later than Jan. 31. No provision made in law for adjustment of tax if stores are added during the year. Period Covered by Tax - Calendar year. Exemptions - (1) Filling stations en-gaged exclusively in the sale of petroleum products. (2) Taxes paid on real property and improvements thereon may be offset against store license fees. Litigation - Upheld by Idaho Supreme Court in 1934, in J. C. Penney Co. v. Diefendorf, 32P. (2d) 784. This Act applies to wholesale stores as well as to retail stores.

Table 14 (continued)

State	Kind of Tax	Rates	Period Effective	Miscellaneous

				(4) Hotels, including restaurants operated in these hotels by hotel management. (5) Persons engaged exclusively in gardening or farming. (6) Liquor stores established and operated by the State Liquor Control Commission.
				
				Litigation - Undertaken via the Institute of Distribution by 22 companies, namely: Benner Tea; A & P; Grant; Green; Goodyear; Graham; Kinney; Kresge; Liggett; Melville; Newberry; Newman; National Tea; Meisner; Penney; Sears; Scott-Burr; Safeway; Thriftway; United Cigar; Walgreen; Woolworth.
				
				Counsel:
				    J. G. Gamble Esquire
				    Gamble, Reed and Howland
				    500 Bankers Trust Building
				    Des Moines, Iowa
				
				History and Result - As originally enacted, the law imposed both the graduated license tax and a graduated gross receipts tax ranging from $25 on a gross receipts not in excess of $50,000 up to a maximum of $1,000 for each additional $10,000 of gross receipts in excess of $9,000,000. On Nov. 19, 1935, the Federal District Court invalidated the entire graduated gross receipts tax provisions, but upheld the per store license tax.

Table 14 (continued)

State	Kind of Tax	Rates	Period Effective	Miscellaneous
INDIANA (Act approved March 11, 1933. Superseding 1929 law.)	Store License Tax	a) Graduated License Fee. 1st store $3.00 2nd-5th stores 10.00 each 6th-10th stores 20.00 each 11th-20th stores 30.00 each All over 20 stores 150.00 each b) Application and renewal filing fee. 50¢ for each store.	Jan. 1, 1934 and thereafter.	Administration - State Board of Tax Commissioners. Licenses - Renewable annually, not later than Jan. 31; those issued after July 1 to be paid at half rate. Applications and Payments - Annually, not later than Jan. 31. Period Covered by Tax - Calendar year. Exemptions - None. Litigation - The 1929 Act was upheld by the U. S. Supreme Court, and furnished the precedent for all subsequent graduated license taxes. (See State Board of Tax Comm. v. Jackson (1931). 283 U. S. 527.)
IOWA (Act approved April 29, 1935.)	Store License Tax	Graduated License Tax. 2nd-10th stores $5.00 each 11th-20th stores 15.00 each 21st-30th stores 35.00 each 31st-40th stores 65.00 each 41st-50th stores 105.00 each All over 50 stores 155.00 each	July 1, 1935 and thereafter.	Administration - State Board of Assessment and Review. Licenses - Renewable annually, July 1, for ensuing year. Period covered by tax - July 1 to June 30. Exemptions - (1) Stores in unincorporated places not over 6 miles from all other stores under the same management. (2) Non-Profit cooperative associations. (3) Stores selling one or more of the following products, if sales of these products exceed 95% of total sales: a) Coal; b) Ice; c) Lumber; d) Grain; e) Feed; f) Building materials (not including hardware, glass and paints.)

Table 14 (continued)

State	Kind of Tax	Rates	Period Effective	Miscellaneous
IOWA (Cont'd)				On appeal by the state from only that part of the decision invalidating the gross receipts tax section of the Act, the U. S. Supreme Court affirmed the decree of the District Court. Thus the collection of the gross receipts tax was permanently enjoined. (Valentine v. Great Atlantic and Pacific Tea Co. (1936) 299 U. S. 32). In another case brought to test the validity in the state courts, the Iowa Supreme Court also upheld the per-store license taxes and voided the graduated gross receipts tax section of the Act. (Tolerton & Warfield Co. v. Iowa (1936) 270 N. W. 427.)
KENTUCKY (Act approved July 3, 1934, amended May 11, 1936 and March 12, 1938; replacing gradu-ated gross re-ceipts tax of 1930.)	Store License Tax	Graduated License Tax. Exempt 1 store $ 27.00 2nd store 25.00 each 3rd-5th stores 50.00 each 6th-10th stores 100.00 each 11th-20th stores 100.00 each 21st-50th stores 200.00 each all over 50 300.00 each	July 1, 1934 and there-after.	Administration - State Department of Revenue. Licenses and Reports - Renewable and due annually July 1; for business begun after July 1, tax is to be prorated for the remainder of the year. Period Covered by Tax - July 1 to June 30. Exemptions - Filling stations, if 70% of business is in petroleum products. Litigation - The validity of the Act was upheld on Oct. 16, 1937 by the Franklin County Circuit Court in Great Atlantic & Pacific Tea Co. v. State.

Table 14 (continued)

State	Kind of Tax	Rates	Period Effective	Miscellaneous
LOUISIANA (Act approved July 12, 1934, superseding 1932 law.)	Store License Tax	Graduated License Tax. Taxpayers classified first according to total number of stores they operate both in Louisiana and elsewhere, and then taxed per Louisiana store at the rate appliable to the classification in which taxpayer falls.	Jan. 1, 1935 and thereafter.	Administration - Collector and Revenue. Licenses - Renewable annually before March 1, on payment of tax. Applications and Payments - Annually, before March 1. Annual Report - To Collector of Revenue due annually by Jan. 31, on number of stores operated in state. Period Covered by Tax - Calendar year. Exemptions - (1) Sales by firms operating under public utility franchises. (2) Gasoline stations where average daily stock carried does not exceed $1,500. Litigation - Undertaken via the Institute of Distribution by 16 companies, namely: Consolidated; Goodyear; Grant; Green; Kinney; Kress; Liggett; Melville; Ward; Newberry; Penney; Scott-Burr; Sears; Wohl; Woolworth; A & P. Counsel - Monte Lemann, Esq. Monroe and Lemann, Whitney Building, New Orleans, La. History and Result - The constitutionality of the Act was challenged in a suit commenced in the Federal District Court. On July 24, 1936, the District Court denied a decree for a permanent injunction, dismissed the complaint and dissolved the temporary injunction previously granted. On appeal to the U. S.

Rates table:

Bracket	Total No. Stores Operated by Co. everywhere	Rate per La. Store
1	Less than 11	$10
2	11 to 35	15
3	36 to 50	20
4	51 to 75	25
5	76 to 100	30
6	101 to 125	50
7	126 to 150	100
8	151 to 175	150
9	176 to 200	200
10	201 to 225	250
11	226 to 250	300
12	251 to 275	350
13	276 to 300	400
14	301 to 400	450
15	401 to 500	500
16	Over 500	550

Table IV (Continued)

State	Kind of Tax	Rates	Period Effective	Miscellaneous
				Supreme Court, the District Court's decree was affirmed and the constitutionality of the Act sustained in a 4 to 3 decision rendered on May 17, 1937. The U. S. Supreme Court, on Oct. 11, 1937, denied a petition for a rehearing of the case. (Great Atlantic & Pacific Tea Co. v. Grosjean 301 U. S. 412.) An appeal from the Louisiana Supreme Court's decision of May 30, 1938, upholding the State's right to attorneys' fees and penalties that accrued during the litigation, has been filed in the U. S. Supreme Court.
MICHIGAN (Passed over Governor's veto July 17, 1933. (Act approved June 6, 1935.)	a) Store License Tax	Graduated License Tax 2nd-3rd stores $ 10.00 each 4th-5th stores 25.00 each 6th-10th stores 50.00 each 11th-15th stores 100.00 each 16th-20th stores 150.00 each 21st-25th stores 200.00 each All over 25 " 250.00 each b) Graduated License Tax. 2nd-10th Counters 10.00 each 11th-15th Counters 15.00 each 16th-25th Counters 20.00 each All over 25 " 25.00 each	July 17, 1933 and thereafter.	Administration - Secretary of State. Licenses - To be renewed annually by March 31; Licenses issued after Oct. 1 may be paid at half rate. Applications and Payments - Annually by March 31. Period Covered by Tax - April 1 to March 31. Exemptions - Outlets selling petroleum products, principally. Litigation - Upheld by State Supreme Court in C. F. Smith Co. et al v. Fitzgerald 270 Mich. 659. Appeal to U. S. Supreme Court Dismissed at request of Counsel of all parties concerned. (Chain "counter" license rates apply to chains of leased departments, stands and concessions.)
	b) Chain "Counters" License			

Table 14 (continued)

State	Kind of Tax	Rates	Period Effective	Miscellaneous
MINNESOTA (Approved July 24, 1937 repealing 1933 law)	a) Store License Tax	**a) Graduated License Tax**	July 24, 1937 to Dec. 31, 1940.	**Administration** - State Tax Commission. **Applications and Payments** - Annually not later than Jan. 20. Payments for stores established or discontinued during the calendar year will be diminished by 1/2 for every full month expired or remaining in the year.
		1st store $ 10.00		**Period Covered by Tax** - Calendar year.
		2nd store 10.00		**Exemptions**
		3rd store 20.00		1. Retail Stores - Selling fuel, lumber, building material, gasoline and oils and grain, when gross sales of these products equal 95% of total sales.
		4th store 20.00		
		5th store 30.00		2. Cooperative associations.
		6th store 40.00		3. Places of business owned and operated by processors for the sale of their own food products at retail.
		7th store 50.00		
		8th store 60.00		
		9th store 70.00		4. Mail order establishments - selling horticultural and nursery products, seeds, books and periodicals, etc. when gross sales of these products equal 95% of total sales.
		10th store 80.00		
		11th store 95.00		
		12th store 100.00		
		13th store 125.00		
		14th store 140.00		
		15th-25th stores 155.00 each		**Litigation** - In a preliminary ruling by the Hennepin County District Court on July 15, 1938, the 1937 law was held valid in C. Thomas Stores Sales System, Inc., v. State. The case will be tried on its merits before the District Court at a later date.
		26th-35th stores 175.00 each		
		36th-45th stores 200.00 each		
		46th-55th stores 225.00 each		
		56th-65th stores 250.00 each		
		66th-150th stores 350.00 each		
		b) Graduated License Tax		
		1st store $200.00		
		2nd store 300.00		
		3rd store 400.00		
		4th store 500.00		
		5th store 600.00		
		6th store 700.00		
		7th store 800.00		

Table 14 (continued)

State	Kind of Tax	Rates	Period Effective	Miscellaneous
MINNESOTA (Cont'd)		Graduated License Tax		A suit to test the validity of the 1933 which imposed both a graduated license tax and a graduated gross receipts tax was undertaken via the Institute of Distribution by 17 companies, namely: Gamble-Skogmo; Grant; A & P; Allied Stores; Kresge; Melville; Ward; National Tea; Newberry; Penny; Red Owl; Scott-Burr; Sears; Walgreen; White Castle; Woolworth.
		8th store $ 900.00		
		9th store 1000.00		
		10th store 1100.00		
		All stores over 10 1200.00 each		
		The term "mail order establishments" means any place, order office, warehouse and reserve depot in which are stored or kept, or orders taken for merchandise and owned by a person engaged in selling same at retail within the state and at least 15% of whose total intrastate sales therefrom are completed in response to orders received through the mails, and which person issues catalogs or price lists to prospective customers describing such merchandise for sale.		Counsel: W. J. Doherty, Esq. Koherty, Rumble & Butler First National Bank Bldg. St. Paul, Minnesota
				History and Result - For the purpose of testing its validity, two suits were brought in a state lower court. The Ramsey County District Court, on Oct. 18, 1937, upheld the validity of the graduated license tax but invalidated the graduated gross receipts tax provision of the 1933 law in National Tea Co. et al v. State. An appeal to the State Supreme Court from that part of the decision invalidating the gross receipts tax has been filed by the state.

Table 14 (continued)

State	Kind of Tax	Rates	Period Effective	Miscellaneous

MISSISSIPPI (Act approved March 26, 1936.)	Store License Tax	Graduated License Tax
		Upon 2 stores $ 3.00 each
		3rd - 9th stores 10.00 each
		10th -14th stores 20.00 each
		15th -19th stores 30.00 each
		20th -25th stores 75.00 each
		26th -30th stores 125.00 each
		31st - 40th stores 200.00 each
		All over 40 stores 300.00 each
			March 26, 1936 and thereafter	Administration - State Tax Commission
				Licenses - Renewable annually not later than January 30.
				Application and Payments - Annually, not later than January 30.
				Period Covered by Tax - Calendar Year
				Exemptions -
				  1. Outlets selling petroleum products principally.
				  2. Gas and electric appliance stores maintained by utilities.
				Litigation - None

MONTANA (Act approved March 18, 1937, repealing 1933 law.)	Store License Tax	a) Graduated License Tax
		  1st store $ 5.00
		  2nd store 50.00
		  3rd store 100.00
		  All over 4 stores 200.00 each
		b) Outlets selling petroleum products, building materials and hardware when gross sales of these products equal 75% of total; and businesses in which sale of merchandise is less than 25% of the gross business, pay the following fees:
		  1st store $ 5.00
		  2nd store 7.50
		  3rd store 15.00
			Jan. 1, 1938 and thereafter.	Administration - State Board of Equalization.
				Licenses - Renewable annually not later than Jan. 30. Licenses issued after July 1, may be paid at half rate.
				Applications and Payments - Annually, not later than Jan. 30.
				Period Covered by Tax - Calendar year.
				Exemptions - Cooperative associations' stores are taxed $5 each.
				Litigation - The validity of the Act was upheld on June 24, 1938 by the Lewis and Clark County District Court in Vaughan & Ragsdale v. State.

Table 14 (continued)

State	Kind of Tax	Rates	Period Effective	Miscellaneous
MONTANA (Cont'd)		$ 22.50 4th store 30.00 5th store 37.50 each All over 5 stores c) Wholesale stores are taxed as individual units at $37.50 each. d) Filing Fee - 50¢ per store.		
NORTH CAROLINA (Act approved May 9. and re-enacted March 9. 1937; amending 1933 law.)	Store License Tax	a) Graduated License Tax. 2nd-5th stores $ 50.00 each 6th-9th stores 70.00 each 10th-13th stores 80.00 each 14th-17th stores 90.00 each 18th-21st stores 100.00 each 22nd-31st stores 125.00 each 32nd-51st stores 150.00 each 52nd-101st stores 175.00 each 102nd-201st stores 200.00 each All over 201 stores 225.00 each b) An additional annual license fee of $4 is payable on each pump owned and leased by distributors or wholesalers through which motor fuel is retailed.	June 1, 1935 and there-after	Additional Taxes - While counties may not levy an additional chain store tax, cities may levy a tax of not more than $50.00 per store. But store in which principle office is located is not to be liable for city tax. Chain Stores Are Defined to Include: 1. Stores separately incorporated but having a common ownership through stock control of subsidiaries. 2. Separately incorporated companies having similar names. 3. Separately incorporated companies having benefit of group purchasing and common management. Chain stores owned by individuals and / or part-nerships are similarly defined. Administration - Commissioner of Revenue. Licenses - Renewable annually by June 1; licenses issued after Jan. 1 may be paid at half rate. Payments - Annually, June 1.

268

Table 14 (continued)

State	Kind of Tax	Rates	Period Effective	Miscellaneous
NORTH CAROLINA (Cont'd)				**Period Covered by Tax** - June 1 to May 31. **Exemptions** - Chain store tax "shall not apply to retail or wholesale dealers in motor vehicles and automobile equipment and supply dealers at wholesale who are not liable for tax hereunder on account of the sale of other merchandise." **Litigation** - North Carolina Chain Store Tax. Act of 1930 upheld by U. S. Supreme Court in 1931; Great Atlantic & Pacific Tea Co. v. Maxwell 284 U. S. 575, affirming 199 N. C. 433. New laws enacted in 1933 and 1935. This Act applies to wholesale stores as well as to retail stores.
PENNSYLVANIA (Act approved June 5, 1937.)	Store License Tax	Graduated License Tax 1st store $ 1.00 each 2nd- 5th stores 5.00 each 6th-10th stores 10.00 each 11th-15th stores 20.00 each 16th-20th stores 30.00 each 21st-30th stores 50.00 each 31st-50th stores 100.00 each 51st-75th stores 200.00 each 76th-100th stores 250.00 each 101st-200th stores 350.00 each 201st-500th stores 450.00 each all over 500 stores 500.00 each	June 1, 1937 and thereafter.	**Administration** - State Department of Revenue **Licenses** - To be renewed annually, not later than May 31. **Exemptions** - (1) News stands; (2) Outlets engaged exclusively in the sale or storage of commodities in bulk. **Litigation** - Undertaken via the Institute of Distribution by 10 companies, namely: Grant; Kresge; Murphy; Newberry; Woolworth; Penney; United Cigar; Melville; McCrory; Kinney. **Counsel:** Harold B. Beitler, Esq. Beitler, Burns & Rosenberger 1421 Chestnut Street Philadelphia, Pennsylvania

Table 14 (continued)

State	Kind of Tax	Rates	Period Effective	Miscellaneous
PENNSYLVANIA (Cont'd)				History and Result - A temporary order restraining the state from collecting this tax from parties to litigation was granted on July 9, 1937 by the Dauphin County Court in American Stores Co. et al v. State. The case has been tried on its merits and a decision is expected in the near future.
SOUTH CAROLINA (Approved April 5, 1930; re-enacted in 1933)	Store License Tax	Graduated License Tax Store Rate Store Rate 1st $ 5 16th $80 2nd 10 17th 85 3rd 15 18th 90 4th 20 19th 95 5th 25 20th 100 6th 30 21st 105 7th 35 22nd 110 8th 40 23rd 115 9th 45 24th 120 10th 50 25th 125 11th 55 26th 130 12th 60 27th 135 13th 65 28th 140 14th 70 29th 145 15th 75 30th 150 Over 30 $150 each.	April 5, 1930 and there-after	Administration - State Tax Commission. Licenses - To be renewed annually, not later than April 1. Applications and Payments - Annually, not later than April 1. Period Covered by Tax. Calendar Year. Exemptions - (1) Gasoline Filling Stations. (2) Stores located outside of incorporated cities or towns. Litigation - The validity of the Act was upheld in Southern Grocery Stores v. S. C. Tax Comm. 55f (2nd) 931.

269

Table 14 (continued)

State	Kind of Tax	Rates	Period Effective	Miscellaneous
SOUTH DAKOTA (Act Approved March 8, 1937)	Store License Tax	a) <u>Graduated License Tax</u> 1st store $ 1.00 each 2nd- 5th stores 5.00 each 6th-10th stores 15.00 each 11th-15th stores 25.00 each 16th-20th stores 50.00 each 21st-30th stores 100.00 each 31st-40th stores 200.00 each All over 40 stores 250.00 each b) Filing fee of 50¢ per store.	July 1, 1937 and thereafter	<u>Administration</u> - State Director of Taxation. <u>Licenses</u>. - To be renewed annually, not later than Jan. 31; licenses issued after July 1 may be paid at half rate. <u>Applications and Payments</u> - Annually not later than Jan. 31. <u>Period Covered by Tax</u> - Calendar year. <u>Exemptions</u> - (1) Establishments selling fuel, lumber, building materials, gasoline, and oils, grains, dairy products, poultry, electric current, telephone service, feeds and seeds, gas, when gross sales of these products equal 90% of total sales. <u>Litigation</u> - None. The 1935 Chain Store Tax Act, imposing both a graduated license tax and a graduated gross receipts tax was invalidated by the State Supreme Court on Nov. 16, 1936 in J. C. Penney Co. et al v. Welsh. The suit to test its constitutionality was undertaken via the Institute of Distribution by 6 Companies, namely: Kresge; Newberry; Penney; Walgreen; Woolworth; Red Owl. Counsel: J. V. Sickels, Esq. Hitchcock & Sickels 206 Commercial Bank Bldg. Mitchel, South Dakota

Table 14 (continued)

State	Kind of Tax	Rates	Period Effective	Miscellaneous
TENNESSEE (Act approved March 5, 1937)	Floor Space Tax	Upon each store in a chain in excess of one, there is levied a tax of $3.00 for each 100 sq. ft. of floor space, or major fraction thereof, in each store.	June 1, 1937 and thereafter	Administration - Commissioners of Finance and Taxation. Licenses - To be renewed annually by June 1. Applications and Payments - Annually by June 1; sworn statement setting forth number of stores operated, square feet of floor space of each store, and the location of each store, including the exempted store, must accompany tax payment. Period Covered by Tax - June 1 to May 31. Exemptions - (1) Store in which chain maintains its general office in Tennessee, or if no general office is maintained, a store to be designated by the taxpayer. (2) Filling Stations. Definitions - "Floor space" includes the total number of square feet determined by the internal measurements as to width and depth of each floor. "Floor space" does not include floors, basements, or separate rooms used exclusively for storage purposes, to which customers are not ordinarily admitted; but counter space, office space, elevator space, etc. is computed as floor space. The Department of Finance and Taxation has ruled that window display space is not to be measured in computing this tax. The act also applies to counters, divisions, departments or leased space operated under a chain store system in a department store. Litigation - None.

272

Table 14 (continued)

State	Kind of Tax	Rates	Period Effective	Miscellaneous
TEXAS (Act approved Oct. 16 1935)	Store License Tax	a) Graduated License Tax 1st store $ 1.00 2nd store 6.00 3rd- 5th stores 25.00 each 6th-10th stores 50.00 each 11th-20th stores 150.00 each 21st-35th stores 250.00 each 36th-50th stores 500.00 each in excess of 50 750.00 each	Jan. 13, 1936 and thereafter	**Administration** - Comptroller of Public Accounts. **Licenses** - To be renewed annually by Dec. 31. Fee for license issued after Jan. 1 to be pro-rated for remaining months of calendar year. **Applications and Payments** - Annually, Dec. 31 **Period Covered by Tax** - Calendar year. **Exemptions** - 1. Distributors selling exclusively lumber and building materials. 2. Distributors selling exclusively petroleum products and motor vehicle services. 3. Places of business used by manufacturers exclusively for distribution of their own products. 4. Vendors of oil and gas well supplies and equipment. 5. Places of business used by processors exclusively for the sale of dairy products. 6. Any business paying an occupation tax-measured by gross receipts. This Act applies to wholesale stores as well as to retail stores. **Litigation** - Undertaken via the Institute of Distribution by 14 Companies, namely: Anthony; Grant; Green; Kress; Goodyear; Kinney; Melville; Newberry; Sears; Scott-Burr; United-Cigar; Penney; Walgreen and Woolworth.

Table 14 (continued)

State	Kind of Tax	Rates	Period Effective	Miscellaneous
TEXAS (Cont'd)				Counsel: G. G. Gannon, Esq. Baker, Botts, Andrews & Wharton, Esperson Building, Houston, Texas History and Result - A permanent injunction restraining the enforcement of the Act was granted by a state lower court on July 3, 1936. An appeal from this decision was taken by the State to the Texas Supreme Court. The Texas Supreme Court, on Dec. 1, 1937, upheld the validity of the Act in Hurt et al v. Cooper et al. A petition for rehearing of the case was denied.
WEST VIRGINIA (Act passed March 17, 1933 without Governor's Approval)	Store License Tax	a) Graduated License Tax 1st store $2.00 2nd- 5th stores 5.00 each 6th-10th stores 10.00 each 11th-15th stores 20.00 each 16th-20th stores 30.00 each 21st-30th stores 35.00 each 31st-50th stores 100.00 each 51st-75th stores 200.00 each All over 75 stores 250.00 each b) Filing fee - 50¢ per store	June 15, 1933 and thereafter.	Administration - State Tax Commissioners. Licenses - To be renewed annually, not later than Jan. 31. Licenses issued after July 1 may be paid at half rate. Applications and Payments - Annually, not later than Jan. 31. Period Covered by Tax - Calendar year. Exemptions - None. Litigation - Act upheld by U.S. Supreme Court in Fox v. Standard Oil Co. of N.J. 294 U.S. 87 (1935). The applicability of the Act to "authorized licensed oil dealers" was upheld by the U.S. Supreme Court in Gulf Refining Co. v. Fox 297 U.S. 381 (1936). This Act applies to wholesale stores as well as to retail stores.

Table 14 (continued)

State	Kind of Tax	Rates	Period Effective	Miscellaneous
WISCONSIN (Act approved Oct. 16, 1937)	Store License Tax	a) Graduated License Tax 1st store — no tax 2nd- 5th stores $25.00 each 6th-10th stores 35.00 each 11th-15th stores 45.00 each 16th-20th stores 55.00 each 21st-25th stores 75.00 each All over 25 stores 100.00 each	Oct. 20, 1937 to July 1, 1939.	Administration - State Tax Commission. Licenses - Issued on payment of tax. Payments - Annually Dec. 31; fees for licenses issued Jan. 1 will be diminished by 1/12 for every full month expired. Period Covered by Tax - Calendar year. Exemptions - 1) Cooperative associations; 2) lumber, coal or building material yards; 3) outlets selling petroleum products when gross sales of these products equal 70% of total sales. Litigation - None.

APPENDIX C

PATMAN FEDERAL CHAIN STORE EXCISE TAX BILL
AS AMENDED FOR INTRODUCTION 2/14/38

H.R. 9464

Providing for an excise tax on retail stores.

Whereas Members of the House of Representatives from a large number of
the States believe that the question of taxing retail stores should be
seriously considered by Congress; and

Whereas Members have been giving careful consideration of the proposal
and have agreed on a draft of a bill to be submitted; and

Whereas the following named Members of the House of Representatives
from the following States are designated co-framers, co-authors and
co-sponsors of the bill:

> Alabama--Patrick; Arkansas--Kitchens; Cravens; California--
> Scott, McGroarty; Connecticut--Citron; Florida--Green, Wilcox;
> Illinois--Fries, Boyer, Sabath; Indiana--Gray, Schulte, Farley;
> Idaho--White; Iowa--Wearin, Harrington, Gilchrist; Kansas--
> Houston, Patterson; Maine--Oliver; Michigan--Sadowski, Engel;
> Minnesota--Bernard, Kvale, Johnson, Buckler; Mississippi--
> Colmer, Collins; Missouri--Zimmerman, Cochran; Montana--
> O'Connell; Nebraska--Binderup; New York--Lanzetta, O'Day; North
> Carolina--Weaver; North Dakota--Lemke; Ohio--Kerwin, Kniffin,
> Bigelow, Sweeney; Oklahoma--Smith, Rogers, Massingale; Pennsyl-
> vania--Dunn, Crosby, Allen, Drew; South Carolina--Gasque; South
> Dakota--Hildebrandt; Texas--Patman, Poage, Dies, Maverick,
> McFarlane, Patton, Sanders, Thomas; Virginia--Flannagan; Wash-
> ington--Hill, Coffee, Leavy, Smith; West Virginia--Ramsay;
> Wisconsin--Gehrman, Boileau, Withrow, Cannon, Schneider; and

Whereas said group instructed one of its members to introduce the bill:
Therefore

> Be it enacted by the Senate and House of Representa-
> tives of the United States of America in Congress
> assembled, That

(new)

> (a) On and after the effective date of this
> Act, every person opening, establishing, operating,
> or maintaining under the same general management,
> supervision, ownership, or control ten or more
> retail stores, or five or more retail stores, shall
> pay annually an excise tax for each fiscal year ending
> June 30, measured by the number of retail stores so
> opened, established, operated, or maintained during
> such fiscal year as follows, except as provided in
> subsection (b) hereof:

For each store not in excess of 15, $50 a store;

For each additional store not in excess of 25, $100 a store;

For each additional store not in excess of 50, $200 a store;

For each additional store not in excess of 75, $250 a store;

For each additional store not in excess of 100, $300 a store;

For each additional store not in excess of 200, $450 a store;

For each additional store not in excess of 300, $600 a store;

For each additional store not in excess of 400, $750 a store;

For each additional store not in excess of 500, $900 a store;

For each additional store in excess of 500, $1,000 a store.

(new)

(b) For the first fiscal year beginning on July 1 following the date of enactment of this Act, the tax under this section shall be one-half of the amount determined in accordance with subsection (a) hereof; and for the second fiscal year, the tax shall be three-fourths of the amount determined in accordance with such subsection.

Sec. 2. If any person subject to the tax imposed by section 1 opens, establishes, operates, or maintains during the taxable year retail stores under the same general management, supervision, ownership, or control located in more than one state, the tax imposed by section 1 shall be multiplied by the number of states (including the District of Columbia) in which any of such stores are located, except that for the first fiscal year beginning on July 1 following the date of enactment of this Act, the tax shall be one-fourth of 1 per centum of the amount determined in accordance with the preceding provision hereof, and that for the second fiscal year the tax shall be one-half of 1 per centum of the amount determined in accordance with such provision or application thereof, shall be held invalid, the validity or application of section 1 shall not be affected thereby.

Sec. 3. (a) The tax imposed by this Act shall be collected by the Bureau of Internal Revenue under the direction of the Secretary of the Treasury and shall be paid into the Treasury of the United States as internal-revenue collections. If the tax is not paid when due, there shall be added as part of the tax interest at the rate of one-half of 1 per centum per month from the date the tax became due until paid.

(b) Not later than July 31, next following the close of the taxable year, each person subject to the tax imposed by section 1 shall make a return of the tax under this Act for such taxable year. Each such return shall be made under oath, shall be filed with the collector of internal revenue for the district in which is located the principal place of business of the taxpayer, or, if he has no principal place of business in the United States, then with the collector at Baltimore, Maryland, and shall contain such information and be made in such manner as the Commissioner of Internal Revenue, with the approval of the Secretary of the Treasury, may by regulations prescribe. All provisions of law (including penalties) applicable in respect of the taxes imposed by section 600 of the Revenue Act of 1926, shall, insofar as not inconsistent with this Act be applicable in respect of the tax imposed by this Act. The Commissioner may extend the time for filing the return of the tax imposed by this Act, under such rules and regulations as he may prescribe with the approval of the Secretary of the Treasury, but no such extension shall be for more than sixty days.

(c) Returns filed under this Act shall be open to inspection in the same manner, to the same extent, and subject to the same provisions of law, including penalties, as returns made under Title 11 of the Revenue Act of 1926.

(d) The taxpayer may (except in case of the taxable period between the effective date and July 1 following) elect to pay the tax in four equal instalments instead of in a single payment, in which case the first instalment shall be paid not later than the last day prescribed for the filing of returns, the second instalment shall be paid on or before the last day of the sixth month, and the fourth instalment on or before the last day of the ninth month, after such last day. If the tax or any instalment thereof is not paid on or before the last day of the period fixed for its payment, the whole amount of the tax unpaid shall be paid upon notice and demand from the collector.

(e) At the request of the taxpayer the time for payment of the tax or any instalment thereof may be extended under regulations prescribed by the Commissioner with the approval of the Secretary of the Treasury, for a period not to exceed six months from the last day of the period prescribed for the payment of the tax or any instalment thereof. The amount of the tax in respect of which any extension is granted shall be paid (with interest at the rate of one-half of 1 per centum per month) on or before the date of the expiration of the period of the extension.

279

(f) The Commissioner of Internal Revenue, with the approval of the Secretary of the Treasury, shall make and publish rules and regulations for the enforcement of this Act.

Sec. 4. When used in this Act—

(a) The term "person" shall include any individual, corporation, partnership, association, joint stock company, or business trust, however organized and whether or not incorporated, but does not include any such person if during the taxable year the gross business of the retail stores opened, established, operated, or maintained by it does not exceed $250,000 or, in case of the taxable period between the effective date and July 1, following, does not exceed such part of $250,000.00 as such period bears to a year.

It starts the graduated tax at $50 per store for all stores over 15, rather than over 10 as in the attached bill.

(new) (b) The term "retail store" shall mean and include any store or mercantile establishment in which goods, wares, or merchandise of any kind or description are sold at retail; but said term shall not include any filling station engaged primarily in the sale or distribution of petroleum products and not engaged in the sale or distribution of automobile tires or tubes, any establishment or facility maintained by a common carrier as part of its transportation facilities primarily for furnishing meals or other commodities to its passengers and employees, or any branch office maintained by a newspaper for the distribution of its papers or for taking subscriptions or advertisements therefor, and shall not include the individually-owned stores, whose revenues in part or in whole are not made available to or inure to the immediate or ultimate benefit of any other person, firm or corporation operating a retail store as herein defined.

(new) (c) The term "under the same general management, supervision, ownership or control" shall include control or direction by one management or association of ultimate management, whether by legal control, direct or indirect, through ownership or control of evidences of indebtedness, physical property, or other assets, through contract, lease, or agency arrangements, through interlocking directors or officers, or through any other means.

(new) (d) The term "effective date" means January 1, April 1, July 1, or October 1, whichever date first follows the date of enactment of this Act. In case the effective date of this Act is a date other than July 1, the period between the effective date and the following July 1 shall be considered as a taxable year under this Act, but the tax for such period shall be such part of the tax imposed by this Act for the first fiscal year beginning July 1 as such period bears to a year.

Sec. 5. If any provision of this Act, or the application thereof to any person or circumstance, is held invalid, the remainder of the Act, and the application of such provision to other persons or circumstances, shall not be affected thereby.

It exempts all companies with annual sales of less than $250,000.

The Effect of the Application of Section 1, (a) and (b), Where All of the Stores Are Located in One State Only

Number of Stores	TAX - 1st YEAR Total	TAX - 1st YEAR Average Per Store	TAX - 2nd YEAR Total	TAX - 2nd YEAR Average Per Store
10	$ 250.00	$ 25.00	$ 375.00	$ 37.50
25	1,000.00	40.00	1,500.00	60.00
50	3,500.00	70.00	5,250.00	105.00
75	6,625.00	88.34	9,937.50	132.51
100	10,375.00	103.75	15,562.50	155.62
200	32,875.00	164.38	49,312.50	246.57
300	62,875.00	209.59	94,312.50	314.39
400	100,375.00	250.94	150,562.50	376.41
500	145,375.00	290.75	218,062.50	436.13
600	195,375.00	325.63	293,062.50	488.45

TAX 3rd YEAR AND AFTER Total	Average Per Store
$ 500.00	$ 50.00
2,000.00	80.00
7,000.00	140.00
13,250.00	176.67
20,750.00	207.50
65,750.00	328.75
125,750.00	419.18
200,750.00	501.88
290,750.00	581.50
390,750.00	651.25

The Effect of the Application of Section 2
Where the Stores are Located in Ten States

Number of Stores	FIRST YEAR		SECOND YEAR	
	Total Tax	Average Per Store	Total Tax	Average Per Store
10	$ 11.25	$ 1.13	$ 22.50	$ 2.26
25	45.00	1.80	90.00	3.60
50	157.50	3.15	315.00	6.30
75	298.13	3.97	596.20	7.94
100	466.88	4.67	933.76	9.34
200	1,479.38	7.40	2,958.76	15.80
300	2,829.38	9.43	5,658.76	18.86
400	4,516.88	11.29	9,033.76	22.58
500	6,541.88	13.08	13,083.76	26.16
600	8,791.88	14.65	17,583.76	29.30

Full Effect of the Application of Sections 1 and 2
For the Third Year and Thereafter Where Stores
are Located in Ten States

Number of Stores	Total Tax	Average Per Store
10	$ 5,000.00	$ 500.00
25	20,000.00	800.00
50	70,000.00	1,400.00
75	132,500.00	1,766.70
100	207,500.00	2,075.00
200	657,500.00	3,287.00
300	1,257,500.00	4,191.80
400	2,007,500.00	5,018.80
500	2,907,500.00	5,815.00
600	3,907,500.00	6,512.50

The J. C. Penney Company, with 1466 stores located in 48 states, would pay the first year under Section 2 only $150,810.00, an average per store of $103.00; and the second year $301,620.00, an average per store of $206.00; the third year under the combined effect of Sections 1 and 2 in full $60,324,000.00, or an average per store of $41,148.00.

A. & P., with 15,000 stores in 36 states, would pay the first year under Section 2 only $1,331,167.50, an average per store of $88.75; the second year $2,662,335.00, an average per store of $177.50; the third year under the combined effect of Sections 1 and 2 in full $532,467,000.00, or an average per store of $35,500.00.

SMALL BUSINESS ENTERPRISE
IN AMERICA

An Arno Press Collection

Bruchey, Stuart Weems. **Robert Oliver, Merchant of Baltimore, 1783-1819.** 1956

Bunn, Verne A. **Buying and Selling A Small Business.** 1969

Bunzel, John H. **The American Small Businessman.** 1962

Carosso, Vincent P. and Stuart Bruchey, Eds. **The Survival of Small Business.** 1979

Carpenter, Walter H., Jr., and Edward Handler. **Small Business and Pattern Bargaining.** 1961

Christensen, C. Roland. **Management Succession in Small and Growing Enterprises.** 1953

Commerce Clearing House, Inc. **Small Business Investment Companies: Law, Regulations, Explanation; New Financing for Small Business.** 1959

Daughters, Charles G. **Wells of Discontent: A Study of the Economic, Social, and Political Aspects of the Chain Store.** 1937

Flink, Salomon J. **Equity Financing of Small Manufacturing Companies in New Jersey.** 1963

Glover, John Desmond. **Public Loans to Private Business** (Doctoral Dissertation, Harvard University, 1947). 1979

Haas, Harold M[ilburn]. **Social and Economic Aspects of the Chain Store Movement** (Doctoral Dissertation, University of Minnesota, 1939). 1979

Hollander, Edward D. and others. **The Future of Small Business.** 1967

Howard, Marshall Chapman. **The Marketing of Petroleum Products: A Study in the Relations Between Large and Small Business** (Doctoral Dissertation, Cornell University, 1951). 1979

Kaplan, A[braham] D.H. **Small Business: Its Place and Problems.** 1948

Konopa, Leonard Jesse. **The Methods of Operation and the Credit Accommodations of a Commercial Bank to Small Business in the Pittsburgh Area** (Doctoral Dissertation, University of Pittsburgh, 1954). 1979

Lumer, Wilfred. **Small Business at the Crossroads: A Study of the Small Business Retreat of 1953-1955.** 1956

McGee, John S[eneca]. **The Robinson-Patman Act and Effective Competition** (Doctoral Dissertation, Vanderbilt University, 1952). 1979

Merwin, Charles L. **Financing Small Corporations in Five Manufacturing Industries, 1926-36.** 1942

Morris, Bruce Robert. **The Economics of the Special Taxation of Chain Stores** (Doctoral Dissertation, University of Illinois, 1937). 1979

Neifeld, M[orris] R. **Cooperative Consumer Credit: With Special Reference to Credit Unions.** 1936

Pepper, Roger S. **Pressure Groups Among "Small Business Men"** (M.A. Thesis, Columbia University, 1940). 1979

Proxmire, William. **Can Small Business Survive?** 1964

Richards, Max Devoe. **Intermediate and Long-Term Credit for Small Corporations** (Doctoral Dissertation, University of Illinois, 1955). 1979

Schor, Stanley S. **The Capital Product Ratio and Size of Establishment for Manufacturing Industries** (Doctoral Dissertation, University of Pennsylvania, 1952). 1979

Still, Jack W. **A Guide to Managerial Accounting in Small Companies.** 1969

Tosiello, Rosario Joseph. **The Birth and Early Years of the Bell Telephone System, 1876-1880** (Doctoral Dissertation, Boston University, 1971). 1979

United States House of Representatives, Select Committee on Small Business. **Effects of Foreign Oil Imports on Independent Domestic Procedures: Hearings...Eighty-First Congress, Second Session Pursuant to H. Res. 22, a Resolution Creating a Select Committee to Conduct a Study and Investigation of Problems of Small Business, Part 3.** 1950

United States House of Representatives, Subcommittee No. 1 of the Select Committee on Small Business. **Monopolistic and Unfair Trade Practices: Hearings...Eightieth Congress, Second Session on the Matter of Problems of Small Business Resulting from Monopolistic and Unfair Trade Practices.** Two Volumes. 1949

United States House of Representatives, Subcommittee No. 1 of the Select Committee on Small Business. **Organization and Operation of the Small Business Administration: Hearings...Eighty-Sixth Congress, First Session Pursuant to H. Res. 51, a Resolution Creating a Select Committee to Conduct a Study and Investigation of the Problems of Small Business, Parts I & II.** 1959

United States House of Representatives, Subcommittee No. 1 of the Select Committee on Small Business. **The Organization and Procedures of the Federal Regulatory Commissions and Agencies and Their Effect on Small Business: Hearings...Eighty-Fourth Congress First and Second Sessions Pursuant to H. Res. 114, a Resolution Creating a Select Committee to Conduct a Study and Investigation of the Problems of Small Business, Parts 1-5, Federal Trade Commission.** 1956

United States House of Representatives, Select Committee on Small Business. **Problems of Small-Business Financing: A Report...Eighty-Fifth Congress, Second Session Pursuant to H. Res. 56, a Resolution Creating a Select Committee to Conduct a Study and Investigation of the Problems of Small Business.** 1958

United States House of Representatives, Select Committee on Small Business. **Problems of Small-Business Financing: Hearings...Eighty-Fifth Congress, First and Second Sessions Pursuant to H. Res. 56, a Resolution Creating a Select Committee to Conduct a Study and Investigation of the Problems of Small Business, Part I & II.** 1958

United States House of Representatives, Subcommittee No. 4 on Distribution Problems Affecting Small Business, Select Committee on Small Business. **Small Business Problems in Urban Areas: Hearings...Eighty-Eighth Congress, Second Session Pursuant to H. Res. 13, a Resolution Creating a Select Committee to Conduct Studies and Investigations of the Problems of Small Business.** 1965

United States House of Representatives, Select Committee on Small Business. **Status of Small Business in Retail Trade (1948-1958): Staff Report...Eighty-Sixth Congress, Second Session.** 1960

United States Senate, Subcommittee of the Committee on Banking and Currency. **Credit Needs of Small Business: Hearings...Eighty-Fifth Congress, First Session on Various Bills to Amend the Small Business Act of 1953, As Amended.** 1957

United States Senate, Subcommittee on Monopoly of the Select Committee on Small Business. **Foreign Legislation Concerning Monopoly and Cartel Practices: Report of the Department of State...Eighty-Second Congress, Second Session.** 1952

University of Pittsburgh, Bureau of Business Research. **Small Business Bibliography.** 1955

Vatter, Harold G. **Small Enterprise and Oliogopoly: A Study of the Butter, Flour, Automobile, and Glass Container Industries.** 1955

Vatter, Paul A. **The Structure of Retail Trade by Size of Store: An Analysis of 1948 Census Data** (Doctoral Dissertation, University of Pennsylvania, 1953). 1979

Weissman, Rudolph L. **Small Business and Venture Capital: An Economic Program.** 1945

Zeigler, Harmon. **The Politics of Small Business.** 1961